A MISCELLANY

ALSO BY E. E. Cummings
IN LIVERIGHT EDITIONS

Complete Poems, 1904–1962

The Theatre of E. E. Cummings

Erotic Poems

EIMI

Selected Poems

Fairy Tales

73 Poems

One Times One

95 Poems

Etcetera

22 and 50 Poems

AnOther E. E. Cummings

ViVa

XAIPE

Is 5

Tulips and Chimneys

The Enormous Room

No Thanks

Self-portrait, 1927

E. E. CUMMINGS

A MISCELLANY

Revised Edition edited by

GEORGE J. FIRMAGE

LIVERIGHT PUBLISHING CORPORATION

A Division of W. W. Norton & Company

Independent Publishers Since 1923

New York • London

Printed in the United States of America
First Liveright Edition 2018

For information about permission to reproduce selections from this book, write to Permissions, Liveright Publishing Corporation, a division of W. W. Norton & Company, Inc., 500 Fifth Avenue, New York, NY 10110

For information about special discounts for bulk purchases, please contact W. W. Norton Special Sales at specialsales@wwnorton.com or 800-233-4830

Manufacturing by LSC Communications Harrisonburg
Book design by Marysarah Quinn
Production manager: Lauren Abbate

ISBN 978-0-87140-653-8

Liveright Publishing Corporation, 500 Fifth Avenue, New York, N.Y. 10110
www.wwnorton.com

W. W. Norton & Company Ltd., 15 Carlisle Street, London W1D 3BS

1 2 3 4 5 6 7 8 9 0

CONTENTS

Introduction *by George J. Firmage* xi

Foreword *by E. E. Cummings* 1

The New Art 3

Gaston Lachaise 11

T. S. Eliot 25

The Soul Story of Gladys Vanderdecker 30

Vanity Fair's Prize Movie Scenario 41

What Our Loving Subscribers Say 49

An Ex-Multimillionaire's Rules for Success in Life 56

A Modern Gulliver Explores the Movies 63

When Calvin Coolidge Laughed 73

William Adams-Wiggley: Genius and Christian 80

Seven Samples of Dramatic Criticism 93

Unexpected Light on the Dawes Plan 98

Jean Cocteau as a Graphic Artist 106

How to Succeed as an Author 114

The Adult, the Artist and the Circus 118

The Very Latest School in Art 125

Helen Whiffletree, American Poetess 131

You Aren't Mad, Am I? 137

"I Confess!" 144
"I Take Great Pleasure in Presenting" 149
The Theatre: I 154
The Theatre: II 158
Coney Island 163
Conflicting Aspects of Paris 168
Vive la Folie! 173
How I Do Not Love Italy 178
The Tabloid Newspaper 184
The Secret of the Zoo Exposed 189
Frenzied Finance 194
Ivan Narb: Abstract Sculptor of the Cosmic 199
The Agony of the Artist (with a capital A) 205
Why I Like America 211
The New Mother Goose 216
Mr. X 222
Miracles and Dreams 228
A Book without a Title 233
Brief Biography 267
A Fairy Tale 269
The Red Front 272
And It Came to Pass 298
Ballad of an Intellectual 301
Weligion Is Hashish 304
In Memoriam 307
Exit the Boob 311
Burlesque, I Love It! 317
Speech from an Unfinished Play: I 322

Speech from an Unfinished Play: II 324
Speech from an Unfinished Play: III 327
Fair Warning 334
What About It? 335
Re Ezra Pound: I 340
Re Ezra Pound: II 341
Foreword to an Exhibit: I 342
Foreword to an Exhibit: II 344
Foreword to an Exhibit: III 346
Foreword to an Exhibit: IV 347
Is Something Wrong? 349
A Foreword to Krazy 351
Words Into Pictures 357
Jottings 358
Videlicet 361
A Poet's Advice to Students 363

INTRODUCTION

The prose and poetry of E. E. Cummings, as well as the life and times of the late poet-painter, have recently received the long overdue attention of several able critics and a biographer.[1] *To add yet another introduction to this body of Cummings criticism is not the intention of the editor nor was it the wish of Mr. Cummings. His own brief foreword to the original edition of this book was all that he wanted said. However, a word or two about this volume's history might not be out of place.*

A Miscellany—*as published in 1958 in an edition limited to seventy-five signed and less than a thousand unsigned copies—contained "a cluster of epigrams," forty-nine essays, a poem and three speeches from an unfinished play. All of these pieces had been written for or first published in magazines, anthologies or art gallery catalogues. A considerable number of them were published under pseudonyms; a few appeared anonymously.*

The original Miscellany *was intended to be a gathering of all the shorter pieces by Cummings that had not previously been published in book form by the author himself. This intention did not fall far short of total realization; only six known appearances were purposely omitted. Three fairy tales, first published in the Harvard* Wake, *were being held for publication*

---

1. Charles Norman, *The Magic Maker: E. E. Cummings* (New York: 1958; revised edition, New York: 1964); Norman Friedman, *e. e. cummings: the art of his poetry* (Baltimore: 1960) and *e. e. cummings: The Growth of a Writer* (Carbondale: 1964); S. V. Baum, *ΕΣΤΙ: ee—E. E. Cummings and the Critics* (East Lansing: 1962); and Barry Marks, *E. E. Cummings* (New York: 1964). *The Prose and Poetry of E. E. Cummings*, Robert E. Wegner, is scheduled for publication in 1965.

in book form[2]*; and three other stories*[3] *were left out at the request of the author who did not consider them successful.*

The publication of A Miscellany Revised *has accomplished three things. First, the many textual errors that inadvertently crept into the first, limited edition of the book have been corrected. Second, the contents have been rearranged to reflect, as closely as possible, the original order of their first separate publication. And third, seven pieces and numerous unpublished line drawings by the author have been added to the book.*

Four of the additions—"Foreword: I," "Re Ezra Pound: I," "Re Ezra Pound: II" and "Is Something Wrong?"—were collected in whole or in part in i: Six Nonlectures. *"Brief Biography" was discovered after the limited edition of this book went to press. And Cummings' book without a title, reprinted here with the illustrations drawn by the author for its limited hardbound appearance, has long been out-of-print and, it was felt, deserved the new audience its publication here might bring it. None of the foregoing needs any further word of explanation.*

The final addition, E. E. Cummings' translation of "Le Front Rouge" by Louis Aragon, was undertaken at the request of the Russian Revolutionary Literature Bureau as "a friendly gesture of farewell," according to Cummings' account of his 1931 visit to the Soviet Union in EIMI. *Cummings was quick to point out that Aragon's political beliefs were not his own*[4]*; but "The Red Front" was not without interest as a poem and its author and the translator had been friends in Paris. Above all else, the translation itself is excellent; it is also one of the few extant examples we have of this phase of Cummings' art. "The Red Front" is printed here for the first time next to the long-suppressed original text.*

The editor is indebted to many people for many kindnesses; but none more so than Mrs. E. E. Cummings. Without her assistance, understand-

---

2. The three tales and a fourth, unpublished one are soon to be issued in an edition illustrated by the young Canadian artist John Eaton.
3. "The King" (*The Harvard Monthly*, July 1915); "Everybody's Mother, Anybody's Mate," by "An Anonymous Author" (*Vanity Fair*, October 1925); and "Little Red Riding Hood," by "Eugene Heltai" (*Vanity Fair*, March 1926).
4. See "A Fairy Tale" in this collection and *EIMI*, in particular pages 142–143 where Cummings analyses certain lines and images in Aragon's poem.

ing and generosity this book would not have been given a second life. A special thanks is due D. Jon Grossman; and to all those who lent a helping hand with the first, limited edition of this book the editor is still indebted.

It is hoped that everyone who contributed to the adventure which this book represents will join the undersigned in dedicating this volume to the memory of the poet-painter who IS E. E. Cummings.

—GEORGE J. FIRMAGE
1965

A MISCELLANY

FOREWORD to the First Edition

This book consists of a cluster of epigrams,forty-nine essays on various subjects,a poem dispraising dogmata,and several selections from an unfinished play.

Play and poem and epigrams need (I feel) no comment.

As for my essays—here grouped under three headings: Etcetera, Appreciations,VanityFair—the earliest is dated 1915 and the latest 1957;but more than half of them (comprising much of A Miscellany's second and most of its third portion) appeared during the twenties in Vanity Fair magazine,having been graciously commissioned by a charming personage named Frank Crowninshield.

Taken ensemble,the forty-nine astonish and cheer and enlighten their progenitor. He's astonished that,as nearly as anyone can make out,I wrote them. He's cheered because,while re-reading them,I've encountered a great deal of liveliness and nothing dead. Last but not least;he's enlightened via the realization that,whereas times can merely change,an individual may grow.

—E. E. CUMMINGS

THE NEW ART

The New Art has many branches—painting, sculpture, architecture, the stage, literature, and music. In each of these there is a clearly discernible evolution from models; in none is there any trace of that abnormality, or incoherence, which the casual critic is fond of making the subject of tirades against the new order.

It is my purpose to sketch briefly the parallel developments of the New Art in painting, sculpture, music, and literature.

I.

Anyone who takes Art seriously, who understands the development of technique in the last half century, accepts Cézanne and Matisse as he accepts Manet and Monet. But this brings us to the turning point where contemporary criticism becomes, for the most part, rampant abuse, and where prejudice utters its storm of condemnation. I refer to that peculiar phase of modern art called indiscriminately, "Cubism," and "Futurism."

The name Cubism, properly applied, relates to the work of a small group of ultramodern painters and sculptors who use design to express their personal reaction to the subject, i.e.—what this subject "means" to them—and who further take this design from geometry. By using an edge in place of a curve a unique tactual value is obtained.

Futurism is a glorification of personality. Every socalled "Futurist" has his own hobby; and there are almost as many kinds of painting as artists. For instance, one painter takes as his subject sounds, another, colours. A third goes back to old techniques; a fourth sees life through a magnifying glass; a fifth imposes an environment upon his subject proper, obtaining very startling effects; a sixth concerns himself purely with motion—in connection with which it is interesting to note the Japanese painters' wholly unrealistic rendering of the force of a river.

The painter Matisse has been called the greatest exponent of Cubist sculpture. At the 1913 exhibition the puzzled crowd in front of Brancusi's "Mlle. Pogany" was only rivalled by that which swarmed about the painting called "Nude Descending a Staircase." "Mlle. Pogany" consists of a more or less egg-shaped head with an unmistakable nose, and a sinuous suggestion of arms curving upward to the face. There is no differentiation in modelling affording even a hint of hands; in other words, the flow of line and volume is continuous. But what strikes the spectator at first glance, and focuses the attention throughout, is the enormous inscribed ovals, which everyone recognizes as the artist's conception of the subject's eyes. In this triumph of line for line's sake over realism we note the development of the basic principles of impressionism.

II.

Just as in the case of painting, it is a French school which brought new life to music; but at the same time, Germany has the honour of producing one of the greatest originators and masters of realism, Richard Strauss.

The modern French school of music finds its inspiration in the personal influence of César Franck. Debussy, Ravel and Satie all owe much to this great Belgian, who (like Maeterlinck and Verhaeren), was essentially a man of their own artistic nationality.

It is safe to say that there will always be somebody who still refuses to accept modernism in music; quoting in his defense the sovereign innovator, Beethoven! On a par with the sensation produced by the painting and sculpture of the Futurist variety was the excitement which the music of Strauss and Debussy first produced upon audiences. At present, Debussy threatens to become at any moment vulgarly common; while Strauss is fatuous in his clarity beside Schönberg; who, with Stravinsky, is the only god left by the public for the worship of the aesthetes.

Erik Satie is, in many respects, the most interesting of all modern composers. Nearly a quarter of a century ago he was writing what is now considered modern music. The most striking aspect of Satie's art is the truly extraordinary sense of humour which prompts one of his subjects, the "sea cucumber," to console himself philosophically for his lack of tobacco.

The "Five Orchestral Pieces" of Arnold Schönberg continue to be the leading sensation of the present day musical world. Their composer occupies a position in many respects similar to that of the author of the "Nude Descending a Staircase." I do not in the least mean to ridicule Schönberg—no lawlessness could ever have produced such compositions as his, which resemble bristling forests contorted by irresistible winds. His work is always the expression of something mysteriously terrible—which is probably why Boston laughed.

I have purposely left until the last the greatest theorist of modern music—Scriabin. Logically, he belongs beside Stravinsky, as leader of the Russian school. But it is by means of Scriabin that we may most readily pass from music to literature, through the medium of what has been called "sense-transference," as exemplified by the colour music of the "Prometheus."

This "Poem of Fire" is the consummation of Scriabin's genius. To quote the *Transcript*: "At the first performance, by the Russian Symphony Society, on March 20, for the first time in history a composer used a chromatic color score in combination with orchestration. . . . At the beginning of the orchestration, a gauze rectangle in about the position of a picture suspended on the back wall became animated by flowing and blending colours. These colours were played by a 'colour-organ' or 'chromola,' having a keyboard with fifteen keys, and following a written score."

III.

The suggestion of an analogy between colour and music leads us naturally to the last branch of the New Art—to wit, literature. Only the most extreme cases will be discussed, such as have important bearing upon the very latest conceptions of artistic expression.

I will quote three contemporary authors to illustrate different phases and different degrees of the literary parallel to sound painting—in a rather faint hope that the first two may prepare the way for an appreciation of the third. First Amy Lowell's "Grotesque" affords a clear illustration of development from the ordinary to the abnormal.

> "Why do the lilies goggle their tongues at me
> When I pluck them;
> And writhe and twist,
> And strangle themselves against my fingers,
> So that I can hardly weave the garland
> For your hair?
> Why do they shriek your name
> And spit at me
> When I would cluster them?
> Must I kill them
> To make them lie still,
> And send you a wreathe of lolling corpses
> To turn putrid and soft
> On your forehead
> While you dance?"

In this interesting poem we seem to discern something beyond the conventional. The lilies are made to express hatred by the employment of grotesque images. But there is nothing original in the pathetic fallacy. No one quarrels with Tennyson's lines.

> "There has fallen a splendid tear
> From the passion-flower at the gate"—

Let us proceed further—only noting in the last three lines that brutality which is typical of the New Art—and consider the following poem by the same author:

"THE LETTER"

"Little cramped words scrawling all over the paper
Like draggled fly's legs,
What can you tell of the flaring moon
Through the oak leaves?
Or of an uncurtained window, and the bare floor
Spattered with moonlight?
Your silly quirks and twists have nothing in them
Of blossoming hawthorns.
And this paper is chill, crisp, smooth, virgin of
  loveliness
Beneath my hand.
I am tired, Beloved, of chafing my heart against
The want of you;
Of squeezing it into little ink drops,
And posting it.
And I scald alone, here under the fire
Of the great moon."

This poem is superb of its kind. I know of no image in all realistic writing which can approach the absolute vividness of the first two lines. The metaphor of the chafed heart is worthy of any poet; but its fanciful development would have been impossible in any literature except this ultramodern.

I shall now quote from a sonnet by my second author, Donald Evans:

> "Her voice was fleet-limbed and immaculate,
> And like peach blossoms blown across the wind
> Her white words made the hour seem cool
> and kind,
> Hung with soft dawns that danced a shadow fête.
> A silken silence crept up from the South.
> The flutes were hushed that mimed the
> orange moon,
> And down the willow stream my sighs
> were strewn,
> While I knelt to the corners of her mouth."

In the figure "Her voice was fleet-limbed," and the phrase "white words," we have a sought-for literary parallel to the work of the "sound painters." It is interesting to compare Dante's expressions of a precisely similar nature, occurring in the first and fifth cantos, respectively, of the Inferno—"dove il Sol tace," and "in loco d'ogni luce muto."

From Donald Evans to Gertrude Stein is a natural step—up or down, and one which I had hoped the first two might enable us to take in security. Gertrude Stein subordinates the meaning of words to the beauty of the words themselves. Her art is the logic of literary sound painting carried to its extreme. While we must admit that it is logic, must we admit that it is art?

Having prepared the way, so far as it is possible, for a just appreciation, I now do my best to quote from the book "Tender Buttons," as follows:

(1) A sound.

Elephants beaten with candy and little pops and chews all bolts and reckless reckless rats, this is this.

(2) Salad Dressing and an Artichoke.

Please pale hot, please cover rose, please acre in the red stranger, please butter all the beefsteak with regular feel faces.

(3) Suppose an Eyes

* * *

Go red go red, laugh white.

Suppose a collapse is rubbed purr, is rubbed purr get.

Little sales ladies little sales ladies little saddles of mutton.

Little sales of leather and such beautiful, beautiful, beautiful beautiful.

The book from which these selections are drawn is unquestionably a proof of great imagination on the part of the authoress, as anyone who tries to imitate her work will discover for himself. Here we see traces of realism, similar to those which made the "Nude Descending a Staircase" so baffling. As far as these "Tender Buttons" are concerned, the sum and substance of criticism is impossible. The unparalleled familiarity of the medium precludes its use for the purpose of aesthetic effect. And here, in their logical conclusion, impressionistic tendencies are reduced to absurdity.

The question now arises, how much of all this is really Art?

The answer is: we do not know. The great men of the future will most certainly profit by the experimentation of the present period. An insight into the unbroken chain of artistic development during the last half century disproves the theory that modernism is without foundation; rather we are concerned with a natural unfolding of sound tendencies. That the conclusion is, in a particular case, absurdity, does not in any way impair the value of the experiment, so long as we are dealing with sincere effort. The New Art, maligned though it may be by fakirs and fanatics, will appear in its essential spirit to the unprejudiced critic as a courageous and genuine exploration of untrodden ways.

A "commencement part," given by the author at Sanders Theatre on the occasion of his graduation from Harvard, and published in the *Harvard Advocate*, June 1915.

GASTON LACHAISE

To get rid altogether of contemporary "sculpture" is perhaps the surest way of appreciating the achievement of Lachaise. This coup of unadulterated intelligence has already been given by Mr. W. H. Wright in four sentences which I lift from the masterly sixth chapter of *Modern Painting*—

> "After Michelangelo there was no longer any new inspiration for sculpture. After Cézanne there was no longer any excuse for it. He made us see that painting can present a more solid vision than that of any stone image. Against modern statues we can only bump our heads: in the contemplation of modern painting we can exhaust our intelligences."

I say masterly, because so long as the author keeps one or more eyes on Cézanne it must be admitted by any intelligent person that his analysis is unspeakably correct. Were the entire book devoted to a consideration of Cézanne our own task would be confined to proving that Lachaise does not produce "modern statues." Unfortunately this is not the case. Elsewhere the author remarks that Swinburne brought the rhymed lyric to its highest development. And at one point he mentions that "the aesthetic possibilities of the human form were exhausted by" his old friend Michelangelo, with which it is a trifle difficult to agree. How about the renowned Pablo? Or, to take two far-from-colossal geniuses: Lembrach, in his lean girl at the Armory Show (1913), and Brancusi, in his Princess Bonaparte at the Independent of is it three years past, did something more than exciting. In the first case a super-El Greco-like significance was pitilessly extorted from the human form, in the second the human form was beautifully seduced into a sensual geometry. In his feeling for his material, moreover, Brancusi showed for some time genuine originality. But he reached an impasse very soon. Judging from the recent bumps and buttons at the De Zayas Gallery he is at present as dead as a doornail.

It must be admitted that Wright is Johnny on the spot when it comes to Paul Manship—a "sound" man, of course, but no slave to the Rodin tradition, nor the Saint Gaudens tradition, nor whatever may have produced those fattish girls helplessly seated on either hand as you enter the Boston Public Library. Manship's statues, including the enlightened Injun at the Metropolitan, remind one a good deal of the remark (which appeared on the back page of I have forgotten which French funny paper while la guerre was still with us) of one *gonzesse* to another—"J'ai un bon truc chez les boches. Je leur dis que je suis française; ça prend toujours." Not that Manship tells us that he is *française* (gender aside) but that in his sculpture he is always *chez les américains*, besides having in everything a *bon truc*, a certain cleverness, a something "fakey." One wonders whether his winning the Prix de Rome accounts for the fact that in the last analysis Manship is neither a sincere alternative to thinking, nor an appeal to the pure intelligence, but a very ingenious titillation of that well-known element, the highly sophisticated unintelligence. At any rate, he was formerly very popular, just as Nadelman (who appeals less subtly to the H. S. U.) is at present supremely popular. Fundamentally Manship is one of those producers of "modern statues" whom Wright's four sentences wipe off the earth's face. His work is, of course, superior to the masterpieces of such people as French, Barnard, Bartlett, the Borglums, and Bela Pratt—in so far as something which is thoroughly dead is superior to something which has never been alive.

Wright is, after all, correct in his main thesis. We have bumped our heads altogether too often on "modern statues." Until recently we gave them a bump every time we passed the celebrated Arc de Triomphe at Twenty-third street. And if we have been caught in the modern sculpture section of the Metropolitan we have received gratis such a massage of bumping as probably could not be duplicated in any one place in America. Let us then turn to Lachaise and exhaust our intelligence for a change, assuming that we can boast thereof.

In the light of contemporary "criticism" this assumption is decidedly daring. Lachaise has, in the past few years, made a large number of artists extremely enthusiastic, and a great many gallery goers very nervous, not to mention the ladies and gentlemen who may have died of anger. But the official "critics," perhaps realizing the disastrous consequences to "criticism" of a genuine reaction on their part to work of overwhelming aesthetic value, have as it were agreed to risk nothing. An exception which proves the rule is Mr. McBride Of The Sun, who on Sunday (February 17, 1918) said, in the course of some hair-raising platitudes, "I like this statue [The Elevation] immensely," generously adding, "If the ribald laugh at it and call it a fat woman they may." In regard to Lachaise's personality The Dealers In Second-hand Ideas (Strictly guaranteed. Good as new.) are content to quote from the preface which Lachaise wrote for the catalogue of the American sculptors' show (Bourgeois Galleries, Spring of 1919). As to his work, the consensus of "critical" opinion seems to be that it has "dignity" and is the "buoyant" product of a Frenchman who was born, and came to America.

This ducking and side-stepping of Lachaise and his work by the "critics" is more than very amusing. It is extremely valuable as drawing a nice line between his personal achievement and contemporary "sculpture." Like some people who have to have their heads rubbed before they can go to sleep, the "critics" must have theirs bumped before they can go to "criticism." But in Lachaise (as we shall, it is to be hoped un-"critically," see) these gentlemen are up against a man who not only refuses to bump their heads for them but demands a profoundly intelligent expenditure of sensitivity.

"Criticism" or no "criticism," to attempt an analysis of Lachaise's personality strikes us as being almost equally futile and impertinent. And yet, given the important negative obscurity in which the "critics" would plunge that significant and essentially positive part of him, a few however random and obvious remarks on the subject may not be wholly without value. Three things Lachaise, to any one who knows him, is and is beyond the shadow of a doubt: inherently naif, fearlessly intelligent, utterly sincere. It is accurate to say that his two greatest hates are the hate of insincerity and the hate of superficiality. That Lachaise is supremely and incorrigibly enthusiastic about his adopted country would appear (in the light of that country's treatment of him) perfectly unreasonable, had it not its reverse side, which is the above-mentioned disgust with superficiality and contempt for insincerity—two qualities which he attributes in a high degree to his native land. As his work proves, he has no use for prettiness. This work of his, a crisp and tireless searching for the truths of nature as against the facts of existence, negates Rodin incidentally, as Cézanne's solid strivings incidentally negate Monet. Temperamentally Lachaise is about as far from the typical Frenchman (more especially from what America likes to believe is the typical Frenchman) as can be imagined; as far, that is, as Cézanne, whose famous hate of contemporary facility and superficiality drove him to a recreation of nature which was at once new and fundamental. Lachaise's perhaps favourite (French) word is *simple*. Applied to his work, it means something quite different from, as in Brancusi, a mere economy of form through the elimination of unessentials; it means form which completely expresses itself, form that perfectly tactilizes the beholder, as in the case of an electric machine which, being grasped, will not let the hand let go.

We confess that in the sumptuousness of certain of his perfectly sensuous exquisitely modulated vaselike nudes we have felt something pleasantly akin to what are known as the least imperfect specimens of Chinese art. This brings up an interesting trait of Lachaise's character. He believes that the Orient fascinated him at one time to the point of hypnotism and is resolved that the experience shall not be repeated. Significantly in contrast to Gauguin, he turns his eyes to the north. There is one thing which Lachaise would rather do than anything else, and that is to experience the bignesses and whitenesses and silences of the polar regions. His lively interest in Esquimaux drawings and customs stems from this absolutely inherent desire—to negate the myriad with the single, to annihilate the complicatedness and prettinesses and trivialities of Southern civilizations with the enormous, the solitary, the fundamental.

Lachaise's work is the absolutely authentic expression of a man very strangely alive.

Every one has read, and no one has heard him boast, that he "studied at the École des Beaux Arts 1898–1903, exhibited at the Salon des Artistes Français 1899, worked with Lalique and Aube 1901," took various prizes, and so forth. What no one knows, outside his immediate friends, with whom he is preternaturally frank, is Lachaise's attitude toward triumphs which would have seduced a mind less curiously and originally sensitive. The fact is that he regards them with something between amusement and disgust. This is not a question of modesty, but of direct and fearless thinking—at which, as had been already stated, Lachaise is a past master. Of the man who in his twenties has captured beyond question every trick of academical technique we ordinarily expect that he will amuse himself for a few years at least, if not for the remainder of his life, by the little game which Mr. Huneker has (if we remember correctly) called "exploding firecrackers on the steps of the institute." If he doesn't do this, it means (to use the conventional argument against art schools) that in the realization of academical ideals whatever originality the pupil may have had at the outset has been, if not entirely eliminated, at any rate irrevocably diluted. Lachaise's personality profoundly negates the possibility of self-advertising. As for the instinctive art thesis, his work makes this answer: that the man who by the gods has been fated to express himself will succeed in expressing himself in spite of all schools; that the greatest artist is the man whom no school can kill.

Even if Lachaise could have enjoyed making chumps of his teachers for the pure fun of the thing, it is safe to say that he would never have done so, any more than his genius would ever have made the mistake which Rodin made, of accepting the technique which it had so easily conquered and with that as a basis proceeding to surpass conventional standards, thereby creating another academy. For a Lachaise, as for a Cézanne, academies hold nothing beyond a knowledge of tools. For this reason both men are intrinsically great geniuses. The significance of their production lies in the fact that it goes not beyond but under conventional art.

Frequent allusions having been made to "Lachaise's work," it is high time that we become specific. Last Spring at Penguin Lachaise had on show, in addition to a bust and an alabaster bas-relief, a thing seventeen inches long which he called The Mountain. It is not the slightest exaggeration to say that, to any one genuinely either cognizant or ignorant of Art As She Is Taught, this thing was a distinct shock. Surrounded by a gurly sea of interesting chromatic trash it lay, in colossal isolation: a new and sensual island. Merely to contemplate its perfectly knit enormousness was to admit that analysis of, or conscious thinking on our part about, a supreme aesthetic triumph, is a very pitiful substitute for that sensation which is impossibly the equivalent of what the work itself thinks of us. It is difficult to conceive any finer tribute to The Mountain than the absence of "criticism" which it created. Bust and bas-relief came in for their customary meagre share, but, so far as can be discovered, The Mountain was never once mentioned: which fact may partially, at any rate, excuse the sentences which follow.

Its completely integrated simplicity proclaims The Mountain

to be one of those superlative aesthetic victories which are accidents of the complete intelligence, or the intelligence functioning at intuitional velocity. Its absolute sensual logic as perfectly transcends the merely exact arithmetic of the academies as the rhythm which utters its masses negates those static excrements of deliberate unthought which are the delight of certain would-be "primitives." Let us as a specimen of the latter take a painter: say Zorach. In being spectators of his work we are charmed, lulled, by the lure of shapes which imitate and we are tempted to say duplicate the early most simple compositions of mankind. Our intelligence is as it were temporarily numbed into inactivity by the work's "emotional appeal"—but only temporarily, since it is obvious that no art which depends for its recognition upon the casting of a spell on the intelligence can, except in the case of an undeveloped mind, endure beyond a few moments or a few hours at best. The spell wears off, the intelligence rushes in, the work is annihilated. Herein is discovered the secret of that "fakey" feeling with which we are inevitably left by the designs of this unquestionably sincere artist.

In contrast to this self-consciously attempted naiveté on the part of a twentieth-century adult there is unself-conscious expression, that of the child who has not yet inherited the centuries and the savage whose identity with his environment has not yet become a prey to civilization, which—eminent aestheticians to the contrary—is of the utmost significance to aesthetics. The stories by Harlow Atwood in a recent number of *Playboy*, which unfortunately caters habitually to the Zorach audience, are a supreme and exquisite example. Two of Denise's paintings that Lachaise has, which she did before sophistication set in, are another. With Harlow and Denise, A.D. 19—, are the authors respectively of that most amazingly beautiful of all American Indian folk tales, The Man Who Married A Bear, and certain forms and colours out of Africa. All these demand for their complete appreciation that, far from being mere spectators, we allow our intelligences to be digested; and not until this occurs do they cease to excite in us amusement or *mépris*, and reveal their significance. That is to say, they require of us an intelligent process of the highest order, namely the negation on our part, by thinking, of thinking; whereas in an "art" which emulates naiveté through intelligent processes the case is entirely different. In the work of Zorach and his ilk our role is that of spectator, never anything more. But the inexcusable and spontaneous scribblings which children make on sidewalks, walls, anywhere, preferably with coloured chalk, cannot be grasped until we have accomplished the thorough destruction of the world. By this destruction alone we cease to be spectators of a ludicrous and ineffectual striving and, involving ourselves in a new and fundamental kinesis, become protagonists of the child's vision.

To analyze child art in a sentence is to say that houses, trees, smoke, people, etc., are depicted not as nouns but as verbs. The more genuine child art is, the more it is, contrary to the belief of those incapable persons who are content merely to admire it, purely depictive. In denying that the child "represents" and substituting for "representation" some desperately overworked word like "expression," these people are only showing their hostility to the academies, just as when they tell us (which is true) that the bad artist is the representational artist. But, as has been sometimes pointed out, the artist who represents is bad not because he represents: he is bad because he represents something which a camera can represent better. This means that he is depicting something that is second, or rather *n*th, hand, which a child most distinctly is not. Consequently to appreciate child art we are compelled to undress one by one the soggy nouns whose agglomeration constitutes the mechanism of Normality, and finally to liberate the actual crisp organic squirm—the IS.

Academies are when everything included in the abstract and therefore peculiarly soggy noun Nature is accepted superficially or as a noun, and as such declined. In this case "art" is technically nothing but an important prepositional connective—Mr. Sargent's portrait OF Some One, Mr. French's statue OF something (to take the worst painter and the worst sculptor in America)—between two nouns: an artist and a sitter (if we may make so bold as to say that Grief is it sat for Mr. French). But painting had its Cézanne, whose incredulous and otherwise energetic intelligence resented the doctrine that walking in the wake of some one who is smoking a cigar is vastly superior to smoking the cigar yourself, and by whom the academies, and their important fattish remarks about facts by means of colours, were significantly undermined with minute sculptural shocks of chromatic truth. Insofar as to understand something is, not completely to taste or smell or hear or see or otherwise to touch it, and to believe something is, not completely to understand it, Cézanne was compelled to mis- or disbelieve and to dis- or misunderstand "Nature"; and he disbelieved and misunderstood it at the age of faith and hope so violently and so carefully as to present us with a significant conjugation of the verb which is just as inherently intense as, from the plastic standpoint, declensions and nouns are inherently flabby. Precisely in this sense Cézanne became truly naif—not by superficially contemplating and admiring the art of primitive peoples, but by carefully misbelieving and violently disunderstanding a secondhand world.

To the vocal gesture which preceded grammar Lachaise is completely sensitive. Consequently, in his enormous and exquisite way, Lachaise negates OF with IS. To say that the 1918 exhibition at the Bourgeois Galleries drew from the "critics" more statements of ungentle unintelligence, and from the gallery-going public more expressions of enthusiastic ignorance, than any one-man show of sculpture previously held on the Avenue, is but to do justice to all concerned, including Monsieur Bourgeois. The Elevation, which, as we have already noted, occasioned, in the case of Mr. McBride, the sole unbiased reaction of "criticism" to this exhibition, was responsible for, on the one hand, more unclever exasperation and on the other more fulsome ecstasy than all the rest of the show put together. Lest any should accuse us of hyperbole, we will quote a sample of each "point of view" and let the reader decide for himself whether or not one is more incredibly meaningless than the other.

> "It might be a satire on the stout woman who pinches her waist and wears high heels that stand her on her toes for life, or it might be an idealization of her. The answer is in the point of view. Mr. Lachaise is himself not very definite on this score. If it is a satire, it is curious that he should employ the figure as a motif so often. Mr. Lachaise is one of those modernists who hark back to the serenity of Greece and forward to new rhythms which shall be more active.
>
> "She is the mother of men, with the scorn of wisdom and dominance on her brow. She is an unathletic—a queen bee-Amazon, different both from the 'clinging vine' or the pioneer companion that her mothers were. She is the creature toward which creation groaneth. She is man's old 'delicious burden,' buoyed by his reverence like a mist above the ground."

Perhaps it should be stated that one "critic," instead of mentioning The Elevation by name, presented the world with a synopsis of what he, she or it is pleased to call "modernism."

> "One regrets that an artist so evidently serious in his aims should sacrifice too often to the extraordinary cult of ugliness which seems to have taken the place of beauty on the altars of 'modernism' *à outrance.* Strength, power, individuality, all of these qualities, must be conceded to Mr. Lachaise, but the tendency to emphasize and glorify the unsightly because it is supposed to represent force and have some deep symbolic meaning, can only lead to the apotheosis of ugliness, a

> consummation scarcely to be desired, even by the most ardent exponents of modernism."

The reason why all official and unofficial "criticism" OF The Elevation fails, and fails so obviously as in the specimens quoted, is this: The Elevation is not a noun, not a "modern statue," not a statue OF Something or Some One BY a man named Gaston Lachaise—but a complete tactile self-orchestration, a magnificently conjugation largeness, an IS. The Elevation may not be declined; it should not and cannot be seen; it must be heard: heard as a super-Wagnerian poem of flesh, a gracefully colossal music. In mistaking The Elevation for a noun the "critics" did something superhumanly asinine. In creating The Elevation as a verb Lachaise equalled the dreams of the very great artists of all time.

On the ground that it leads us to a consideration of Lachaise's new show at the Bourgeois Galleries, which event is after all the excuse for this article, we ask the reader's pardon for boring him with a final specimen of "criticism." The author is a distinctly official "critic," Mr. Guy Pène du Bois of the *Evening Post,* of whom it may fairly be said that he succeeds in taking himself more seriously than all the other members of his very defunct profession put together. He is speaking of the exhibition of American sculptures before mentioned.

> "Indeed, in the instance of many of these exhibits, when one has said that they are amusing, full credit has been done to their creators. This is entirely true neither in the instance of Lachaise nor of Diederich. It is true that they are of the ultra-fashionables of sculpture, but it is also true that they are more than this—that they are exceedingly intelligent men, endowed, moreover, with more than the usual allotment of talent. Just now they reach for a very small and very particular audience, one jaded by experience in art, and demand-

> ing certain definite shocks, rare expressions, in order to be aroused. Lachaise's figure of a woman is a real contribution to the so slowly growing gallery of portraits of her."

Unless all signs err, Mr. Guy Pène du Bois is due to get—or should we say has already got, since by the time THE DIAL appears the new Bourgeois show will be in full swing—what may without exaggeration be called the surprise of his "critical" life, when he looks over the menu of the latest Lachaise exhibition. For in contrast to the previous show, in which the titles (Rhythme, Anéantissement, etc.) were chosen by Monsieur Bourgeois, the elements of the present show are, as we trust, to be named by Lachaise himself; in which case the "critic" of the *Evening Post* will find himself confronted by at least two titles which not only knock his "reach for a very small and very particular audience, one jaded by experience in art, and demanding certain definite shocks, rare expressions, in order to be aroused" thesis into a cocked hat, but will, we are confident, give him an attack of goose flesh into the bargain—*id est,* Love and Home. And why? because while any one except Lachaise might stand accused of insincerity in applying these stand-bys of morality to work whose inherent—which is to say ultimate—significance is purely for aesthetics, Lachaise has never stood and never will stand, apropos either his personality or his work, accused of this particular thing. Were it possible so to accuse him, Mr. Guy Pène du Bois would in our opinion be incurring considerable personal danger in so doing. It looks to us as though the gentleman is in the extraordinarily painful, not to say peculiarly undignified, position of being up a tree. At least we may expect of our "critic" that in this predicament he will comfort himself with the last line of that most popular wartime song, America I Love You, which goes, "And there're a hundred million others like me."

Unless some unforeseen accident occurs, the present exhibition should include a number of drawings (which totally negate the favourite contention of "criticism," to the effect that Lachaise's work constitutes the doing of one thing over and over), the bas-relief Dusk (already reproduced in the January DIAL), two reclining figures (Home and Portrait), a diving figure, the colossal Love, and last—and to our thinking best—The Mountain. We have already, in all probability, talked too much and said too little (to use a peculiarly conventional phrase) about The Mountain; yet it is without shame that we are guilty of a parting word, for which Lachaise's infrequently paralleled mastery of stone is wholly responsible. In The Mountain as it appears in this exhibition Lachaise has completely enjoyed an opportunity to work directly in the stone Himself as he calls it. He has enjoyed it as his contemporaries to whom stone is not a tactile dream, but a disagreeable everyday tangible nuisance to be handled by paid subordinates, can never enjoy it. In the transformation from the patina'd plaster (which was at Penguin and later, unofficially, at the Bourgeois Galleries) to the stone now on view, several vastly minute and enormously significant changes have occurred—changes dictated purely by the superior medium. To speak accurately, now for the first time The Mountain actualizes the original conception of its creator; who, in contrast to the contemptible conventionally called "sculptor," thinks in stone whenever and because stone is not, and to whom the distinction between say bronze and alabaster is a distinction not between materials but, on the contrary, between ideas. In The Mountain as it IS Lachaise becomes supremely himself, the master of every aspect of a surface, every flexion of a mass, every trillionth of a phenomenon.

The reader who expects an analysis of the other work which we have mentioned as being included in the exhibition (Dusk, Portrait, Love, etc.) is due for a pleasant disappointment. The very good reasons for our not attempting such an analysis (or rather analyses, since, once again—the whole tribe of Defunctives to the contrary—Lachaise's "point of view" never repeats itself) are briefly: first, we do not feel that we are up to the job; second, if this *essai* means anything whatever it means that the only very great sinners are the Gentleman Dealers In Secondhand Thoughts. God knows that in the course of the preceding pages we have sinned deeply enough. Rather than despicably to descend into mere praise of an artist who, if only for the reason that we profoundly admire him, does not merit from us a so conventional insult—a man in relation to whose extraordinary achievement praise cannot but constitute a sumptuous impertinence—we prefer to maintain or perhaps to regain silence.

From *The Dial*, February 1920. E. E. Cummings had long championed the artistry of Gaston Lachaise. For an exhibition of the sculptor's work at the Weyhe Gallery, N.Y.C. (December 27, 1955–January 28, 1956), Mr. Cummings wrote: "It was many years ago that The reborn Dial saluted Gaston Lachaise. Those years comprise (among other drolleries) a complete reversal of public untaste; 'nonobjective art,' once anathematized, being now de rigueur. By contrast, the achievement of Lachaise remains passionately and serenely itself—a marvel and a mystery: the spontaneous and inevitable expression of one fearlessly unique human being."

T. S. ELIOT

The somewhat recently published Poems is an accurate and uncorpulent collection of instupidities. Between the negative and flabby and ponderous and little bellowings of those multitudinous contemporaries who are obstinately always "unconventional" or else "modern" at the expense of being (what is most difficult) alive, Mr. T.S. Eliot inserts the positive and deep beauty of his skilful and immediate violins . . . the result is at least thrilling.

He has done the trick for us before. In one of the was it two Blasts skilfully occurred, more than successfully framed by much soundless noise, the Rhapsody and Preludes. In one of the God knows nobody knows how many there will be Others, startlingly enshrined in a good deal of noiseless sound, Prufrock and Portrait of a Lady carefully happened. But "this slim little volume" as a reviewer might say achieves a far more forceful presentation, since it competes with and defeats not mere blasters and differentists but τὸ ἕν -s and origins and all that is Windily and Otherwise enervate and talkative.

Some Notes on the Blank Verse of Christopher Marlowe are, to a student of Mr. T.S., unnecessarily illuminating:

> ". . . this style which secures its emphasis by always
> hesitating on the edge of caricature at the right
> moment . . .
> . . . this intense and serious and indubitably great

> poetry, which, like some great painting and sculpture, attains its effects by something not unlike caricature."

Even without this somewhat mighty hint, this something which for all its slipperiness is after all a doorknob to be grasped by anyone who wishes to enter the "some great" Art-Parlours, ourselves might have constructed a possibly logical development from Preludes and Rhapsody on a Windy Night along J. Alfred and Portrait up the two Sweeneys to let us say The Hippopotamus. We might have been disgracefully inspired to the extent of projecting as arithmetical, not to say dull, a classification of Eliot as that of Picasso by the author of certain rudimentary and not even ecclesiastical nonsense entitled The Caliph's Design. But (it is an enormous but) our so doing necessarily would have proved worthless, precisely for the reason that before an Eliot we become alive or intense as we become intense or alive before a Cézanne or a Lachaise: or since, as always in the case of superficial because vertical analysis, to attempt the boxing and labeling of genius is to involve in something inescapably rectilinear—a formula, for example—not the artist but the "critic."

However, we have a better reason. The last word on caricature was spoken as far back as 1913. "My dear it's all so perfectly ridiculous" remarked to an elderly Boston woman an elderly woman of Boston, as the twain made their noticeably irrevocable exeunt from that most colossal of all circuses, the (then in Boston) International. "My dear if some of the pictures didn't look like something it wouldn't be so amusing" observed, on the threshold, the e.B.w., adding "I should hate to have my portrait painted by any of those 'artists'!" "They'll never make a statue of *me*" stated with polyphiloprogenitive conviction the e.w.o.B.

> "Sway in the wind like a field of ripe corn."

Says Mr. Eliot.

In the case of Poems, to state frankly and briefly what we like may be as good a way as another of exhibiting our numerous "critical" incapacities. We like first, to speak from an altogether personal standpoint, that any and all attempts to lasso Mr. Eliot with the Vorticist emblem have signally failed. That Mr. E. Pound (with whose Caesarlike refusal of the kingly crown we are entirely familiar) may not have coiled the rope whose fatal noose has, over a few unfortunate Britons, excludingly rather than includingly settled, makes little or no difference since the hand which threw the lariat and the bronc' which threw the steers alike belong to him. Be it said of this peppy gentleman that, insofar as he is responsible for possibly one-half of the most alive poetry and probably all of the least intense prose committed, during the last few years, in the American and English language, he merits something beyond the incoherent abuse and inchoate adoration which have become his daily breakfast food—merits in fact the doffing of many kelleys; that insofar as he is one of history's greatest advertisers he is an extraordinarily useful bore, much like a riveter which whatever you may say assets the progress of a skyscraper; whereas that insofar as he is responsible for the overpasting of an at least attractive manifesto, "Ezra Pound," with an at least pedantic war cry, "Vorticism," he deserves to be drawn and quartered by the incomparably trite brush of the great and the only and the Wyndham and the Lewis—if only as an adjectival garnish to that nounlike effigy of our hero by his friend The Hieratic Buster. Let us therefore mention the fact, for it seems to us worthy of notice—that at no moment do T.S. Eliot and E.P. propaganda simultaneously inhabit our consciousness.

Second, we like that not any of Poems' fifty-one pages fails to impress us with an overwhelming sense of technique. By technique we do not mean a great many things, including: anything static, a school, a noun, a slogan, a formula: These Three For Instant Beauty, Ars Est Celare, Hasn't Scratched Yet, Professor Woodbery, Grape Nuts. By technique we do mean one thing: the alert hatred of normality which, through the lips of a tactile and cohesive adventure, asserts that nobody in general and some one in particular is incorrigibly and actually alive. This some one is, it would seem, the extremely great artist: or, he who prefers above everything and within everything the unique dimension of intensity, which it amuses him to substitute in us for the comforting and comfortable furniture of reality. If we examine the means through which this substitution is allowed by Mr. Eliot to happen in his reader, we find that they include: a vocabulary almost brutally tuned to attain distinctness; an extraordinarily tight orchestration of the shapes of sound; the delicate and careful murderings—almost invariably interpreted, internally as well as terminally, through near-rhyme and rhyme—of established tempos by oral rhythms. Here is an example of Eliot's tuning:

> "Apeneck Sweeney spreads his knees
> Letting his arms hang down to laugh,
> The zebra stripes along his jaw
> Swelling to maculate giraffe."

Here is a specimen of his compact orchestration:

> "I have seen them riding seaward on the waves
> Combing the white hair of the waves blown back
> When the wind blows the water white and black.
>
> We have lingered in the chambers of the sea
> By sea-girls wreathed with seaweed red and brown
> Till human voices wake us, and we drown."

Here is Eliot himself directing the exquisitely and thoroughly built thing:

"His laughter was submarine and profound
Like the old man of the sea's
Hidden under coral islands
Where worried bodies of drowned men drift down
  in the green silence,
Dropping from fingers of surf."

To come to our final like, which it must be admitted is also our largest—we like that no however cautiously attempted dissection of Mr. T.S.'s sensitivity begins to touch a few certain lines whereby become big and blundering and totally unskilful our altogether unnecessary fingers:

"The lamp hummed:
'Regard the moon,
La lune ne garde aucune rancune,
She winks a feeble eye,
She smiles into corners.
She smooths the hair of the grass.
The moon has lost her memory.
A washed-out smallpox cracks her face,
Her hand twists a paper rose,"

At the risk of being jeered for an "uncritical" remark we mention that this is one of the few huge fragilities before which comment is disgusting.

From *The Dial*, June 1920.

THE SOUL STORY OF GLADYS VANDERDECKER

Heiress to Tin King's millions finds love in humble surroundings

By the Society Editor of *Vanity Fair*

Editor's Note: So many New York debutantes, and heiresses at large, have of late been marrying their chauffeurs, butlers and other workers in the humbler industrial vineyards (and, what is more, finding the adventure greatly to their liking) that this absorbing story of how an heiress found married happiness with a chauffeur ought to be of interest and help to our more youthful readers. It teaches a wholesome lesson and is commended to them without reserve. The interview is the work of our Society Editor.

Snobbishly speaking, the year 1913 was a series of quite unparalleled social triumphs, among which the *fête champêtre* of the Baroness Zabaglione and the Orage-Delamorde wedding protrude with particular brilliance; but, of all the thrilling spectacles of fashionable frivolity which occurred that year, we believe the debut of Gladys Vanderdecker rankled deepliest in the souls of those unhappy many upon whom no invitation had seen fit to alight.

Possibly never in the annals of New York society did beauty, wealth and prestige conspire among themselves to create so sumptuous, so throbbing, and so perfect an occasion.

The great ballroom of the Ritz literally disappeared in an overwhelming deluge of flora, through which, here and there, the fortunate guests floated like bright bits of spray in a monster wave. Thither and hither—along corridors whose carefully subdued lights yielded a subtle and luxurious almost-darkness, occasionally violated by the crashing radiance of a tiara—glided skilfully the rich and radiant debutantes of 1913.

Nebulae of confetti from time to time descended slowly through the atmosphere, bedewing with a billion trivial and flickering petals the gesturing flesh, the exquisite arms, hinting shoulders and bodies voluptuously yearning to the rhythms of an ever-splashier jazz, which squirted from the simultaneously burbling saxophones of eleven gorgeously apparelled Negroes, each slenderer than an ebony Apollo.

When morning brought an end to these unparalleled festivities, she in whose honour all these splendours had occurred bade her proud parents good night, and wearily betook herself to her canopied couch, there to snatch a brief slumber before facing the arduous social duties of the day. If—as the little figure paused a moment, framed in the doorjamb—there glimmered in the long-lashed eyes a strange sadness, it is certain that no one noticed it. Not even her queenly mother, far less her rubicund father, could have guessed what disillusionments filled the mind of Gladys upon the occasion of her official entry into social life.

And when, a few hours later, the awakened debutante allowed herself to be dressed and motored to the Colony Restaurant for luncheon with the dashing Count Unamuno, no one remarked that a new expression dwelt at the edges of her slim lips. The young nobleman himself may have thought that she was more charming than usual, but he might never guess the secret of this increased attraction. Only we, who are privileged spirits, may look into the very soul of Gladys Vanderdecker, where we shall find strange and most disturbing things.

I say that we are privileged—and I mean it. Did the present writer possess a mere dollar for each time that a reporter, an editor, an owner of a newspaper, vainly climbed the five flights of partially demolished stairs leading to the snug little pair of rooms where Mrs. Bullinski (nee Gladys Vanderdecker), her children and her husband now live, he would be as rich, or richer than father Vanderdecker himself. Since he has not any of those dollars, he must be content with a triumph which, after all, outranks any mere monetary success—and which, albeit due quite as much to good fortune as to sagacity, contributes a new and startling chapter to the history of human ingenuity. I refer to the fact that, where better men than myself have failed, I have succeeded: and by "succeeded" I mean that a great and difficult task undertaken in behalf of the readers of *Vanity Fair* has been definitely accomplished: that now, for the first time, the entire, palpitating, intimate heart-story of Gladys Vanderdecker (now Mrs. Frank Bullinski) is unfolded before the eyes of a breathless public!

How did we accomplish this miracle?

To begin at the beginning—we took precautions. And justly so; for the last story-hunter at the Frank Bullinskis' home had received, from the toe of Mr. Frank Bullinski (Gladys' lovemate) a kick which, according to the testimony of competent witnesses, was of sufficient force to propel the recipient down the five flights of stairs and out of the door into the middle of the street, where he had the misfortune to be run over by a taxicab and instantly killed. We desired no such fate, and accordingly took pains to sound the immediate neighbours of this redoubtable defender of his hearthstone on the topic of the strong man's hobbies. For weeks, months even, no information could be obtained; then one day—subsequent to the bestowing of a five dollar bill upon James Reilly, garbage man, it developed that Gladys' terrible husband had no passions at all, save a possibly singular but nevertheless authentic passion for his wife and little ones. Instantly we began our campaign, constructed for ourselves a slight disguise, and boldly essayed the tumble-down stairs at number 104 Patchin Place, New York.

A knock—and the decayed door opened abruptly.

In the doorway stood a decidedly matronly figure of massive proportions, more or less completely attired in batik pyjamas. The figure surveyed us with frank distrust. "Who instructed you to come here?" she asked severely. We replied that we sought an interview.

As we had suspected, the once Gladys Vanderdecker possessed, for all her gilded upbringing, a simple heart. "I'm sorry," she murmured, with downcast eyes, "but my husband is unfortunately absent. Were it otherwise, I am certain that he would thank you for calling on us."—At which very moment a terrible voice, larger and deeper than a cannon-shot, pronounced from below-stairs the horrifying monosyllable "WOT?" and the tramp of enormous feet was distinctly heard ascending the quaking stairs. Our heart sank.

"Oh, there he is," the pyjama-clad lady emitted gaily.

The next we knew, a hand whose grip resembled that of Dempsey himself, had seized, by the collar, ourselves and was dangling them in mid-air. Realizing, at this awful moment, the utter futility of resistance, we relaxed, and closing our eyes, began to recite our favourite passage from Ward McAllister's "Society as I Have Found It."

"WOTZ DISS?" the cannon-like voice thundered, directly behind us.

"A poor workman who admires you, Frank, and seeks an interview," Mrs. Bullinski stated, simultaneously answering her husband's question and explaining the presence of ourselves.

Mr. Bullinski opened his hand, and we fell in a heap at the feet of his spouse. "Is dat so?" he growled hugely. He stooped, and as he did so, we saw him for the first time: a truly picturesque figure, made entirely of muscle, dressed in a waiter's false shirt front, Paris garters, and B. V. D.'s, his feet (which, under the circumstances, we particularly noticed) being ensconced in a pair of colossal wooden sabots, and his smallish head adorned with a collapsible opera hat.

This was our moment—we rose and bowed. "Mrs. Bullinski," we said, in perfect English, "to interview your husband and yourself were all too great a pleasure."

As, rising, we turned, Mr. Bullinski came forward gently, almost timidly, and without a word extended his enormous hand, which, with all our strength, we managed to shake slightly. His wife followed, weeping with happiness, and throwing her pyjamed self upon our rags and tatters, kissed us effusively in any number of places. "So you're not an insurance agent, after all, you clever thing!" she sobbed.

Covered with caresses, we allowed ourselves to be placed in the seat of honour, an aged rocker, from which point of vantage ourselves were surveying an interior remarkably dirty, as well as incredibly cluttered with semi-artistic junk (not excepting a mammoth reproduction of Washington Crossing the Delaware) when we noticed—no—impossible—our heart stopped beating for an instant—in one corner, upon a little table, which stood all by itself and which bore no other burden, a copy of the refined periodical for which we had undertaken this very interview.

Absoutely unable to accredit our eyes, we stared and stared.

"Duh wif's favourite readin'," Mr. Bullinski volunteered affably.

His helpmeet nodded, smiling through her tears. "Frank likes the pictures," she added whimsically.

Choking down an involuntary sob, we turned to the former heiress of the Vanderdecker millions. "Madame," we stated, "the public has long worshipped you and I ardently desire to furnish the intelligentsia of five nations and seven seas with the burning story of your romantic marriage: and now, after profound meditation on the part of my editor, he has irrevocably decided to send to your door a gifted author whose loftiest mission is to record your every word and gesture for the benefit of a spellbound public which is panting with expectancy." We bowed, to indicate that the messenger was ourselves.

"Youse?" was the potent monosyllable which leaked from Mr. Bullinski's ample vocal orifice.

Turning to him, we again bowed.

"If Frank doesn't mind," Mrs. Bullinski murmured, radiantly.

"Go to it, goylie," the husband counselled heartily.

We produced a notebook and a fountain pen. Mr. Bullinski, stretching considerably less than all of himself upon a mutilated bed near the door, fell immediately into a resounding slumber. The once Gladys Vanderdecker tiptoed to a cupboard, extracted therefrom a sheet of flypaper, moved noiselessly to her husband's side, laid the flypaper, sticky side up, over his gigantic face, and returned to us. Seeing no other, we offered our chair, which she refused in a whisper, at the same time gracefully sitting down on the floor with her back against the wall. Then, with half-shut eyes, she spoke: softly, musically, reminiscently . . .

"As you probably know, I was brought up to be a social butterfly, fluttering my tiny wings for a single day, without thought of the morrow." Ok-k-k-k (this from the supine and dormant Mr. Bullinski: fortissimo). "My coming out ball at the Ritz Hotel was the gossip of everyone, everywhere, for months. Even a whole year after it had occurred, it was still talked about here and there. We—papa and all of us—had a darling house at Aiken, a horrid big one at Newport, a really comfy one near the Piping Rock Club (you know the kind I mean—seventy-two rooms), besides daddy's home in New York which Stanford White had once designed. But you really should have seen our *hôtel* in Paris, it was the smartest thing: do you know, I simply adore Paris. Of course we used to go abroad every year and it was such fun. Rome, and London, and everything. Well, daddy simply kept on making money: I never saw anything so perfectly stupid. He tried and tried, but he just couldn't stop making money. It had become a habit or something, I guess. Anyway, we had our box at the opera, you know, and awful dinners at home with ever so many people, and of course millions of luncheons, and bridge parties and all that kind of thing. You can't imagine how boring it all was. And never being able to take a step without having a chauffeur wave you into a motor, and being dressed and undressed like a doll, and everything—my dear, it was really terrible. I can't begin to tell you how I hated it all.

"Well, I knew I should go mad, or something, unless something happened. And something did. We were forbidden to read vulgar magazines, but I bribed Cholmondley—that was daddy's first chauffeur—to bring me a copy of the Illustrated News. My dear, I lay in bed all day reading it: I can't tell you how thrilled I was by all those wonderful murders and poisonings and everything. I decided really to live. It was awfully exciting. I jumped out of bed and dressed in my oldest clothes. I packed a bag and told Mortimer—my own chauffeur—to drive me to the Grand Central Station, and he was too scared to refuse.

"At the station I hopped out and ran in and took a subway. Meantime I'd decided to become a working girl, desert my family and forgo the rigmarole of society. I got out somewhere and walked a long distance and found myself at the river front. I walked into the queerest looking house and hired a furnished room for a month. Then I felt hungry. So I went out and wandered along till I came to an Automat restaurant, and as I walked in through the door, I saw . . . sitting there" . . . the speaker's voice trailed off, her eyes drooped: a lovely flush gradually suffused her brow, her cheeks, her neck—then, in a slightly trembling tone, she resumed: "him . . ."

Something, instinct perhaps, told us that by "him" Gladys Vanderdecker Bullinski referred to the sonorous figure on the bed, whose vocal detonations were, by this time, shaking the whole house to its none-too-secure foundations. A furtive glance—deliciously shy—which she directed toward the flypaper-covered face, confirmed our suspicions. We leaned forward, putting our hand to our ear, resolved not to miss a syllable of what should follow.

"He beckoned me to a . . . seat beside him in the Automat," the former pampered pet of society blushfully continued. "He was eating ham and spinach. He caught my eye and recommended to me the ragout of which he had just consumed two portions. There was something . . . I mean . . ."—she paused, deeply, entirely, moved. We felt our own throat strangling with a strange and overwhelming emotion: it was as if, through some lucky accident, the gates of a great and enthralling romance had swung wide, permitting our dazzled eyes to feast upon the intrinsic flames of virginal passion.

"And then . . . that night . . . he took me to a . . . burlesque show," she murmured. "It was on Fourteenth Street. The play was called . . . The Kissing Kuties, and was enacted by the Girls de Looks. Between the act he—proposed."

A perfect thunder surged from the bed. "Yes?" we interrogated breathlessly, at the top of our voice.

"Of course I—accepted him. It turned out that he was a chauffeur. He drove a motor truck for the Berelzheimer Brewery with headquarters in St. Louis. Well, we were married at City Hall, by a nice old man. Then we walked up to Fifth Avenue, because I'd insisted on having a bus ride for a honeymoon. At Washington Square we were just getting on a beautiful big bus, when father and a lot of detectives jumped out of father's Rolls Royce and made for Frank. My dear, I was never so thrilled. Frank simply murdered father: he took him by the throat and father's eyes stood out *inches,* like balloons or something, because of course he couldn't breathe. Then Frank hit father twice between the eyes, but father is very strong. He got away and gave Frank a nasty kick in the shins. At the same time, one of the detectives jumped on Frank and bit him in the ear. Two others were between his legs, trying to trip him up, but they couldn't. Frank was wonderful. He then hit father so hard that father went through a plate glass window right into the lap of a saleslady in Schwartz's toy shop, carrying all sorts of toys along with him. You can't imagine how funny father looked, with tin battleships all over him, and tiny steam engines, and automobiles, and dolls, and canaries, and everything!"

Mrs. Bullinski paused and, throwing back her head, laughed melodiously. Then a sudden kindliness crept into the hazel eyes; around the mouth, lines of pity formed themselves: "I was almost sorry for father," she murmured.

"Then what happened?" we shouted, above the din of her sleeping hero.

"Why, we left them there," she answered: "father in Schwartz's, being taken care of by a lot of people because he was pretty well shaken up, and the four detectives lying on the sidewalk, gagged with their own caps, and tied, hand and foot to one another, with shoelaces which Frank had bought from an old blind man who came along just then. Frank signalled to a taxi, and we got into it all right, but a policeman asked Frank, through the window, who he was, and of course that made Frank terribly angry because he thought the policeman was trying to insult him. So he asked me for my umbrella, and of course I gave it to him, and Frank poked it into the policeman's mouth which happened to be open, and we drove away. Since that day, I've never once stopped being awfully proud of my husband," the pyjamad narratrix, casting in the direction of the bed a glance of prettily mingled enthusiasm and adoration, concluded softly.

"May I ask . . . the public always wants to know . . . if there are any little ones?" I hazarded timidly.

As the innocuous epithet "little ones" left my lips, a titanic snore (by comparison with which all previous specimens were as whispers) issued from the nose of Mr. Bullinski—followed by a complete silence: then—as, somewhat alarmed, I turned—"ARE der!" boomed a gigantic voice: the sleeper had awakened.—"ARE der!" the mammoth larynx repeated as, rising to its full height, the colossal equivalent of several average human beings cautiously removed from its microscopic head the collapsible opera hat which, until that moment, that head had unflinchingly worn—"ARE der!" it reiterated, with one vast paw extracting from his pocket a huge key . . . "I'll say der are!"—and, while Washington Crossing the Delaware shuddered with the vibration of the final Are der; while the china rattled, while a light novel—dislodged from a bookcase—fell to the floor with a heavy thud, Mr. Bullinski—reaching at one stride the wall opposite ourselves—inserted, in that portion of it which constituted a hitherto unnoticed means of egress or ingress, the key: then, as ourselves stared, trembling hysterically, not knowing what to expect from so extraordinary a procedure, a door flew inward—and our eyes beheld a vision of such extreme loveliness as would baffle description by the most inspired pen which ever touched paper: a spectacle at once so gripping and so peaceful that the least tribute to its unbelievable beauty were no better than a profanation.

For the benefit of our subscribers, we have investigated the entire vocabulary of the English language with the idea of finding one phrase, one group of words, one idiom which should express, perfectly and for all time, the precise aroma of that unforgettable instant when the wall unexpectedly opened; and revealed the transcendent contents of that inner room of the Bullinski household. Our search for words seemed futile, hopeless.

But mysterious are the ways of fate! After some months' intensive study, while we were lying in the endopsychic ward of a prominent local hospital, suffering from a combination of shingles and acute anemia, we were overtaken by a delirium in the course of which we confided our most cherished aims to O-la-la, the Chinese night nurse at the hospital, who immediately quoted what—even in our somewhat exceptional mental state—we recognized as a justly celebrated passage from the Calendar of Happy Hours by Tsa-Tsi, the Chinese poet and philosopher (4th Century, B.C.). With a cry of sheer pleasure, we sprang from the bed, and, fleeing through the backdoor, reached the street, where, attired only in a paper napkin, we hailed a taxi. Three minutes later, we were seated before an astonished stenographer in the offices of *Vanity*

Fair, dictating from memory the elegant, but at the same time literal, translation of the Chinese epic by Mrs. Gertrude Waters, which runs:

> "In ruined nest robins build never.
> Flower without smell, marriage without children."

The appropriateness of this selection becomes apparent only when the reader understands a supremely important fact, i. e. that, coincident with the throwing open of the secret door by Mr. Bullinski, our astonished eyes beheld—side by side in a single soapbox—no less than five offspring, all males and all in a state of Nature and graduated as to diminutiveness.

"Jackie, Jamie, Johnny, Jimmie, and my youngest, Joey," crooned their mother, in quiet ecstasy.

The father fell upon his enormous knees playfully, and began poking and punching the infants one by one in a delightfully affectionate way. A perfect chorus of ahgoos and dah-dahs greeted his efforts.

Something told us that we were not needed here. We paused an instant, contemplating the entire beauty of the scene; then, with tears in our eyes and joy in our heart, tiptoed out. We went slowly down the five flights, and into the sunny street—happy in the happiness of Gladys Vanderdecker and her stalwart hero-husband; proud in the conviction that, so long as true love marriages between the rich and the noble, the smart and the good, continue in this country, and as long as institutions like the Bullinski home persist, the destiny of America and of the human race is more than secure.

From *Vanity Fair,* December 1924.

VANITY FAIR'S PRIZE MOVIE SCENARIO

Contest closes triumphantly with winning manuscript—"A Pair of Jacks"

by C. E. Niltse, A Master of Screen Continuity

Editor's Note: *Vanity Fair*'s Scenario Editors are broken reeds. For days, weeks, months, they have been swamped by a stream of manuscripts, all competing for the magnificent cash prize (running into several dollars) which, as we announced in a recent issue, would be awarded to the author of the moving picture considered, by our judges, the scenario best qualified to carry on the popular traditions of Art on the Silver Screen. Manuscripts have poured in from every corner of the world; from rich and poor, from hemstitchers and importers of isinglass; from the busy marts of finance and even from Milady's boudoir. Everyone, it seems, is writing for the movies!

For the selection of the prize winning manuscript, we appointed a committee of judges comprising some of the most glittering and glamorous names in the country, including Stronghart (the movie star), Dr. Traprock, the Russian Lilliputians and heaps and heaps of others. Accommodations were secured for them at Atlantic City's most luxurious hostelries, where they repaired for the period of perusal, brows in hand. Since that day, the wires have been humming with an account of what they have jokingly called their "doings." It is estimated that two of them, in one week, rode farther, and faster, in roller chairs than any other visitors to America's playground in the past twenty years; while another—an eminent litterateur who modestly requests that his name be withheld—won a large pewter cup on his first night in Atlantic City for dancing the Charleston at Evelyn Nesbit's "Silver Slipper" cabaret.

Now, however, their work is done, and *Vanity Fair* is happy to announce the winner of its epochal Scenario Contest, Mr. C. E. Niltse, whose manuscript, "A Pair of Jacks," received (practically) the unanimous vote of the judges in the contest. "A Pair of Jacks" is perhaps the most perfect example of the "popular" type of movie, such as may be found at almost any theatre in your own town. It carries to a fine point the sentiment, passion and human interest which are such important factors in our current cinema productions.

It may be interesting to our readers to learn a little something about Mr. Niltse himself. He is, it seems, a hot embosser by profession, residing in Scranton, Pa., where, fortunately for American letters, the demand for hot embossing is for the moment practically nil. Mr. Niltse thus finds more and more time to devote to literature—his first love. We take great pride and pleasure in presenting this perfect scenario of his for the first, and last, time.

A PAIR OF JACKS

FADE IN TITLE: *In the sleepy province of Zinacantepec, Northern China, not far from the picturesque valley of the Tlaxcala, and near the Apetatian Mountains, lounges the drowsy village of Xochilhuehuetlan.*

SCENE 1. Exterior Coutryside. FADE IN, on a LONG SHOT of a lovely African landscape, the foothills hazy in the background, and a one-horned Indian rhinoceros nursing its young in the foreground.

TITLE: *Mother love is mother love, no matter where it occurs.*

SCENE 2. Exterior Town. A FULL SHOT of the otzolote pee, or mayor, of Xochilhuehuetlan. He is a young woman, with a centripetal red beard. He is between ninety-eight and ninety-nine years old, a type of the typical centrifugal hermaphrodite of the country. His face is large and small, he has the muscular fragility of a sixteen year old baby; there is about him the inherent inebriety of a recently cauterized factotum. He is deep, but also he is round—the mendacity and the propinquity of the Celt lie side by side in his down-right Iberian make-up. He is sucking a snake bite in his ear, and waiting for death.

TITLE: *Tamanlipas Guerrero, whose fingers are five in number, was not afraid to die.*

Back for a glimpse of the official as he sucks his snake bite. There is a flicker of scorn for the snake's treachery on his face.

SCENE 3. Exterior Deck. FADE IN on a SEMICLOSEUP of a young girl. She is a mature, manly Negress, with a jade nose-ring, protruding lips, and a wooden leg, dressed in a middy blouse and hip rubberboots over which is thrown carelessly a pair of silk stockings. She is standing wildly by a ventilator and gazing throbbingly over the entire ship, on which everyone else is seasick, as vast breakers dash fiercely from time to time over the entire ship, and as a baby rolls at intervals into the scuppers she stoops and gives the little one a kiss.

TITLE: *In the meantime, Elizabeth Bilge, the girl who held Jack Waters' esteem, is peacefully cruising homeward.*

SCENE 4. Interior Home. IRIS IN on a New England Homestead, in the foreground Granny is knitting as a mischievous kitten is playing with the yarn, while Mother reads aloud to father, Kitty and Tom, who are both obviously overinterested in each other. In the background, a glimpse of snowcovered Mount Chocorua, named after an old Indian chief and 3,540 feet above sea level.

TITLE: *But the spirit of the hour and the old traditions are not the same like they was once when Mother was a girl.*

SCENE 5. MEDIUM SHOT of a perfectly terrible storm at sea. Even the captain does not know what to do. It is terrible. They will all be drowned. Terrible waves are dashing over the poor ship which is sometimes underneath the top of the water, smashing all the lifeboats. With a terrible crash the unhappy ship strikes a submerged cliff.

TITLE: *Jack Clinton, gentleman garter salesman, had a way with him, and with the ladies.*

SCENE 6. Interior Cabin. CLOSEUP of Jack. The water is pouring in, but he is awake in his pyjamas. The ill-starred ship is sinking. He unwinds the alarm clock with a smile. The bed with everything on it collapses without warning, as, without meaning to, he picks up a telephone. CUT TO

SCENE 7. The Bottom of the Sea, 9:55 A.M. Interior Cabin. Exterior Town. A shot of a submarine cable winding and unwinding along the valleys of the mountainous sea bottom. Simultaneously each side of this shot recedes toward the middle, discovering, on the left, Jack at his telephone, on the right, Tamanlipas at his telephone, until the cable disappears wholly and Jack and Tamanlipas confront each other in one scene. Dissolve out the telephone. From this point on the two men play their scene as if back to back against a neutral foreground.

SCENE 8. Interior Cabin. Water pours in deluging Jack who, smiling, hangs up the phone. As he does so—

SCENE 9. The Bottom of the Sea, 9:56 A.M. Interior Cabin. Exterior Town. The scene breaks in the middle, going back on each side, cutting off the shots of Jack and Tamanlipas, discovering the submarine cable along the bottom of the sea once more.

SCENE 10. Exterior Town. Tamanlipas Guerrero, nursing his snake bite, puts down the telephone to die.

TITLE: *And the sun's last rays reflected the passing of a good Indian.*

SCENE 11. Exterior Deck. Shot of Jack Clinton with Elizabeth Bilge in his arms lowering himself from the rail to the open sea on a pair of Boston garters which he has tied to the rail with his free hand as waves pour all over the entire ship and everyone is very sick.

SCENE 12. Exterior Home. MEDIUM SHOT of Grandma standing gracefully on a piano stool in the middle of the front yard. Above her head is the limb of an apple tree in full bloom. About six inches from the old lady's nose is a nest into which she is looking, as the excited mother bird beats her wings frantically.

SPOKEN TITLE: *"Don't worry, birdie, Granny won't hurt your babies!"*

SCENE 13. The Middle of the Ocean. IRIS IN on Jack Waters

standing in his twelve-cylinder Ford sedan, as he spies the scene at one glance of the naked eye. He is a clean-cut, well-dressed, happy-go-lucky will-o'-the-wisp with a bad record at Yale to the credit of his twenty-three years as a rich man's pampered and only son, holding under one muscular arm a tennis racquet. There is something about him which courts dangers of every sort. He laughs and says:

SPOKEN TITLE: *"Give me the binoculars, Captain, it looks like a cane rush!"*

SCENE 14. Interior Heaven. LONG SHOT of the gates of Heaven: God, angels, cherubim, seraphim, etc. The soul of Tamanlipas Guerrero is walking toward a little house. It is dressed in a crêpe-de-Chine nightie, a straw hat with a fraternity band, and is smoking a pipe. God turns to Michael for information about the unknown visitor. Michael says it is a good Indian.
God speaks:

SPOKEN TITLE: *"Bid him welcome, then, in the name of all that is good."*

SCENE 15. Exterior Deck. Jack Clinton's eyes flash black lightning as, with an oath, he falls into the sea with Elizabeth Bilge in his arms as the garters break, and is drowned.

TITLE: *But for once in his life, the clever salesman of a next-to-indispensable commodity found his match in a watery grave.*

SCENE 16. Interior Nest. CLOSEUP of five eggs as one of them begins to hatch.

TITLE: *"Peep, peep."*

Back for a look at Granny's wrinkled smiling face as it regards the hatching progeny. Over the tired eyes comes an expression of broad laughter.

SCENE 17. The Middle of the Ocean. FADE IN on a CLOSEUP of Captain Black of the Ford Sedan, as he hands Jack Waters the binoculars. He is rugged, rough, robust, uncouth, short-spoken, good-hearted, horny-handed, two-fisted, ten-toed specimen of master mariner with a father complex.

SPOKEN TITLE: *"Here they be, God bless you, Mister Jack!"*

SCENE 18. Exterior Deck. MEDIUM SHOT of Elizabeth Bilge who struggles with the waves, supported by her wooden leg. About to go down for the first time, she shouts:

SPOKEN TITLE: *"Save me!"*

SCENE 19. Interior Heaven. CLOSEUP of the soul of Tamanlipas Guerrero. Its eyes are fixed on the little house, at a point just over the door, where there is a sign in large letters: Caballeros. Tamanlipas Guerrero's soul does not read or write. What a terrible predicament! Just then along comes Michael. The soul hails him and asks him something. Michael nods and smiles. The soul starts to hurry off in the direction of the house, when Michael lays a detaining hand on its arm, saying:

SPOKEN TITLE: *"I am instructed to bid you welcome, spirit. You are now in Heaven."*

SCENE 20. The Middle of the Ocean. LONG SHOT of Jack Waters looking through the binoculars. As he sees something, the glasses fall from his nerveless hands. At the same moment he falls himself but is caught by Captain Black, who works over him for some time with a stomach pump, until the young man's eyes open. Gazing indistinctly at the Captain, the youth of whom Elizabeth Bilge held the esteem murmurs:

SPOKEN TITLE: *"Full speed ahead!"*

SCENE 21. Exterior Home. MEDIUM SHOT of Granny as she gracefully descends from the piano stool. (Hold long enough for human interest.) Shutting her umbrella she enters the house, whereupon it stops raining and the sun comes out.

SCENE 22. Cross section of the Ocean. CLOSEUP of the descending binoculars, which have fallen overboard, as they start toward the bottom of the sea. Some local colour: a frightened fish or two, for instance.

(Note: if we could rent an octopus, or something, it would be good here.)

TITLE: *Meanwhile, giving free rein to their intrinsic curiosity, a pair of lenses spontaneously traverse the dim domain of Neptune.*

SCENE 23. Interior Heaven. LONG SHOT of the soul of Tamanlipas Guerrero, as it exits from the little house registering blissful contentment. It says to Michael, touchingly:

SPOKEN TITLE: *"Heaven is right."*

SCENE 24. IRIS IN on a YIDDISH PICNIC IN THE CATSKILLS. About a fire of driftwood made by girl scouts are seated thousands and thousands of Hebrew maidens, their faces are chewing gum and smileless. A slight dark slip of a feminine thing in the foreground investigates a recently-opened can of sardines.

TITLE: *Lizzie Finklestein, who plays the violin beautifully.*

SCENE 25. The Bottom of the Sea. MEDIUM SHOT of binoculars as they come to rest on the volcano-strewn sea bottom. (Perhaps a whale passes, pursued by another whale, or almost anything to give local colour.)

SCENE 26. Interior Home. The old mother falls down a flight of stairs and breaks both her legs simultaneously as Jack Waters, torn between his devotion to his parent and his love for Elizabeth Bilge, does not hesitate a moment, then turns the rudder of the Ford sedan backward and is soon carrying the delighted old lady in his aeroplane to Captain Black's half-brother's expensive sanatorium, while Lizzie Finklestein plays her instrument so lovely, until all the picknickers fall one by one asleep, then gets into a breeches buoy and in that terrible predicament rescues Jack Clinton who was not drowned as we all thought, but at this moment a birth certificate is discovered proving that the ghost of Tamanlipas Guerrero is a fourth cousin to Dr. Marie Stopen, whereupon a lawn party is given for no reason whatever by Mrs. Harry Payne Whitney and everyone dances to general hilarity, as

SCENE 27. Exterior Moon Night. CLOSEUP of a cloud. It nears the moon. It passes over the moon. The moon disppears. The cloud moves on. The moon reappears. A tree appears in front of the moon. A nest appears upon a limb. In the nest are five eggs. Thunder and lightning. All hatch suddenly.

TITLE: *"Poems are made by fools like me, only God can make a tree."*

VERY SLOW FADE-OUT

From *Vanity Fair,* January 1925.

WHAT OUR LOVING SUBSCRIBERS SAY

A few diverting epistles, published only with our most profound apologies

No sooner had *Vanity Fair*—as usual, in a spirit of pure bravado—invited its subscribers to express their unfettered opinions of the magazine, than a cloudburst of letters, telegrams, cables, and post cards descended upon our heads. Stunned by the impact, we take pleasure in publishing a handful of these responses.

> *Cupples, Missouri*
>
> *I have read your challenge to express a frank view regardless of all costs and would beg to say that next to the Gettysburg address W. Shakespeare and Dr. Frank Crane I think Vanity Fair is in every way a better kind of magazine.*
>
> *I always read it to my pupils (both boys and girls) between the ages of 6 and 19 who find it extra stimulating.*
>
> *The pictures, too, are pleasing.*
>
> *Cordially yours,*
>
> CORNELIA F. ZERG

Girlish enthusiasm is always welcome, especially when wafted to us from far off.

Zeus, Virginia

What simply marvelous pictures in Vanity Fair! ! ! ! (sic) My heart it just stops beating when I see some of them. That deliciously vague one in your next to the last number of the danseuse with the boyish figure in the distant foreground holding something wonderfully indefinite was perfectly adorable. I want more—more—more—

SAPHO SMITH

A ringing greeting:

Tangerine, Orange, California

Just a single month without your magazine were worse to bear than a whole year without Christmas. How I know not but you always manage to reflect the very internal essence—sparkling, vivacious, electric—of the hour. My husband, with whom I lived for some time, we were separated in 1906, always particularly enjoyed The Well Dressed Man and, as for me, my motto has been and will ever remain in spite of all: Carpe Diem! Keep up your wonderful work!

Faithfully,

(MRS.) ELIZABETH B. ATKINS

In happy contrast to the preceding, a perfectly soul-mated spouse speaks to us from

Cream, Minnesota

I think your stage department most illuminating. The Dolly Sisters I love. Never having seen them, which is which? Also Heywood Broun. Who runs the Hall of Fame? I dote on it. My husband is a candidate for alderman and he is sure he will be elected. He is thirty-eight, tall, strong, handsome, and worked hard all of his life like anyone else. He is terrible popular with the people. Speaks languages, etc. I enclose a photo which does not come near to doing Jim justice.

MRS. BUCHEWETSKI

A brief apology for the absence (necessitated by exigencies of space) of Mr. B's lineaments, and we turn our expecting countenances toward the banks of the tranquil Charles, whence emanates this quaintly cultured expression of scholarly opinion—proving that Fair Harvard is alive to the needs of the hour:

Cambridge, Massachusetts

I am a professor, well advanced in years, and, as is, under the circumstances, not unnatural, completely, so far as is humanly possible, absorbed in the inexhaustible possibilities of my endearing subject (Cryptogamic Botany).

Some time ago, the Cambridge police proceeded to enforce an absurd ordinance prohibiting the riding of bicycles on the sidewalks and I was on several occasions arrested. During the war, my son Richard did very well, as we are told, in the army or navy, I forget which. He as well as my wife and I, believe that the menace of the Ku Klux Klan should awaken a throbbing response in the heart of every true American, be he man, woman, or child.

Faithfully yours,

N. G. BAXTER

P.S. My wife, whose knowledge of such matters is irrefutable, informs me that your valued periodical has been on our parlour table for a number of years, and I look forward to perusing it in the near future.

A lady dentist says:

Quidnick, Rhode Island
To the Editor of Vanity Fair
Dear Sir, or Madam,

as a bibliophile of standing I naturally resent your unnecessary illusions to authors of undying reputation which, from time to time, you permit a superficial mind to incur. Life is not a mere flicker of the butterfly's wing, as you seem to think. It is (as the hymn says) Earnest: then why slight the more sober and enlightening aspects of humanity at large? Despite all your limitations you do well to feature Douglas Fairbanks and Mary Pickford each month. I would also criticize (since you demand a candid judgment) the preference for a scantily, over the normally, clad Human Form Divine, symptom of the neurotic industrialism which has run rampant amongst our era. What the Creator designed is, truly, too beautiful to be lightly dealt with. Witness the Venus de Milo, etc. (The Greeks knew this better than we.) I merely suggest, in the hopes that you will take seriously what I have felt called upon to say.

(DR.) GERTRUDE L. CONLY

Refreshing:

Big Lump, Texas
Go 2 it!

WILLIE MERANGUE, Y BAR O RANCH

P.S. the fellows out at Chew, Bobo, and Big Paint, all say the same.

With which brilliant specimen of vers libre should be immediately compared a prose poem, the voluptuous simplification of whose spelling and the luxurious paucity of whose syntax (not to mention the small eye) would indicate that E. E. Cummings, the modernist poet and orthographer, is writing to us, under an olfactory pseudonym, from the scented quietude of

Sugar, Idaho
i will not be apt too like yr pichurs butt the articels is grate ps my aunt rote this as i do not rede neither right inglich ownly frensh
very truely,
JACQUE ROQUEFORT

And while we are on the subject of modern art—the inobvious obscurity of the following synthetic ecstasy makes Ulysses, by James Joyce, seem nearly intelligible:

Oxketzcab (sic) Yucatan
dear sir:
never possible to enjoy more of pure spectacle high life wine with real bouquet of New World you are read hear in english school by Lovingly,
PEDRO MANYANA

Written in lead pencil on birch-bark:

Ishawoo via Cody, Wyoming
dear gents
i was only once in n. y. with the 101 ranch wild West and no what i am saying. That was enuf! out here the flyz is fierce & I don't hardly reckon the boys could stick it out without Vanity Fair. Wel, a 1000 pardons for this intrueshun. bye bye
JO SMITH

Here let us pause a moment. So far, we have inspected responses whose principal interest unquestionably lies in certain formal peculiarities: a second class now claims our attention—viz., communications from subscribers to *Vanity Fair* who are also world-renowned names. It is indeed a tragedy that spatial limitations (before referred to) inhibit the reproducing of more than a trio of these Gracious Missives From Great Minds—but let us, instead of reviling the unavoidable, get down to business and decide which masterpiece shall have the honour of appearing on this page. It may as well be this brief but stirring tribute. Translated from the German by Kenneth Burke.

> *Gentlemen—*
>
> *The manifold activity of the second dream system, tentatively sending forth and retracting energy, must on the one hand have full command over all memory material, but on the other hand it would be a superfluous expenditure for it to send the individual mental paths large quantities of energy which would flow off to no purpose, diminishing the quantity available for the ululation of the sex cells.*
>
> SIGMUND FREUD, L.L.D.

Other more or less celebrated personages, who responded with enthusiasm to our invitation are: Lloyd George, Edna St. Vincent Millay, H. R. H. The Queen of the Belgians, Zip (the What-is-it?), Ma Ferguson, Paul Painlevé, Paul Manship, Paul Rosenfeld, Paul Morand, The Grand Duchess Cyril, Al Jolson, Einstein, Trotsky, Governor Charles W. Bryan, Jack Dempsey, Charles Chaplin, Dorothy Dix, Tristan Tzara, King Haakon of Norway, Barbara La Marr, Henry Ford, Cholly Knickerbocker, General Ludendorff, Lita Gray, Aunt Prudence Heckleberry, William Wrigley, Thelma Morgan Converse, Ezra Pound, The Answer Man, Paavo Nurmi, Texas Guinan, Ring Lardner, C. Bascom Slemp, Lionel Strongfort,

Elizabeth Arden, the Four Marxes, Frank Crane, Gilda Gray, Edsel Ford, Mathilde McCormick Oser, Paul Swan, Joe Leblang, and everyone who has ever contributed, in any way, shape or manner, to *Vanity Fair,* including a tousle-headed mite of a sub-errand boy inappropriately entitled Albert Rose.

From *Vanity Fair,* February 1925. The author's only anonymous appearance.

AN EX-MULTIMILLIONAIRE'S RULES FOR SUCCESS IN LIFE

How a modern Midas sank, by his own efforts, to the lowest rung of the social ladder

By C. E. Niltse, Success Editor of *Vanity Fair*

One evening, ten years ago, while along the Bowery haggard-faced men were wandering by thousands toward their twenty-five cent beds, a high powered Rolls Royce slithered noiselessly from its glittering garage and tiptoed softly to the portals of a mansion situated in New York's ultrafashionable residential district. As the machine stopped, a gorgeously liveried footman leaned toward a similarly attired chauffeur: "What's on for tonight, Gaston?" he whispered. "Eat ease hease birt'-day," Gaston, the chauffeur, replied.

Scarcely had the words been pronounced when a lacquey in cloth-of-gold threw open the immense doors, from which an immaculately (albeit unostentatiously) apparelled individual gracefully emerged to view—descending with the elastic tread of youth a flight of marble steps; entered his perfectly appointed limousine—and, with a sheerest sigh of ennui, fled smoothly toward an exclusive haunt of pleasure.

That youth in that limousine was one of the outstanding social figures of the America of ten years ago: everywhere people on the street stopped to stare at him, very little children knew him by sight and greeted his appearance with an admiring "dah-dah," his life and wealth were on the front page of a thousand newspapers, wherever he moved men and women made way in awe, and a million voices whispered simultaneously, "It's Bugg!"

Small wonder!

In addition to a hundred million dollars which his dying father, Herman Bugg (internationally loved as the white vaseline king) had bequeathed to Charles, his only child, outright at the latter's birth, baby Bugg inherited from his mother (Emily Bugg, nee House)'s grandmother a series of railroads and steamship lines too numerous to mention, plus a controlling share in half a dozen of the largest corporations in the world, three of which his maternal uncle, the far-famed financier William Knutt House, had created in the late fifties for his own private emolument. Born into such truly unheard of luxury, it goes without saying that nothing was denied little Charles, until, at twenty-one, we see him perhaps the most brilliant figure in New York's most exclusive social set—a demigod: frank, charming, endowed with that natural and carefree buoyancy which only wealth and culture can bring, lapped in splendor and riches, encircled by influential friends, adored by beautiful women—the perfect apotheosis of gilded youth.

To ask of the ordinary person, who has suffered and struggled in terms of crude everyday reality, that she or he form a definite mental picture of the life of twenty-one year old Charles would be worse than ridiculous. And yet, a fleeting sensation of what it must feel like to be born and to grow up a Bugg, comes over all of us occasionally. I myself enjoyed such a feeling only the other afternoon, while more than doubtfully standing before one of those decayed, dismal, dilapidated, decrepit, ultra-squalid edifices known—by some bitter irony—as "hotels," with whose miserable exteriors and unhygienic interiors the word "Bowery" is inevitably associated. Again and again I had assured myself that this was the right address, a thousand times I had started to enter the reeling doorway, from which a rickety flight of stairs lifted itself . . . each time, the vision of a groomed youth gracefully descending a flight of marble steps had paralysed my every motion. Panting, awe-struck, I whispered: "It *cannot* be!"

A voice, spontaneous and shaggy, growled at my elbow: "Wot's de chances uv gettin' uh cup uv coffee?"

I turned abruptly—to find myself surrounded by "bums" of various kinds, but unanimous in considering my lack of uncouthness as a personal affront. Hastily choosing the lesser of two evils, I fled through the doorway and up the stairs, at the top of which I encountered a large, untidy, ill-smelling room filled with such a motley collection of vagrants, ragamuffins and down-and-outers as baffles all description. "Out of the frying pan into the fire!" flashed through my disordered mind; but since there was nothing for it now but to go through with the business, I made straight for the nearest group of loafers and, buttonholing what looked to be a peculiarly unpromising specimen of depravity, asked politely but firmly: "Can you tell me where I can find a Mr. Bugg?"

The person addressed—a true "hobo" if ever one existed, his costume being a threadbare stiff-bosomed shirt, plus one violet polka-dot suspender, plus unbelievably ancient misfit, ninety-ish pantaloons—regarded me with a look of infantile astonishment, which contrasted agreeably with the expression assumed by his associates' faces, viz. a solemnity suggestive of hibernating woodchucks.

"Charles A. Bugg," I expanded boldly.

My vis-à-vis reacted to the once compelling and still sumptuous cognomen by making a circular gesture in his ear. Thinking that this might be a purely personal method of indicating deafness, I proceeded more loudly: "I am the Success Editor of *Vanity Fair*," I explained in a shout. "The magazine wants me to interview Mr. Bugg. Do you know where I can find him?"

The unwashed visage of my silent interlocutor registered something like anguish as he murmured: "Come with me." Considerably puzzled, I followed him into a little alcove which, with great difficulty, contained an ancient bed, a broken chair, and a twisted washstand. "Sit," my guide directed in a gentle but resonant voice. I did so, cautiously, on the bed. "I," he stated, appropriating the chair, "am that man."

Stupefaction seized me—could this—this mere tramp—shoeless—unshaven—filthy—illclad—ever have been the elegant creature who sank back nightly amid the scented pillows of New York's most exclusive resorts? Was this spectre, seated before me, in reality Charles A. Bugg Himself? Might such a thing be possible in this era of miracles?—Almost fainting, I produced a package of cheap cigarettes and offered them to him.

"I'll tell you how it all happened," he unconcernedly murmured, extracting a cigarette with great eagerness and immediately striking a match on the hornlike sole of one bare foot.

"Thank you," I managed to articulate, as my cigarette was lighted.

"Father," he continued, lighting his own and tossing away the match, "was no bally nitwit—and mother," he paused then spoke proudly, "mother was a House." I bowed. "I had everything," he resumed, "wealth, power, riches, influence. I looked like Lawford Davidson, the screen star. And yet," he paused, "somehow I felt something was wrong somewhere." This penetrating analysis was followed by the modest statement: "I only guessed dimly, at first." He puffed speculatively. "Then one night—morning, rather—when a party of us were celebrating my birthday in Jack's Underground Attic, it came to me like a thunderbolt: I knew, for the first time, what was wrong." He regarded me sternly. "As you will never guess, I shall tell you."

His eyes—small, acute, dark—hypnotized the very core of my being.

"I was unhappy," he stated, scratching himself.

"Unhappy," I breathed.

"There was only one thing to do that night, and I did it. I got up from the table in the middle of the festivities and walked home without paying the check. It was the turning point in my life. I resolved from that moment on, whatever sacrifices it might involve, that I would BE MYSELF.

"Early next morning, I sold my two yachts and three of my railroads, and, with the proceeds, started a company in Rhode Island to exploit the dried pansy industry. Do you read Henley?"

"Invictus?" I hazarded.

"Correct," he beamed. "And Edna Millay? You are familiar with her Renascence? Excellent. Where were we?"

"Among the pansies—"

"Of course. The company, after a highly dramatic career of some weeks, failed for ninety millions. Never, never can I begin to tell you, or anyone else, what that failure meant to me! It was as if my spirit had been reborn: as if new and wider vistas were opening on every hand.

"After that first, unforgettable disaster, you may believe that failure followed failure in rapid succession. Meanwhile, my relatives were either committing suicide or suing to have me committed to an institution. At all the best clubs on Fifth Avenue—the Union, the Knickerbocker—I was refused admittance by my fellow members—my main office included a group of specially trained private secretaries, not a few of whom became afflicted with dementia praecox while attempting to answer a daily average of slightly over three hundred telegrams, letters and postcards, from every nook and cranny of the civilized globe imploring, pleading, begging me to return to my senses.

"It is no small thing to feel that you are fighting a lonely fight against stupendous odds—but to know that you are going to win that fight, no matter what happens or who loses, is a wonderful thing. It makes you stand up straighter and look every man woman and child in the eye. It gives you an honest feeling in your heart, that makes troubles turn tail.

"I kept right on, in spite of everything, failing and failing; until one day I found I had nothing left but my biggest steamship line. The end of my endeavours, the goal of my ambitions, was in sight! Almost delirious with joy, I pawned the company, and, with the cash, established a full-fledged group of model factories, in Arkansas, capable of turning out five hundred and thirty million ping-pong balls per day—I need scarcely tell you that there proved to be no market for my product. Imagine (if you can) my ecstasy when, shortly afterwards, the business exploded to the tune of one hundred and fifty millions, leaving me (at last!) a free man—."

As I regarded this face, the nameless beggar, the bleary nondescript, whom a few moments before I had accosted, faded gradually from my mind—before me I beheld, poised with easy grace upon the ruined chair, a figure in the full heyday of disaster, whose firm simplicity and quiet dignity proclaimed to all the world Hamlet's apostrophe to Horatio: "This was a man!" I stared, fascinated.

Then, restraining with difficulty a wild impulse to fall on my knees, I produced a package of slightly more costly cigarettes, and, trembling, handed it to him without a word. As his fingers closed upon my gift, he smiled: a little child's smile. His eyes lowered themselves slowly. Down the grimy cheek a tear of pleasure stole from beneath a tired eyelid. "Thank you," he whispered.

We cleared our throats together. "That isn't all," he explained, taking a half smoked cigarette from behind his ear, and lighting it again. "I was a free man—yes: a happy man—but still I was not perfectly happy," he went on. "Not until something, as beautiful as it was unexpected, occurred . . ." and his virile visage emitted a mysterious smile.

Conscious of the pounding of my heart: "May I ask," I ventured, timidly, "who . . . ?"

The smile narrowed to a threadlike line. "A woman," he murmured, leaning toward me. "She was all the world to me . . . we believed entirely in each . . . two hearts which beat as . . . ah, the bliss! . . . and then, one night—as I was leaving her apartment—her maid handed me a derby which didn't fit me in the least . . ."

There was a pause. I did not breathe.

"After that," he murmured, "my illusions shattered, my faith in women annihilated, I became a bum. . . ." He straightened, proudly. "I'm just thirty-one," he vouchsafed modestly. "At twenty-one I started out to live my own life, to be true to myself: I am now thirty-one: one from one leaves nothing, two from three leaves one. Ten. Is that correct?"

I nodded, spellbound. The flexibility of his intellect was baffling.

"That makes ten years in which I struggled, through thin and thick, with but a single end in view: TO BECOME A SELF-MADE MAN." He smiled, quietly. "And I have achieved that end."

Quite overcome by this burst of frankness, I rose to go: but he detained me with a glance. "The readers," he said, huskily, "of your magazine—I want you to tell them how I did it."

"If you will be so kind—" I stammered, blushing.

"The secret of my failure is contained in three precepts."

"Three little precepts," he crooned. "The first is nothing more nor less than a very practical bit of advice—Never hit a woman with a child: always use something else. The second has proved helpful to all sorts of people—In case of fire, lie down: do not walk to the nearest, if any, exit. The third really sums up, in a few words, all that the poets, philosophers, and teachers have tried, since the beginning of time, to tell us—" he paused: then in a deep, rich, velvet whisper, distinct with passion, he spoke: "Any man who will be unkind to his mother, a horse will bite."

Speechless with emotion, dizzy with a realization of the man's invincible sincerity and unimpeachable happiness, I gropingly put out my hand—and found Bugg's.

From *Vanity Fair*, March 1925.

A MODERN GULLIVER EXPLORES THE MOVIES

A famous movie studio on Long Island is discovered by an intrepid traveller

By Sir Arthur Catchpole, *Bart.*, D.C.L., K.C.B., R.S.V.P., etc.

Editor's Note: In this article, the elderly and intrepid British explorer (who recently received the Nobel Peace Prize for his elucidation of the little known man-eating inhabitants of the Andaman Islands) presents the world with his almost incredible meanderings among the hitherto undiscovered Gobos, or blood-drinking motion picture actors, scenic directors, camera men, forty year old ingenues, society "extra" ladies, and publicity artists at Astoria. To say that *Vanity Fair* is happy to be the vehicle of so significant a communication is to insult the intelligence of its readers—but let the aged Sir Arthur's story of the Gobos on Long Island speak for itself.

Faced by a truly momentous task (so momentous that, instinctively, I hesitated to imagine that least of a thousand miracles which its accomplishment would entail for humanity in general and the world in particular) it was with a sense of responsibility well nigh crushing that, at approximately seven o'clock in the morning of the fourteenth of October, with a bag of peppermints in my left jacket pocket, I found myself one of the scrambling myriad who, for one reason or another, inhabited at that hour the irrevocable purlieus of the Grand Central Station.

Ordinarily I should have paused to contemplate a scene in

which pity and terror strove for the mastery; now I found myself to be the frenzied protagonist, the fanatical traveller whose one and only aim was to locate, with the least possible delay, a not infrequently imaginary unit of conveyance. Having to the best of my ability explored passage after passage of the marble labyrinth (during which Odysseys I narrowly escaped having my shoes shined, buying a book, eating a dinner, and similar unforeseen perils) I succeeded, by appealing to a considerable number of persons of diverse sexes, in establishing beyond the shadow of a doubt the far from unimportant fact that the particular train whose presence I so ardently desired was to be boarded only upon a level differing from that on which I found myself at the moment. Further inquiries had scarcely revealed the fact that this level was directly attainable, at intervals of from one to three minutes, by means of a lift—when before me doors shot open, and I found myself confronted by two Negroes combining gigantic size with less than the ordinary quota of intelligence. Having (not without some trepidation) entered the machine, I was whisked downward to a substratum or sunken *promenoir* containing, to be sure, a train differing in no essential respect from the ordinary electrically operated conveyance, but which, to my great spiritual comfort, I ascertained to be marked "Astoria."

This circumstance, trivial in itself, considerably heartened me: so much so, indeed, that I immediately boarded the train; which thereupon to my no small satisfaction made off through a tunnel under the river, without other ill effects to myself and—if I may presume—the other occupants, than a slight discomfort to the eardrums coincident with the encountering of a sudden difference in air pressures not unnatural under the circumstances.

During this, the submarine, portion of the journey, I had ample time to pass in review the motives and methods of my truly astonishing expedition; such introspective tendencies as were natural to my personality being reinforced by the complete (except for an occasional cough or sneezing) absence of any factor of external interest. As the train rushed on through darkness I found myself little by little becoming hypnotized by the prospect of treading in person the soil of that fabulous corner of the world from which so many fantastic myths, so many gruesome legends, have emanated, Astoria!—extraordinary principality, mysterious kingdom, unreal domain, inhabited by half-human, half-imaginary creatures! What by comparison was Africa or India or Egypt? What were the secrets of the pyramids, the mutterings of the fakirs, the darknesses of the Congo? Myself appeared to me as one who is both foolhardy and presumptuous: true, I had weathered inconceivable perils, I had wrestled barehanded with the pigmy hippopotamus and crossed the Amazon in a fig leaf—but what, after all, were these dangers, or a thousand times worse than they, compared with the vivid and perpendicular Unknown against which I was being hurled by an elemental force at a velocity truly merciless? My heart quailed. And then a realization of the dignity of my mission—a vision of the sublimity of endeavour—crossed my mind: instantly I was comforted, and murmuring, "Thy will is my law, Scientia!" I clenched the bag of pink peppermints.

At this very moment, with a slight jolt, we emerged into the light of day; and on every hand an (to say the least) awe-inspiring spectacle unfolded itself. What a scene! Before the beholder stretched, literally *à perte de vue*, an inimitable panorama of unparalleled desolation, consisting of acres upon hideous acres of dump heaps, some smoking, others smokeless, all cruelly illuminated by the clear air of morning. The tonality of the whole—a drab mixture of acid browns and constipated greys—was, to be sure, occasionally relieved by the inspired occurrence of some ordinarily humble fraction of objectivity; as when, for instance, a tin can, snaring the sun's rays, tossed into the eye a jet of violet brightness. Occasionally, too, the olfactory contribution of a recently emptied refuse barrel, wafting through the open windows of the train, greeted the nostrils with a far from timid salutation.

But aside from such accidents, it is no exaggeration to say that

B 303

the fatality of disintegration was everywhere strictly observed. Be it understood that I am recounting a first impression, and that I am by temperament abnormally, even peculiarly, susceptible to Nature in her various moods and tenses, in which respect I differ radically from the vast majority of human beings—as is well illustrated by the present situation; a glance to left and right sufficing to persuade me that my fellow travellers were, to all intents and purposes, inured to the desolation of a scene which, so far as I could judge, presented no novel features to their possibly somewhat limited apparati of sense perception; whereas I must candidly admit that from the moment of their exit from terra firma my own eyes and nostrils were busy defending themselves against innumerable onslaughts of, to put it mildly, unwelcome phenomena. But what, after all, is ugliness? Probably not more than a few minutes later I found myself, if not positively enjoying, at least disinterestedly appraising, the extraordinary landscape which forms a stepping-stone from civilization to the awe-inspiring Gobo Land.

Presently the train stopped—not, however, before I had begun to experience a curious sensation in the top of my head. I felt for the peppermints: they were safe. What was this place? I promptly produced from my hat a number of large and inaccurate maps of the district and discovered, with great difficulty, that we had attained the little station of Bee-Bee-Ave. from which point my destination was only a few minutes distant.

Startled by this revelation, I had scarcely time to put away my maps and straighten my necktie when we were off with renewed vigour. In vain I tried to collect my senses, to form some definite plan of offense or defense—my wits had deserted me—I could concentrate upon nothing whatever; and, to my horror, found my own voice humming a popular catch, or ditty, of a distinctly (unless I greatly err) reprehensible nature, its title being "Red Hot Mamma" as I recall.

I rose from my seat just in time to receive the full shock of the train's abrupt stopping, which error resulted in my nothing short of velocitous propulsion into the arms of an elderly female from whose embrace I extricated myself with a difficulty which must have appeared remarkable but for the unassailable fact that, in the flurry of the moment, we had thrown—as it were—our arms around each other.

Just as I was making elaborate apologies for this acrobatic courtship, a door opportunely opened; whereupon I "saved myself" (to employ the French expression) and with such good effect that, a jiffy later, all of me was standing upon the station platform of Astoria, breathless, but intact even to the last peppermint.

A cursory inspection of my immediate environment having failed to display the presence of anyone whose appearance might encourage a stranger to demand the exact whereabouts of the Palace, I was on the point of giving way to despair, when—quite by accident—my eyes perceived, only a short distance away, a magnificent and colossal edifice surpassing in elaborate simplicity the temples of archaic Ethiopia.

Immediately I set out hotfoot over hill and dale, and very soon arrived without interference before a pair of stunning marble gates, behind which was seated a brilliantly uniformed doar-mahn, or bouncer, of whom I politely inquired—employing the dialect of the district with which eighteen years' intensive study had made me slightly familiar—where I was. "Faymoo splay-hoor zlahskee" (you are at the King's own house, stranger) the doar-mahn answered in a drawling, dangerous voice. Unabashed by the menacing tone of the answer, I stated that I desired to be conducted through the edifice, and mentioned by name a certain baron of whom I had been told that he stood very near his sovereign. Courteously but definitely I was assured that the great man was out; whereupon, without more ado, I handed the Cerberus a peppermint, which he immediately tasted, and which so far altered his opinion of myself as to cause him to press a button—at which, as if by magic, an office boy named Gee-hoar-j appeared.

A brief conversation between the doar-mahn and the office

boy now took place: and at its conclusion the latter offered to show me around for two peppermints, which I immediately bestowed upon him. I then shook hands affectionately with the doar-mahn, and followed my enthusiastic guide down a corridor and into a garage, where he called in a loud voice for his car: a glistening, twelve-cylinder Minerva swept up, driven by an elaborately attired chauffeur, and I was ushered into the tonneau. As we sped away, cocktails were served by a Japanese butler, which occurrence considerably increased my already far from negligible bewilderment anent the economic structure of a society in which office boys own limousines; and it was with a positively foreconscious embarrassment that I managed to ask why an inspection of the palace should begin with an automobile ride. My host, without mincing matters, informed me that the enormous size of the royal house made any other procedure ridiculous, further explaining that for a pedestrian adequately to explore the intricacies of the king's ménage would require a continuous promenade of from sixty to ninety days and nights, depending on the speed of the walker.

Inoculated by this statement with a dim realization of the vast scale on which everything in Astoria (including salaries) occurs, I glanced around me with a new interest, while the billionaire emptier of wastepaper baskets, Gee-hoar-j, pointed out—to left and right—various fleeting departments or offices of the palace. After a half-hour's furious drive we slowed down and entered an elevator, which took us up several thousand feet or more (as I should guess) before we stopped rising. I now emerged from the car: my host followed. A door opened—revealing a huge plain, perhaps a hundred acres in area, which, I was informed, constituted only one of a number of "sets" connected with a romance then in the course of production.

For, incredible as it may appear, the king of the Gobos amuses himself by producing from time to time a sinn-ee-mah or picture game, in which all the inhabitants of the royal mansion mingle their efforts, and whose occurrence frequently consumes as much as a whole month. I was in the midst of a thousand tumultuous doubts and fears when I became aware, for the first time, of figures moving (as if in obedience to a master will) hither and thither upon the surface of the plain. At this very instant an attendant came up and, bowing to the ground, displayed for my approval two pairs of diabolical-looking machines, very distantly resembling our roller skates. Gee-hoar-j explained that if I would be good enough to don one pair, he would do the same with the other, and we would examine together the spectacle then in the course of being created. Knowing no way of refusing, I permitted the attendant to secure my feet in the contrivances, and allowed him to place in my right hand a switch whereby the speed of the skates was regulated. Then, as he bowed once more, I gave him three peppermints, and he withdrew joyously. Gee-hoar-j started forward: I closed my switch and felt my feet moving away with my body—a sensation at first somewhat uncanny, but soon positively pleasant.

A few minutes sufficed to enable me to master the operation of my skates; I then followed my guide, and presently found myself approaching a group of actors, all moving by electricity like myself, who were in the midst of interpreting a love scene. Indeed, just as I arrived, the hero and heroine, skating from points several miles apart, met at gigantic velocity and—after promulgating several truly incredible acrobatic exercises—indulged in a kiss lasting, by my watch, just over eleven minutes: upon the conclusion of which highly mercurial act bells thundered, fish horns blew, cannon of large calibre were discharged, and a voice, speaking by radio, shouted above the din a statement which I may roughly translate, "Next scene the rustic swing, mother and child, make it snappy everybody"—whereupon there was a rushing sound, as stagehands, electricians, actors, and managers began simultaneously skating toward a corner of the plain some twenty-three miles distant.

Gee-hoar-j and I followed at top speed, and very soon sighted a forest five hundred feet high built entirely of cardboard, through which celluloid birds flew by electricity uttering phonograph records by famous artists. Having tipped a policeman four peppermints, I made bold to penetrate the wood, and presently came upon a swing, and in it seated a young child of perhaps three years, whose arms were around the neck of a maternal and extremely ill-looking woman. The same voice which I had previously remarked—and which (as Gee-hoar-j informed me in a whisper) belonged to the king of all Gobos—shouted "Kahm-air-ah" (begin) and a great many curiously complicated machines began turning as the infant drew down the woman's ear and whispered something in it. This process was repeated until, in spite of myself, I grew abnormally desirous of knowing the content of the mysterious message—for a long time I restrained my curiosity; but in the end rashness conquered discretion: I gave a house detective five peppermints and, throwing away the empty bag, fell on my hands and knees, in which position I entered the underbrush at its densest point.

For several miles I crept along, making as little noise as possible, without other guidance than a pocket compass: eventually I began to see a dim light, which told me that my objective was near: finally, panting, exhausted, having completed a perfect circle forty-two and five-eights miles in diameter, I arrived at a point directly beside the adult and unhealthy ear into which the mysterious message was about to be whispered by the flourishing and childish lips. At this very moment, the child and woman began to move: the former's baby hand reached up (as if actuated by clockwork) and took hold of the latter's grown-up auditory appendage, which (as previously described) it proceeded to draw downward until the sonal apparatus of the undernourished female was on a level with the oesophagus of the robust little one—until, in other words, the vocal region of the babe and the listening organ of the parent coincided.

Now was my moment!—breathless, perspiring, inchoate, I

stretched every nerve: I closed my eyes, opened my larynx, counted to one hundred and thirty-five (in seven languages), and—as in a dream—heard the tiny tot murmur:

"Do not spoil your eyes with crying, Mama. Daddy will perhaps tire of the lady and come home to you and I. And, if Providence is kind, it may bring you and he together again. See, Mother, there is light at the window. It is the dawn!"

From *Vanity Fair*, March 1925: line drawing by the author.

WHEN CALVIN COOLIDGE LAUGHED

A true account of the world-shaking consequences of a hearty laugh

Calvin Coolidge laughed.

Instantly an immense crowd gathered. The news spread like wildfire. From a dozen leading dailies, reporters and cameramen came rushing to the scene pell-mell in high-powered aeroplanes. Hundreds of police reserves, responding without hesitation to a reiterated riot call, displayed with amazing promptness a quite unpredictable inability to control the ever-increasing multitude, but not before any number of unavoidable accidents had informally occurred. A war veteran with three wooden legs, for example, was trampled, and the non-artificial portions of his anatomy reduced to pulp. Two anarchists (of whom one was watering chrysanthemums at Salt Lake City, Utah, while the other was fast asleep in a delicatessen at the corner of Little B and 12½ Streets) were immediately arrested, lynched, and jailed, on the charge of habeas corpus with premeditated absence. At Lafayette Square, a small dog, stepped on, bit in the ankle a beautiful and high-strung woman who had for some time suffered from insomnia, and who—far too enraged to realize, except in a very general way, the source of the pain—vigorously struck a child of five, knocking its front teeth out. Another woman, profiting by the general excitement, fainted and with a hideous shriek fell through a plate glass window.

On the outskirts of the throng, several nonagenarian members of the Senate, both Republican and otherwise, succumbed to heart trouble with serious complications. A motorcycle ran over an idiot. A stone-deaf nightwatchman's left eye was extinguished by the point of a missing spectator's umbrella. Falling seven stories from a nearby office building, Congressman N. G. Knott of Tennessee (Dem.) landed in the midst of the crowd absolutely unhurt, killing eleven persons including the ambassador to Uruguay. At this truly unfortunate occurrence, one of the most promising businessmen of Keokuk, Iowa, Aloysius Q. Van Smith (a member of the Harvard, Yale, and Racquet Clubs) swallowed a cigar and died instantly. Fifty plainclothesmen and two policewomen with some difficulty transported the universally-lamented remains three and three-fourths miles to a waiting ambulance where they were given first aid, creating an almost unmentionable disturbance during which everybody took off everybody's hat and the Rev. Peter Scott Wilson, of the Eighteenth Anabaptist Church of Paragould, Ark., received internal injuries resulting in his becoming mentally unbalanced and attempting to undress on the spot.

Needless to say, the holy man was prevented by indignant bystanders from carrying out his ignominious intention, and fell insensible to the sidewalk.

Calm had scarcely been destroyed, when a lovesick sailor from the battleship Idaho was seized with delirium tremens. In still another part of the mob, a hydrant exploded without sufficient warning, causing no casualties and seriously damaging an almost priceless full-length portrait of ex-President Theodore Roosevelt kissing ex-Admiral Hashimura Togo on both cheeks by John Singer Sargent in the neighbouring chapel of the Y.W.C.A. Olaf Yansen, Klansman and plumber, and a floorwalker, Abraham Goldstein, becoming mutually infuriated owing to some probably imaginary difference of opinion, resorted to a spontaneous display of physical culture, in the course of which the former (who, according to several witnesses, was getting the worst of it, in spite of his indubitably superior size) hit the latter with a brick and vanished. Mr. Goldstein is doing well.

While quietly playing with a box of safety matches which his parents, Mr. and Mrs. James B. Fitzroy, of 99 Hundredth Street, Omaha, had given to their little son James Jr. to keep him quiet, the infant—in some unaccountable manner—set fire to forty-one persons, of whom nine and thirty were burned to ashes. A Chinese, Mi Wong, who exercises the profession of laundryman at 17 Sixteenth Street, and Signor Pedro Alhambra, a millionaire coffee planter, who also refused to be interviewed but is stopping at the New Willard, are the survivors. Havoc resulted when one of the better-liked members of the young married set (whose identity the authorities refuse to divulge) kissed Tony Crack, iceman extraordinary to the White House, on the spur of the moment, receiving concussion of the brain with two black eyes. In the front rank of onlookers, a daughter of the people became so excited by the Chief Executive's spectacular act, hereinbefore referred to, that before you could say Jack Robinson she presented the universe with twins.

But such trivial catastrophes were eclipsed by a disaster of really portentous significance. No sooner had Wall Street learned what Mr. Coolidge had done, than an unprecedented panic started, and Coca Cola tobogganed in eight minutes from nine hundred decimal point three to decimal point six zeros seven four five, wiping out at one fell swoop the solidly founded fortunes of no less than two thousand two hundred and two pillars of society, and exerting an overpowering influence for evil on wheat, and sugar, not to mention that ever-mobile commodity, castor oil, all three of which tumbled about in a truly frightful manner. At Detroit, Mich., the president of the India Rubber Trust Co., hatless and with his white hair streaming in the wind, tore out of the Soldiers and Sailors' Saving Bank at a snail's pace carrying in one hand a hat belonging to the president of the latter institution, James B. Sears, and in the other a telephone which the famous first had (in the frenzy of the moment) forgotten to replace on the distinquished second's desk.

A hook and ladder, driven by Augustus John (coloured) at an estimated speed of sixty-eight miles an hour, passed over the magnate longitudinally as he crossed Edsel Avenue and left a gently-expiring corpse whose last words—spoken into the (oddly enough) unbroken mouthpiece of the instrument, only to be overheard by P. Franklin Adams, a garbage man—were: "Let us then, if you please—"

So unnerved was the Jehu of the Henry Street Fire Station by this totally unexpected demise that, without pausing to consider the possible damage to life and limb involved in a purely arbitrary deviation from the none-too-ample thoroughfare, he declined the very next corner in favor of driving straight through the city's largest skyscraper, whose one hundred and thirteen stories—after tottering horribly for a minute and a half, during which negligible period several thousand suspicious characters left town—thundered earthward with the velocity of light, exterminating every vestige of humanity and architecture within a radius of eighty leagues including one billion six hundred and forty nine million five hundred and thirty eight thousand two hundred and seven Ford sedans.

This paralysing cataclysm was immediately followed by a fire of stupendous proportions whose prodigiously enormous flames, greedily winding themselves around monuments, cyclone cellars, and certain other spontaneous civic structures, roasted by myriads the inhabitants thereof, while generating a heat so terrific as to evaporate everything evaporable within an area of fourteen thousand square miles not exclusive of the Missouri river—which, completely disappearing in fifteen seconds, revealed a giltedged submarine of the U-C type containing (among other things) William Jennings Bryan, William J. Burns, William Wrigley Jr., Strangler Lewis, the Prince of Wales, Senator Richard O. Thimble of California, Babe Ruth, Major Arthur B. Good, Humphrey Ohm, emeritus professor of radio at Johns Hopkins University,

Rear Admiral George Monk, K. C. B. etc., Nicholas Murray Butler, Sir Arthur Conan Doyle, T. S. F., Harold Bell Wright, Clive Bell, the honorable Robert W. Chambers, the Amir and Amira of Afghanistan and their hosts, Mr. and Mrs. Harold S. Packingbox of Philadelphia and Newport, Al Jolson, Luther Burbank, Ben Ali Hagin, Alfred Stieglitz, Howard Chandler Christy, Daniel Chester French, Paul Manship, George Gershwin, Houdini, Thomas A. Edison and Dr. Frank Crane, the last of whom (being only incompletely intoxicated) promptly shuffled off this mortal coil with the Star Spangled Banner upon his lips and was buried by six or seven stalwart bootleggers on the exact spot where he did not fall.

A moving picture of the preceding historical catastrophe was thereupon instigated by the usual genius of Mr. Griffith who, with unerring judgment if not tact, invoked Rudolph Valentino at a salary of two hundred and seventy-five thousand dollars per week, less nineteen cents war tax, to impersonate simultaneously both George Arliss and Napoleon, whereas Lillian Gish played to imperfection the thankless part of the old mother who—after being bitten by sharks—kills the villain with a knitting needle on horseback and escapes out of the crater of Vesuvius in a brown paper bag, causing a strike among the white paper bag manufacturers, which spread all the way from Tuscaloosa to Yazoo.

Suddenly—unexpectedly—in the midst of all this infrahuman and ultranational pandemonium, compared with which such trivial incidents as solar eclipses, earthquakes, the battle of Aegospotami, Sheridan's ride, the fall of Babylon, the Declaration of Independence, and Pepys' Diary, were as an inelegant globule of H_2O beside the tempestuous entirety of the Dead Sea—in the centre of doom, debauchery, and dissolution—in the naked heart of tintinnabulous chaos—a miracle, a thing unknown, unanalysable, a phenomenon irremediably acatalectic, indubitably unbelievable, and totally indescribable, occurred.

Over the whole country there swept (as sometimes sweeps,

o'er the sickbed of some poor delirious sufferer, a spontaneous sweetness—purging the spirit of its every anguish, uniting the multifarious moods and aspects of the human heart in a triumphant arch through which, with flags flying and bugles blowing, the glorious armies of the soul go marching as to war)—there thrilled—there burgeoned—a mysterious and invincible ululation of utter, absolute, unperforated silence.

So stunning, so irrevocable, was this silence, that the beasts of the field, the fowls of the air, and the fish of the sea, felt, and (each in his own peculiar and characteristic way) responded to, its thunderous intensity. The prairie dog of Kansas and the armadillo of Texas emerged from their burrows hand in hand, bent on satisfying at all costs an unquenchable curiosity as to its occult cause—united by a common inquisitiveness, the moose of Maine and the codfish of Massachusetts (abandoning simultaneously their respectively foliate and aqueous habitats) put their heads together, and listened—the versatile mockingbird of Kentucky started from his sleep and mingled his mellifluous paeans of inquiry with the more staccato queries of the cynical rose-breasted nuthatch—even the mayor of Kankakee, Ill., fired by an overwhelming curiosity, leaned out of a superb gothic aperture in the pre-Romanesque I.O.O.F. hall, dropping a half-smoked Chesterfield into the exact middle of a passing load of hay, with the remark: "Is cigarette taste changing?"—in short, all America, which (but a moment before) had been convulsed to its very roots by unparalleled spasms of massacre, machination, and mayhem, closed its weary eyes . . . and sank suddenly into a profound swoon of unadulterated ecstasy, a delicious coma of inexpressible bliss . . . as through the entire nation, from sea to sea, completely surged that sublime and unmitigated titillation of telepathic tranquility, of rapturous reintegration, of perfect peace . . .

Calvin Coolidge had stopped laughing.

From *Vanity Fair*, April 1925. This was the first prose work of E. E. Cummings to appear in *Vanity Fair* under his own name. It was later shortened and otherwise altered for its appearance as "Chapter I" of a contribution without a title in *The New American Caravan* (New York: The Macaulay Co., 1929). The entire "contribution," illustrated by the author, was published in a limited edition by Covici, Friede in 1930. This book without a title will also be found in this collection.

WILLIAM ADAMS-WIGGLEY: GENIUS AND CHRISTIAN

Minutes of a speech delivered on the birthday of America's great gum magnate.

Reported by C. E. Niltse, S.P.C.V.[1]

Editor's Note: The following are the remarks of the Honorable Humphrey Halitosis, director of the Department of Domestic Propaganda of the Adams-Wiggley Gum Society Inc., at a grand banquet tendered Mr. Adams-Wiggley in honor of his thirty-sixth birthday, by the Y.M.C.A. and the S.P.C.V., under the distinguished auspices of the Harvard Business School; from which festive, albeit sober, gathering the guest of honor was (unhappily) absent, rumor having it that he had embarked for Paris with the preconceived idea of espousing Mrs. William Adams-Wiggley number nine.

Gentlemen: I stand before you tonight endowed with the proudest mission which I dare say it has been the lot of a human mind to accomplish, a mission so deep, so spiritual, and so real, that the soul trembles at its very proximity. I am here to express my appreciation of beauty, of genius, of benevolence, of philanthropy, of Christianity, of every awe-inspiring and uplifting element which can be found in the character of man; and the personage who embodies these singular and lofty traits, and who is the subject of my little discourse to you folks, is no other than he whose name has become

1. Society for the Prevention of Cruelty to Vegetables.

a symbol for clean living and high thinking wherever hearts beat, a byword fondly quoted by billions upon billions of grateful mouths in every country of the world at this moment. I refer to that almost divine benefactor of the human race, whose masterful invention may aptly be called the mainspring of mastication and the father of reflection: William Adams-Wiggley.

I don't need to tell you folks who Adams-Wiggley is. I see by your faces that you're all of you intelligent people who can read and write and do addition and subtraction, and that's the kind of audience that puts William Adams-Wiggley's name in the same pigeonhole with names like Julius Caesar, Abraham Lincoln, Alexander the Great and all the big heroes and great statesmen and mighty generals and illustrious presidents who have ever lived. As I look at you, I see something else: I see your mouths move, your jaws move, your faces move, your ears move, your souls move, rhythmically, musically in tune with the universe, in time to the music of the spheres—and I know who is responsible for that. No, gents, I'm not here to try to describe a superman whom you all of you, consciously or unconsciously, worship: I'm here to give you my idea of that man (if he be a mere man) and I want you to excuse me at the outset for whatever injustice the limitations of my intellect may do the magnificent quality of his rare and indefinable spirit.

In the first place, I want to disillusion you about one thing. I want to tell you, in plain simple language so you'll all of you understand it, that I myself am nothing but a man like any of the rest of you. If I was selected for this task it was not for any qualities of eloquence and intelligence which I might have, but rather because for thirteen years I have lived and moved and had my being in the colossal shadow of the gigantic personality above referred to. Or, to put it differently, I was raised with William Adams-Wiggley, I went to school with him, I grew up with him, I loved him, and I admired him. He was a shy lad when I knew him first—a blond-haired blue-eyed little chap with a dreamy look hovering about his oval face; but under that dreamy look there dwelt an energy, a determination, a sticktoitiveness, which made me feel (even in those early days) that the world would hear from him some day. We were always inseparable: if one did something, the other had to do it. I remember very well when he was taken with mumps and I came down with jaundice the next afternoon—in fact, no closer bond probably ever existed between two spirits than between his and mine, which is why I am here tonight to tell all I know about the man.

William was born in my home town, Mobile, Alabama, at five o'clock in the morning of Irish-German parents, on March seventeenth, eighteen-eighty-eight, making him thirty-six years of age. His father, Mike Wiggley, was the village blacksmith, exactly as he is described in Longfellow's famous poem except he was a consumptive. His mother, Gretchen Adams, was descended from a very old royal family which had a coat of arms. A remarkable woman in every way, she bore twenty-three children in twenty-four years, of which William was number twenty-three and the most intelligent. Being, from his birth, a delicate and sickly child, he distinguished himself by winning a spelling match at the tender age of four and three quarters: in short, he was precocious, so precocious that when I first knew him he used to do the lessons for his brothers and sisters, six of whom died, while one went insane.

The feverish atomosphere of this high-strung and numerous family, combined with the humbleness of his surroundings, could not but cause agony to so sensitive a child. Accordingly, William left home on his sixth birthday never to return, and came to New York after riding the bumpers for eleven days and twelve nights, where he soon made enough money selling newspapers to enable him to start a mining concern, which, however, failed, bankrupting all concerned. Shortly after, penniless, at the age of ten, he wired me to join him in the big city, which I did; and we hunted around for some way of clearing expenses. William was at this time living in a tiny little ramshackle hall bedroom on the Bowery, which I shall never forget, with next to no furniture but a broken bed, and an enlarged photograph of his mother on the wall, to whom he sent two dollars twice a week with a regularity that was positively touching.

We used to eat in Chop Suey joints together, and talk over prospects. One evening (it was ten below zero outside and somewhat colder within) William leaned over the tumble-down table and his face lit up like it was electrified as he cracked me on the back, crying: "Eureka!" I didn't know what that meant, but, as I started picking the wooden dishes off the concrete floor whither his excitement had sent them, something about his wonderful blue eyes and his lively bright smile told me that he'd had an idea. And a few seconds later, after he'd whispered a few words in my ear, I knew that the world was his.

That's how the marvellous and truly wonderful product which we all know today—the industry that ranks second to none throughout the length and breadth of this fair land of ours—had its birth: as we two lingered over a half portion of chow mein and two portions of an Egyptian Deity cigarette which a bum gave us and I broke in two, giving William the longer half as I always did, for I was very fond of him. Today I am well-off and have my own limousine and eat the best of food, while he is a millionaire with a country house at Piping Rock where he entertains such noted celebrities as Gabriele D'Annunzio, Ben Ami, King Albert of Belgium, Lady Duff Gordon, and others too numerous to name. And that, gentlemen, is a romance of American business life which I will now leave in order to consider, in greater detail, the genesis of the actual invention itself.

When I questioned William as to how he came to have the idea which revolutionized contemporary manners, he explained to me, with characteristic frankness, that he had been daydreaming. For no apparent reason, he had had a kind of vision of himself standing at an open window and looking into his empty hand. As he looked, he saw something: rubber. You could do that. I could.

Anybody could. But that isn't all—no. William was a dreamer, but he was also a genius. A dreamer is somebody who goes to sleep, while a genius is somebody who notices what you and I can't see. William Adams-Wiggley's eye observed; and his whole frame trembled, his face contracted, his jaw dropped, for he had noticed an invisible something else: rubber was lonely.

What is a man without a woman? Nothing. What is a bowstring without an arrow, a ship without a rudder? Worse than nothing. Vegetables are just the same. They are like anything else; like us. Rubber was lonely and rubber wept: rubber cried out in its loneliness, and William Adams-Wiggley, bending his pitying head, and applying his incredibly keen and miraculously sympathetic left ear to the unhappy substance which cowered in his benevolent palm, heard that cry. Still he did not quite understand. "What do you wish?" he breathed softly. And a small voice answered with the almost unheard-of monosyllable—"mint."

Right here I should like to utter a well-intended and not unnecessary warning. It seems very simple and obvious, now, to regard mint in its true light as a glorious and salutary and disease-annihilating and health-inspiring plant: an unbelievable cure-all which mother Nature has thrown into our ungrateful laps, making it possible for our otherwise overworked and nervously exhausted organisms to breathe and live. But let us, after all, not avoid the truth; for the truth is always more beautiful than any substitute, however graciously and intricately concocted for our easy and insipid delectation. Let us never forget to remember that it was a man like you and me, folks, only somehow different—somehow strong where we are weak, courageous where we are cowardly, inspired where we are uninspired, prophetic where we are dull—in short, a superman—who lifted mint for all time out of a shameful mire of injustice and obliquity into the perpetual radiance of everlasting renown. That man wears clothes like you and me, has his hobbies, loves his wife and children to distraction, takes a bath regularly, works, laughs, smiles, plays, weeps, like we do—but he is somehow a genius: and his name (which, like the affectionate components of his earth-shaking invention, boasts a proud plurality of parts) is William Adams-Wiggley.

I could go on about this intellectual giant all night, but circumstances over which I unhappily have no control prevent me. What is the use of mincing matters? None. To put it frankly and fearlessly: our time is short, gentlemen; so let us, without more ado, turn to rubber.

There has recently been circulated a vile and insidious rumour which is absolutely without foundation of any sort, to the effect that rubber is dangerous if completely swallowed. I want to squash that rumor now, if it's the last thing I do on earth; and I want to squash it dead. I want to brand it as an infamous, uncalled-for, irresponsible falsehood; a damnable, dirty, inexcusable, unjustified, cowardly, mean, sneaking, outrageous lie. It is NOT true that rubber is harmful to the human organism in any way, shape or manner. Not only is rubber not harmful, but rubber is positively and always beneficial and helpful to the organism. If we do not eat rubber instead of bread, if our systems do not crave rubber in place of cheese, if (at the present comparatively low stages of human evolution) rubber is not actually nourishing, you may be sure of one thing, which incidentally is an absolute fact: that it is the human body's fault; it is our fault, yours and mine, for which we should hide our heads in shame forever—but it is not rubber's.

Now that I have wiped that filthy lie out of existence, I will come back to my subject with renewed vigour.—Fired by the magnetic spark of his electric genius, William (in a kind of dream) took in his strong right hand a piece of rubber. And just what does that mean? What is rubber, gentlemen? Commercially, of course, rubber is important; it is even more than important: it is—thanks to the ingenuity of one man's brain—a mammoth industry. But I am not speaking commercially. Because I am a businessman, the business point of view doesn't limit me. If I were a crack-brained Ph. D., with a warped mind chuck-full of rusty ideas and musty languages and dusty theories—if (to put it briefly) I were a doddering nitwit, an obsolete flapdoodle, or a denatured, book-bitten kewpie-above-the-ears—I would be so balled up in my own particular existence that I couldn't step outside my subject and touch the real, throbbing vital things of life. But I am no professor, gentlemen: far from it. Those things may worry some old dubs but not yours truly. The tragedies of Sophocles do not keep me awake. Dante may have invented Hell but he doesn't cut any ice with me, no sir. I am just a plain simple businessman, and therefore an unprejudiced man, a liberal man, a wide-awake, two-fisted, American go-getter of a human being who doesn't view the life of this day and time through the foggy spectacles of the misty past, and who doesn't go to a dinner party without his necktie, and who doesn't forget his wife's name when he wants to introduce her to a friend. That's the kind of a fellow I am. And being that kind of a fellow I face the music. With a supreme effort, summoning all my strength, spurning the purely commercial aspects of the topic, I look straight into its very essence with an unforgiving eye. Clenching my teeth, I say to myself: William Adams-Wiggley took a piece of rubber in his hand—and since we all know what Adams-Wiggley's hand really is, there remains for us (if we are conscientious, open-minded, out-spoken, free-thinking beings) only one course: and that course is, to ask ourselves—what is really rubber? There lies the question, the gauntlet, the challenge: rubber. What is it? You may seek to dodge, to prevaricate, to equivocate, to pick up your traps and slink out the back door, but you cannot, you shall not, evade me. I repeat, I reiterate, I place before you for the last time the burning question in its lowest terms: what is rubber?

Gentlemen, if we are sincere, if we are honest, and (above all) if we are Americans, there can be for us only one answer. Let us not, then, be afraid. Let us rather look the thing bravely in the face; let us stand firm; let us lift our heads high, and answer, in one unanimous and fearless voice which can be heard all over the entire civilized and uncivilized globe: "Rubber is almost nothing!" It is used upon our lowest extremities, the feet. It is associated with such disagreeable and abnormal phenomena as sleet, slush, and mudpuddles. In common parlance, "to rubber" is a term of frank opprobrium. As a material substance, rubber is humble, debased, downtrodden. And yet the seer, William Adams-Wiggley, in his vision took rubber.

When we have recovered from our astonishment at this colossal condescension, such as only a truly and really big and great man would have been capable of, let us endeavour to pursue the subject further, with a view to ultimately approaching that mysterious and enchanted island, that dazzling bourne, that Ultima Thule of all mortal observation—a Great Man's Soul. Let us curb our surprise, lest we miss yet larger surprises. Let us collect ourselves: let us ask, is that all? I answer, no. That is indeed not all. Rubber, that despised product, is far from all. William took in his right hand rubber, but in his left hand what did he take?

He took mint.

What, mint?

Yes, mere mint. Unbelievable, but true. And what is mint? An incomplete, partial, weakly thing—the final syllable of "peppermint." A fragile partner in that verbal marriage whereof "julep" is the better half. A vulgar mispronunciation of "meant." Look at it any way, from any angle, any side: the verdict is inescapable—mint is unquestionably and unutterably the mental and spiritual and moral and physical inferior even of rubber. If rubber were something, mint would be nothing; but since rubber is nothing, folks, mint does not exist: mint is less than nothing.

When William took rubber in his right hand—poor, humble, abused, foolish, worthless rubber—the vegetable kingdom swooned with a legitimate pleasure in all its infinitely variegated interstices. The skunk cabbage turned to the summer squash and whispered—what is this? The poison ivy vine forgot to poison. The heart of the lemon stood still. I am very sure all these things happened and many more. But when Adams-Wiggley extended his other, or left, hand—and (with a smile gracious and benign) picked between his merciful third finger and his gentle thumb a piece, a leaf, a fragment, of unutterable, common, merest mint—then, gentlemen, it is no exaggeration to say that there occurred an unforgettable moment in human history.

I will leave you with that idea. Since words are, at best, futile things, I will not try to describe the indescribable. But I cannot refrain from mentioning one more point, in connection with the lovely marriage of mint and of rubber: I must needs call to your attention the final dilemma with which William was confronted, and how he found the way out as no one else could have found it. After the process of rubberizing mint and minting rubber had been carefully perfected, Adams-Wiggley gazed with a proud eye upon the product of this unique combination, and pondered the question of a name for his wondrous invention. Well, what did he do? Did he brand it with a complicated, sophisticated, unpronounceable title, like the Greek and Latin teachers do their stick-in-the-mud treatises? Did he endow it with a jaw-breaking appellation, a big word, which nobody but three men in all God's creation could understand? Not he! He wasn't that small. He knew humanity, and he loved it, just as he knew nature and loved her. He wanted to find a name which everybody—no matter what language they spoke, what creed they subscribed to, how much their income was—could understand and speak: and, above all, he wanted to be downright fair. Rubber and mint had appeared to him in a vision, robbing him of his deepest gloom. He was grateful, and he was a gentleman. He wanted to be perfectly fair and square with rubber and with mint. He wanted to represent them equally, and not to slight either of them. You and I would not have thought of so delicate a point, but he did. In his heart of hearts, pulsing with a love for all created and uncreated things alike, there gushed that sublime and almost unattainable ambition. I say "almost," since for genius nothing is unattainable. Genius can walk erect where lesser minds crawl on all fours, and fly where others limp. The works of

Harold Bell Wright, Edna St. Vincent Millay, and Elbert Hubbard, are a proof; but William Adams-Wiggley is the greatest proof of all. For, after infinite researches, involving the best power of his accumulated mind, upon the practically insurmountable problem—in a lightning flash of blinding intuition he discovered the solution of the supposedly impregnable difficulty, the just and equal way out of the awe-inspiring dilemma: the double cognomen which would make both mint and rubber rejoice forever—Chewing Gum!

Now just a word about the actual effect of chewing gum on the world at large: chewing gum has improved living conditions all over the world fifteen per cent, has given the rudiments of education and culture to thousands upon thousands of workless and ignorant aborigines, has created in the midst of the impenetrable jungle a series of model communities equipped with every outlet, orifice, comfort, and even luxury, which our twentieth-century super-civilization can invent—pianolas, phonographs, radios, electric lights, automatic garbage cans, telephones and telegraphs, sane dance halls, hygienic soda fountains, collapsible bungalows, and stropless safety razors. But to enumerate these trifling benefits is to convey only an atom, a molecule, an ohm, of the actual truth. Chewing gum has done these things, of course, but (as everybody from the illiterate savage of the Peruvian pampas to the most highly cultured savant of the Académie Française knows) chewing gum has done more—a million times more. Chewing gum won the last war, and will win the next. If the sticks of chewing gum which are manufactured in just one of the Adams-Wiggley factories during an ordinary eight-hour day were put end to end, they would form a highway to the furthest star which the most powerful telescope has ever perceived. But statistics are merely statistics, so let us rather turn to the man himself.

William Adams-Wiggley, at the age of thirty-six, has made thousands of millions of millions of billions of lips, jaws, and mouths—all over the entire planet, throughout the five nations, the seven seas, the neutral air, the kindly earth—move in rhythmic sequence and keep time perfectly all together without one single error or mistake, just like they were the countless feet of heros advancing into battle. Yes, gentlemen, that's what Adams-Wiggley has really accomplished. In a word, in a nutshell, in a *je ne sais quoi*, he has put into people's mouths, everywhere, in all weathers—into my mouth and your mouth, gentlemen—what had hitherto been considered only suited to an old pair of shoes on a nasty day. Isn't it beautiful? Doesn't it simply prove what genius really is? Genius doesn't despise a thing because it looks lowly or has been maltreated and spat upon—no. A genius isn't going to take anybody's word for something: he's going to go right to the bottom of the problem, and find out for himself what the facts are. That's what Shakespeare did, and Beethoven, and Edison, and Einstein, and all the real geniuses. And that's what William Adams-Wiggley—last but not least—did.

In closing, I call upon you to consider this man's achievement from the standpoint of Christianity: I want you to ask yourselves, what is the highest duty which a person conscious of The Master's teachings can possibly perform? There is but one answer: to raise up, to comfort, to pity. That being understood, let us now—with bated breaths and heads reverently bowed—consider for the last time William Adams-Wiggley, and let us ask, in a devout whisper: is William Adams-Wiggley a Christian?

Is he, gentlemen?

I'll say so. I'll say there are mighty few folks living or dead who can compare with him in that respect. Think it over for yourselves—you'll see what I mean. You'll see, for the first time, how—as a Christian—William looked about him; how his mild, fearless, honest, noble, Christian eye searched everywhere for not just one but *two* altogether humble and utterly unhappy and entirely miserable specimens of plant life. Because he himself was a big, blue-eyed, strong-minded, broad-shouldered, right-thinking, clean-minded Christian man, he wanted to discover the only completely despised twins of the vegetable world—and, because he was a Christian, he did.

But that, my friends, isn't all. Adams-Wiggley wasn't one of those fly-bitten, moth-eaten, idealistic Christians who never got into any action for fear of dirtying their cowardly hands: not he. When William found an intolerable injustice rankling right under the very nose of countless generations of purblind humanity, he wasn't content with wringing his hands and making a fuss—no sir: he *did* something about it. In other words, he had the *real* Christian spirit, and he showed it. I'll say that's a big thing to do; and I'll say that the man who did that thing is a big man and a big Christian. I'll say that—if to pity and to comfort and to raise up the fallen are the real Christian virtues—no man ever breathed who had more of the real Christian virtues than William Adams-Wiggley; and that's what I mean when I tell you that, although he is a noble and wonderful man and a great and exalted genius, he is first of all, and *par excellence*, a Christian. So long as the sun and the moon persist, gentlemen, so long as a fact is a fact and a lie is a lie, there can be no getting away from the truth and, in this case, the plain, unvarnished, unadulterated, ineradicable, irremediable, unalterable, absolute truth is simply this: mint and rubber were in trouble, and—just because he was a Christian—Adams-Wiggley pitied rubber and pitied mint. That, gentlemen, is the utterly naked truth.

But let us not forget something else. Because the inventor of that practically blessed substance, that almost sacred commodity, that miraculous substitute for deviltry and idleness, that glorious panacea for all human and inhuman ills—chewing gum—is not an ordinary, humdrum, noncommittal, happy-go-lucky, nonchalant Christian like you or me, but a Christian who takes his religion seriously, who practises his lofty aims and lives his unimpeachable ideals—because, in short, William Adams-Wiggley is that extraordinary, far-sighted, richly gifted, unshakable, almost extinct kind of Christian to whose alert and luminous and vibrant being the slightest injustice of whatever variety constitutes an irrevocable challenge—only because of this, gentlemen—the superman, the genius, the Christian of Christians, William Adams-Wiggley, did something which common-or-garden men and lackadaisical Christians such as you and me would not, and could not, do—he raised up mint: he comforted rubber.

From *Vanity Fair*, April 1925.

SEVEN SAMPLES OF DRAMATIC CRITICISM

In the best and most highly approved Metropolitan manner

Editor's Note: When *Vanity Fair* suggested to Mr. E. E. Cummings that he give us his impressions anent the current American drama, the author of "&" replied—with a startling absence of subterfuge—that he would be happy to accept our invitation on one condition: viz., that he should not be expected to go to see any of the seven plays we wished reviewed, adding that he had never attended the theatre in his life and could not find any particular reason for doing so now, particularly as he studiously read all the New York dramatic critics and knew the *métier* thoroughly. Incredible as such a purely medieval statement may appear in the renaissance of this ultra-enlightened epoch, its veracity is irrevocably substantiated by the infra-mendacious tidbits which follow.

I. BOOM BOOMED

How Much Assassination is a play which is surely worth going to see. My throat specialist was particularly moved, and spent half the last appointment describing to me exactly why the production is a human document. As nearly as I can make out, I agree with him; although it seems he was in the air forces. No one who ever went over the top, which neither of us did, can fail to be amused by the dialogue between Rinehart and Belasco, or is it between Buffalo Bill and General Pershing? We forget which, unfortunately. Anyhow, the idea is there; and that man who did the ape in *All*

God's Chillun Got Wings is a remarkable actor in every way, and some of the slang just makes you want to stand up and say, "Let there be no more war!"

II. CLAPTRAP BEARNAISE

Pink Thunder from start to finish is a gripping melodrama in which frankly tropical lust is forcefully contrasted with intrinsic spiritual affection. The action—which reaches a heart-rending climax on the summit of Popocatepetl—is essentially a struggle between two women, one of whom is certainly no worse than she should be, for the possession of Peter Thomson, a missionary who is torn by conflicting emotions. Thrill-ridden scenes succeed each other with an agonizing rapidity, until Lucille Stingray (played to almost unendurable perfection by Mischa Elman) bribes a bloodthirsty tribe of Peruvian headhunters to abduct the sleeping heroine, for whom, until this dreadful moment, Peter—absorbed in the excruciating convolutions of his own ubiquitous conscience—had cherished merely a vague, unrecognizable emotion. The crisis, however, precipitates love; and the apostle is supplanted by the man. In a delirium of perspicuity, scarce knowing what he does, Michael Arlen as Peter rescues Isabel who faints with pleasure in his arms: whereupon, overcome—in what would appear to be the supreme moment of his life—by mingled inhibitions, the young man turns his back on temptation, gives himself (in an agony of remorse) to Lucille, and promptly jumps into the infernal fires of the volcano, which go out, causing the superstitious aborigines to hail him as a god. This sacrilege brings the devotee to his true senses—a fascinating psychological twist, for which the author (Miss Marianne Moore) is to be unstintingly congratulated—and he immediately, to everyone's relief, inherits sixteen million dollars, kisses June Walker, embraces the American flag, and lives happily ever after as innumerable spectators swarmingly exeunt from New York's best ventilated theatre.

III. STRUT YOUR STUFF

Strut Your Stuff is a typical revue with Ethel Barrymore and the costumes—consisting of paper napkins, accurately and painstakingly designed by Claude Bragdon, beautifully photographed by Alfred Stieglitz, and capably produced by Edward Royce.

IV. LOVE'S COMING OF AGE

Hairy Jones' *Desire under the Elms* is a play in the manner of Greek tragedy about a monkey who is also a Negro in which little is left to the imagination. Hairy Jones (not to be confused with Robert Edmond Jones who did his level best with the somewhat slanting elms) after being born (in New England) becomes "dif'rent." During all the rather long next, or third, act, the heroine alternately dabbles in incest and hides peanuts under a rug to amuse her doting grandfather who, we are given to understand, hangs himself in a shop window on the corner of Fifth Avenue and 42nd Street to the dulcet thuddings of a tom-tom, as the curtain falls and subscribers exchange looks all over the Provincetown Theatre. But this is not the point of the production by any means, for the author is far from being one whom mere mute inglorious melodrama satisfies. Rather are we presented with a continuous cross section of the Oedipus complex as it occurs in a mixture of the African galley slave with the gorilla who has become a typical citizen of New Bedford, Massachusetts, during those old whaling days when might made wrong. The cast is excellent, Mary Garden excelling in the difficult part of Liz, while Sir Al Forbes-Robertson Jolson's portrayal of the ambigeneric hero is a triumph of tact, vigour, and nuance; and profusely illustrated brochures, entitled "Anthony Comstock's Reminiscences, or Tramping on Life" are distributed (gratis) to members of the audience, at each and every performance which I myself enjoyed very much.

V. THE GREAT AMERICAN DRAMA AT LAST

Mickey's Yiddisher Tulip: Several million dollars have already flowed into the ermine-lined pocketbook of her who is, to put it mildly, the authoress of *Mickey's Yiddisher Tulip*, and small wonder! For sheer blitheness of sentiment, gaiety of situation, sublimity of pathos, and general inventiveness, no story, since *Uncle Tom's Cabin* thrilled our immediate ancestors, has enshrined so many genuinely laughable and authentically weep-able moments, making of the human heart a sensitive and responsive instrument at the beck and call of alternate terror and joy. It were indeed difficult to imagine what could be more wholly touching, and at the same time funnier, than a juxtaposition of the Icelandic and Assyrian temperaments; yet precisely this feat has won for the inspired progenitor of *Mickey's Yiddisher Tulip* an everlasting seat among the geniuses of all time. (Standing room only.)

VI. CORN BEEF AND CAVIAR

Once again, after its triumphant tour of Athens, Constantinople, and Pekin, *The Bohemian Ballet* is with us. The only fault which your reviewer can find with this invariably extraordinary ballet organization, whose ranks are this year enriched by two dancers of international renown—Gretchen Fahrenheit and Mike Frost—is that it somehow just misses being neither the Swedish nor yet the Russian Ballet. Nevertheless, there are some far from wholly unpleasant moments; as when, for example, the superb curtain by Wable Wicasse falls (after the third scene of *La Princesse Enceinte* is somewhat less than half over) on the by no means negligible occiput of Igor Ivanovich Vladimir Skipski; or when Lucy Goeblum (that most astute of Lithuanian *terpsichoristes*) executes the banana dance of the Fiji Islands to a witty, if slightly posthumous, nocturne by Chopin—or during those few utterly inspired, absolutely unforgettable instants, when, against the molecular meanderings of Strapfka Fooking, are agreeably silhouetted the cerebral somersaults of Serge Kapoot.

VII. POLLYANNA AESTHETICS

The Black Suspenders is, as its name frankly implies, an evanescent folk tale of corrupt peasant life done into verse by Edna St. Vincent Millay and translated from the Algerian by Mrs. John F. Hylan. George Smith, the hero, ably interpreted by Mr. John Howard Lawson, is put to sleep by a fairy named Sylvio, and remains in a state of coma during the entire performance, parts of which (especially the twelfth and twenty-sixth tableaux) might be omitted to advantage without violating the delicate spirit of Arthur Hopkins' conception. Aside from this minor error, the plot deals with Smith's subconscious reaction to three characters—Geraldine Glumb, a future mother; Dorothy Dumb, a telephone girl, and Creichton Crumb, a painter of marine animals—all of whom are obviously in search of the author, Yudenich Pilsudski Numb, who remains off-stage, however, occasionally singing *Nearer My God To Thee* to the accompaniment of an ancient African instrument shaped somewhat like a cross between beggar on horseback and the mandolute. An audience (composed, last Saturday night, of a sprinkling of Danish plumbers and a scattering of Norwegian bank messengers) loudly booed the far from discreditable work of Philip Widget Moeller in the role of Philip Moeller Widget, and expressed almost unjustified approval whenever—as not infrequently happens—Geraldine hits Creichton with a stuffed cat in the middle of Dorothy's wedding. On the whole, we are reluctantly forced to admit, we can congratualte Miss Millay, Mr. Pilsudski Numb and Mayoress Hylan.

From *Vanity Fair*, May 1925.

UNEXPECTED LIGHT ON THE DAWES PLAN

An exclusive interview with General Von Memmling, Pan-German Unionist

By N. G. Archibald, PH.D., L.L.D.

Editor's Note: So many contradictory reports on the working of the Dawes Plan have lately appeared in our journals of opinion that we are glad to publish the following revelation by Professor Archibald—the eminent authority on World Peace, International Law, and other dubious subjects. He has just returned from the other side with this well-earned "scoop." The thrilling account of his exclusive interview with the German General is told with characteristic frankness and a simplicity of diction which renders its veracity unimpeachable.

To begin with, on arriving in Germany, I spent five weeks and three days in solitary confinement at a little town called Liederkranz, this course having been decided upon with a view to protecting such perfect foreigners as myself from the cannibalistic tendencies of a starving populace. While deeply engaged in fighting rats and perfecting my German, I was taken out by thirteen soldiers and an officer; and given, in rapid succession: a letter of introduction to General von Memmling (Chairman Pro Tem. of the pan-German Committee on the Practical Application of the Dawes Plan), a hot bath, and a birth certificate.

Somewhat dazed, I found myself dressed in the uniform of a Hessian soldier and placed on a box car with twenty-three other members of the Associated Press, including the Editor of *Forest and Stream*, in which condition we all started under double lock and key for Berlin, being fed from time to time (through a triangular hole in the semicircular roof) two mouse omelets and a glass of water apiece. Just sixty-one hours later the door was thrown open, in Berlin, and Mr. George B. Harris of the *Herald Tribune*—who, being a chronic sufferer from insomnia and other things, happened to be leaning against it—fell into the middle of the Leipziger Bahnhof and was taken away to a hospital, while the rest of us were locked up for the night on the fifth floor of the former Kaiser's palace, after someone had said (in English) that we would undoubtedly be received by General von Memmling at three o'clock next morning.

Such were a mere tithe of the precautions with which the Committee had generously seen fit to surround our entrance into the capital; and I may add that only by appreciating to the full their real significance can the average reader hope to understand how tense was the situation, in Germany, at the moment when—as if by a miracle—the Dawes Plan solved at one blow that Gordian knot whose innumerable strands combined such difficulties as World War, Famine Prevention, and the Occupation of the Ruhr.

But to continue: bright and early we were all aroused from our sleeplessness by the firing of revolvers close to our ears. We were then heavily blindfolded and arrived in taxicabs exactly three hours later at General Headquarters. I was the first to be received, possibly because my name begins with A, in contrast with Mr. George Van Antwerp's of "True Stories," which (as might not be expected) leads off with a V. At the point of a bayonet, then, I entered a narrow passage; presently the towels were whisked from my eyes—and I found myself standing before a tall, angular, forbidding man, somewhere between thirty-nine and forty years of age, who was seated in pyjamas, embroidered with a Royal order, before a combination cook stove and escritoire working a crossword puzzle and gorging himself (with almost animal ferocity) on a frozen banana.

Von Memmling, for it was indeed no other, rose; and, having greeted me cordially in a thunderous voice, ignored further ceremony by offering me a bite of the full-blown fruit, which I politely but firmly refused—pleading (in somewhat inadequate German) that I had suffered from continual stomach-aches since arriving in his country. But I soon regretted my frankness; for I was immediately clapped on the back, tied hand and foot, and placed practically upside down, in a straight jacket; in which condition I began my interview with the daring but necessary question, "Herr von General, just what *is* the Dawes Plan?"

My interlocutor frowned pityingly a moment; and then replied with Spartan brevity, "Simplicity itself."

I countered, with dignity, that I was absolutely sure he was right; but that we in the United States craved to know the exact details—whereupon General von Memmling started violently, and regarded me with something very like admiration. "Do you know," he muttered through the depths of his gigantic moustache, "that you are the first and only magazine man who has ever made, in my hearing, an even semi-intelligent remark?"

I blushed, as was not unnatural under the circumstances, and explained that I could not be considered an ordinary magazine man; since *Vanity Fair* was the organ which I had the honour to represent—but here the Chairman Pro Tem. of the pan-German Committee on the Practical Application of the Dawes Plan uttered a tremendous cry which quite upset the sentinel at the door, who tumbled over backwards in sheer amazement and narrowly missed colliding with both von Memmling and myself; the former of whom, placing one huge foot on his prostrate sentinel's abdomen, supplemented the ululation as follows: "You need say no more. I will tell you all. Your magazine is" (here I translate freely) "the political mainstay of the illustrious bowsprit of glorious America's progressive forefront."

I tried to bow.

"Turn *that* right side up," von Memmling added, to a second sentinel (who had automatically taken the place of the first)—and he pointed to the present writer. Instantly the command was obeyed: my head and feet changed places as if by magic. "Decorate him!" the general bellowed—whereupon six orderlies in undress uniform entered, each carrying upon a plum-coloured cushion a different emblem of heroism: and, marching straight up to me, respectfully placed the variegated tokens one by one on my breast.

"Now," the military genius stated, as the last decorator withdrew, salaaming profoundly in my direction, "we can begin"; adding, with a touch of delicacy which I had scarcely anticipated, "make yourself perfectly comfortable."

"Good," I answered, overcome.

"You have doubtless read many newspaper accounts, purporting to explain the origin and significance of the Dawes Plan," the General prefaced, "but there is not a word of truth in any one of them, for two simple reasons: first, no one except myself and nine other people really knows anything about it; second, Mr. Dawes himself had nothing whatever to do with it." My surprise upon hearing these bits of news caused me to redden visibly.

The General continued: "Now as to the precise contents of the Dawes Plan: would it interest you to hear the unvarnished truth on that subject?"

"Yuh-yuh," I gasped.

"The Dawes Plan," my informant continued, "the hope of the whole world, the salvation of the German People, is divided into five parts, each of which deals with something else.—You're sure you're not catching cold?"

I shook my head, overcome by mingled emotions.

"Very good," he pursued. "In that case, I will read to you verbatim the original manuscript, which I always carry for reference." (I bowed in appreciation of this condescension, and the General produced from his coat a volume, most of the pages of which were blank, but which otherwise bore a striking resemblance to the Social Register.)

"Part one," his clarion voice trumpeted, as he adjusted a pair of horn-rimmed spectacles on his eccentric nose, and took a dark Havana from his fatigue cap after the manner of policemen the world over. An orderly having lit the prodigious weed for him with an immaculate salute, von Memmling proceeded—"Habeas Corpus: whatever is imported must first have been exported, since it is a well-established principle of economics (*vide* Taussig) that nothing can go into any country unless it has first come out of the country. Exceptions to this rule are—all narcotics, fireworks, dogs, stomach pumps, cabarets, guinea pigs (for medical purposes), gunmen, and umbrellas."

I sneezed my appreciation.

"So much for imports," the General remarked caressingly. "Let us turn to exports—Part Two: Quid pro quo. Nothing whatever, including postage stamps, elephants, and diplomats, shall be permitted to leave Germany until further notice, either with or without the special permission of the Allies. Duly elected members of the Reichstag to the number of twelve thousand, armed with willow whistles and wearing silk hats, shall from time to time enforce this rule."

I smiled understandingly.

"That settles the pernicious question of exports—just like *that*," the General cried enthusiastically, snapping his enormous fingers. "Now as to the problem of food supply—Part Three: Status Quo. Article One: since people are starving by hundreds of thousands, everyone shall be compelled to eat less for the good of the majority. Article Two: at the same time, the majority shall be intensively instructed as to the highly nutritive properties of certain well-known and easily obtainable substances, among which may properly be counted—sawdust, carpet tacks, all kinds of nails, rubber boots, and stove polish. Article Three: the masses shall be incessantly encouraged, by music, propaganda, and machine guns, to eat much and often of the unquestionably digestible and meticulously health-giving items hereinbefore enumerated; and offenders shall be punished with the utmost vigour. Note: Policemen shall set the crowd a good example whenever necessary by sucking their billies."

The General smiled, then, clearing his cavernous trachea and pulling one ubiquitous ear, he read on—"Part Four: Quo Vadis. Each and every male child or part thereof between the ages of 0.0007 and 2.318 (months) shall be restricted (during the calendar and fiscal year) to the production or possession of five battleships, eight armoured cruisers, twenty submarines, fifty-six aeroplanes, and one Zeppelin. If more than the prescribed amount of each or any element or armament of disarmament herein described, prescribed, inscribed, or proscribed, be found in his possession, whereabouts, or vicinity, said male child of said age or ages shall be forthwith compelled to submit in writing to the police commissioner of his district an apology, signed by the mayor and sub-mayor, as well as by his parents (if any); and moreover this questionnaire or affidavit shall be received by said commissioner not later than the first Thursday of the month immediately preceding the discovery of said extraneous element or elements, otherwise said child shall be declared extraneous, and taken on a Lithuanian warship to The Hague for trial on the charge of corrupting the youth of Germany. In the case of a female child, the armaments or disarmaments in her vicinity, whereabouts, or possession shall be limited to 0.31415 per cent of the sum total produceable, or possessable, or both, by any male child; and the punishment for infringement of this decree shall be the same. Adults must positively not own, purchase, steal, manufacture, have, or play with, anything whatever of a warlike nature, exception being made in the case of the cap pistol on Allied holidays, such as the seventeenth of March."

"Don't be restless," von Memmling admonished gently, "we are almost through. Listen to Part Five, And Last." He rolled his mastodonian eyes, and an orderly entered to relight his general's ebbing cheroot. "Part Five: Mirabile Dictu," the master resumed, as the servitor vanished. "The railroads of Germany shall be completely reformed, and their present inefficiency shall be remedied, as follows—in the first place, the already inhibitory prices of all seats shall be quadrupled, with a view to eliminating unnecessary traffic, and no animals whatever (except captive canary birds on leash) shall be allowed: secondly, all trains of whatever nature must be equipped with automatic conductors, must on no account ever whistle except when invited to do so, must have square wheels made of window glass, must be lighted with paraffin candles, and must run forwards and backwards at the same time; thirdly, the Allies shall have the inalienable right, at any hour of the night, day, either, or both, to search all locomotives for steam—if the slightest trace of which be discovered (whether with microscopes, thermometers, or crowbars) the guilty locomotive shall be pronounced null and void, sealed with particoloured sealing wax, drawn by two snow-white oxen into the town hall of the nearest village, city, or hamlet, and demolished by dynamite in the presence of the entire population."

General von Memmling pocketed the volume; and his eyes adopted a musing, dreamy, far-away expression, as he half-bellowed and half-whispered, "the Dawes Plan—in whose five paragraphs lies the salvation of my country and the peace of the uncivilized world."

Then, removing his feet from the by-this-time breathless abdomen of the continuously supine sentinel, he added as an afterthought, "Get up!"—and when the obedient soldier had done so, "Let all those other dumbbells be given a glass of beer and returned to New York in good condition," von Memmling directed, pithily referring to the twenty-three waiting American interviewers—"but treat this gentleman—the representative of a moral and refined family paper—as if he were the Kaiser's own brother!" At these momentous words, I was rolled out, untied, put into a twelve cylinder Fokker and sent over the border with Mrs. Ebert's seventeen bottles of French champagne, and a distinguished danseuse from the Moscow Art Theatre, to whom I was properly introduced, but whose name I unfortunately did not quite catch.

That, in a nutshell, is the result of my interview, on behalf of this magazine, with General von Memmling.

From *Vanity Fair*, May 1925. The Dawes Plan, prepared by a committee of American and European experts headed by Charles G. Dawes, fixed the total of German reparations payments to the Allied and Associated Powers of World War I and indicated the methods by which such payments were to be made.

JEAN COCTEAU AS A GRAPHIC ARTIST

The French critic, novelist and poet "unites writing" with surprising originality

Whatever the words "Jean Cocteau" may convey to readers of *Vanity Fair*, to which he has occasionally contributed his masterpieces, it is highly probable that "modern French writer," or "poet, satirist and dramatist," is all that most Americans associate with this well-known name. I must confess that to me "Jean Cocteau" meant (until very recently) even less: to wit, "gilt-edged literary flaneur." I must also confess that my only definitely agreeable contact with Cocteau's work had been established with his ballet *Les Mariés de la Tour Eiffel*; which articulate spectacle, alone and of itself, seemed to justify the existence of the otherwise deaf-and-dumb Swedish Ballet. As a final confession, I must state, that having been more amused by *Les Mariés* than by anything else in Paris—more, even, than by the police—I entertained a wish to meet the author of this excellent satire, but that my wish died an unnatural death. For at the apartment of Lewis Galantière (who has brilliantly translated several of Cocteau's works) a militant *superrealist* writer and one of the most charming of people, by name Aragon, described his distinguished contemporary, Jean Cocteau, in terms so vivid as to convince me that, coming after such a portrait, Cocteau himself would be a distinct anticlimax.

On this occasion Aragon (in his best form) made several enormous assertions; the smallest of which was, that the renowned poet and author of such novels as *Thomas l'Imposteur, Le Grand Ecart,* etc., etc., did not know how to write French. My surprise when Aragon uttered this very superrealist statement was by no means negligible; but I was infinitely more surprised to learn that Jean Cocteau—doubtless overhearing, from the Eiffel Tower radio station, or in some even more obscure manner, those terrible words—had been moved to produce a volume, not of poems, nor yet of prose, but of drawings. My third surprise came when I opened this book and read the first words of the dedication to Picasso: "Poets don't draw."

Cocteau continues: "They (poets) untie writing and then tie it up again differently. Which is why I allow myself to dedicate to you a few strokes made on blotters, tablecloths and backs of envelopes. Without your advice I'd never have dared put them together."

Judging by this profound and brittle bow to the greatest living draughtsman, and knowing Cocteau's predilection for satire, I anticipated a mass of imitative pretense. And once again I was surprised. For *Desseins* (as this collection of more that 200 of Cocteau's drawings is modestly entitled) reveals itself as a rather lengthy and random concoction of portrait sketches, scenes, caricatures, scrawls, imaginings—or what you will—strictly by a "poetic ironist" of this day and time, and possessing so much originality that if M. Picasso be to blame for its publication the world owes him a new debt of gratitude.

PICASSO. *A brother-artist caricatured. Cocteau's album is dedicated to Picasso, one of the greatest of the living painters.*

But let us take a few examples of Cocteau's drawing (the book is on sale in most of the New York book stores)—why not the person with the pipe, called *Picasso*, for instance?

Nobody, I am sure, will deny one thing: meeting him for the first time, the flesh-and-blood Picasso is a troll who has just sprung out of the ground. He is not a man. Picasso himself, I reiterate, is a troll—tightly made, genial, clinched, eyeful, and moreover (as E. O. once remarked, descending the Elysées with me one fragile and immortal evening) "with little velvet feet such as dolls *should* have." Returning now to what I shall call this portrait of Picasso by Cocteau—let me assure any interested person who has not found him- or herself face to face with the original, that what Cocteau's drawing expresses, first of all, is an uncouth aliveness which Picasso's actual presence emanates. In other words, this sketch apprehends—in a spontaneous, acutely personal way—the tactile stimulus which a glimpse of the Spaniard, creature, or genius, called "Picasso" involves: the feathery jolt or, so to speak, shock of confrontation.

Now let us consider a bit the drawing by Cocteau which is

COMRADES. *The artist, Picasso, in conversation with the composer, Stravinsky. Cocteau's drawing shows skill and subtle penetration. He is a first-rate psychoanalyst of graphic art.*

called *P. Picasso-Igor Stravinsky.* In this drawing, Jean Cocteau (the poet, the satirist, the Parisian, the literary idol) stands off—politely, maliciously portraying two celebrities of the "aesthetic renaissance" of modern Paris, both of them foreigners, who happen also to be the world's greatest living painter and the world's greatest living composer. The extremely trenchant characterization admits of no tricks—the observer's vision is direct—here again, we are refreshed by that rarest of all virtues: spontaneity.

MILLERAND. *A conservative estimate of the former President of the French Republic without the usual cruelty of political satire.*

The President of the French Republic, in itself a compelling delineation (which I reproduce) of M. Millerand, of contemporary politics, and of politicians in general should be compared with another drawing of the same personage, (not reproduced here) entitled "M. Millerand leaves Toulon" (in a wonderful gollywog automobile, with too much flunkeyism and too many salutes); just as the Picasso-Stravinsky drawing should be compared with "Stravinsky playing the *Sacre du Printemps*" (a portrait not only of Stravinsky in action, but of his music as well—for from the piano issue wire-ghost materializations, angular weirdnesses, remarkably suggestive of this composer's unique combinations of timbres). And now, if one contrasts Cocteau's version of the president of the French Republic with "caricatures" having for their parody our own

Coolidge, one begins to realize how insensitive most of the pictorial satire is which is being perpetrated in the U.S.A.—not that one can't mention Bob Minor, Covarrubias (via Mexico), Gropper, Frueh—and also, if one is peculiary wide-awake, one begins to suspect that whereas Art is mobile, all mere classifications are stationary. (Take for instance, the following specimen of classification, which adorns an article on caricature in the Encyclopaedia Britannica:

> "Few traces of the comic are discoverable in Egyptian art—such papyri of a satirical tendency as are known to exist, appearing to belong rather to the class of ithyphallic drolleries [*sic*] than to that of the ironical grotesque."

If this means anything it should be shot at sunrise.)

To proceed further with Cocteau's drawings: I wonder just how any classification would effect Cocteau's extraordinary mobile interpretation of Georges Auric, the bright particular star in that singularly unluminous constellation of composers known as *Les Six*? Less intuitive, coarser, than the ectoplasmic *Auric*, but still a notable achievement, is another of Cocteau's satires called *L'Expressioniste*—a roly-poly personage, lolling over backward and dangerously warping the unhappy piano in a hey-day of unordered ecstasy.

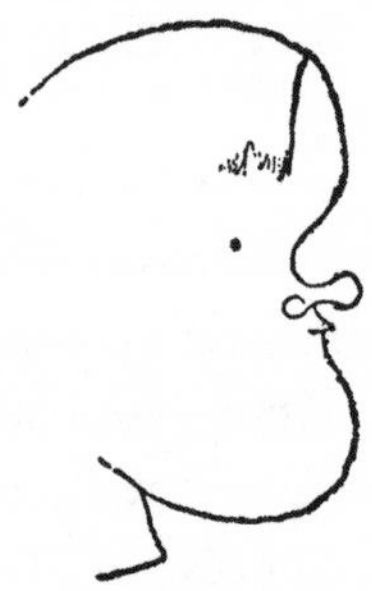

AURIC. *A drawing of the French modernist of music and member of "Les Six" who appears several times in Cocteau's Book.*

PIANO PLAYER. *One of the most extravagant of the Cocteau drawings, satirizing the composing methods and execution of the French Expressionists of music.*

Next we come to the portrait of Pierre Loti. Primarily, this drawing is the creation of an extremely sensitive individual: secondarily, it is the reaction of a "modern" (though by no means "super-realistic") writer to the "great literary figure of established reputation," the (defunct) "national genius," the over-worshipped narrator of exotic and iridescent tales. Anybody even superficially acquainted with the work (play would be a better word) of Loti, or with his literary-naval career, or with both, cannot fail to be impressed by the cruel delicacy, the unpitying skill, with which he has here been snared.

And now (at a dreadful risk) I should like to make a very few general remarks. The drawings from Cocteau's book selected here for reproduction give a fairly accurate idea of what Cocteau means, when he says that a poet "unties writing and ties it up again differently," in so far as such a statement means anything whatever (or in so far as writing resembles a necktie). The point, however, is this: a writer, assisted by "blotters, tablecloths and backs of enve-

LOTI AT HOME. *An admirable thrust at the Loti tradition. Cocteau has caught the mood and spirit of the author of "Madam Chrysanthème" in what one may call a caricature of his psyche.*

lopes," has presented us with a collection of what he prefers to call "strokes," certain of which are—to employ the most abused word in our language—beautiful. A number of these "strokes" (like the Picasso-Stravinsky sketch) may, if properly cued, roll into the pocket of "caricature"; whereas others, like a superb line drawing of two sumptuous horses, which Cocteau fortunately calls *Les Rimes Riches*, refuse to occupy any pigeonhole, except the meaningless one of "Art." Moreover, in the course of perusing this book of *Desseins*, we encounter a variety of drawings which insist on falling into several categories at once; which is why I stressed, a moment ago, the dangerous futility of classification. Finally, there is a thing (no better term suggests itself) called *Le Chant du Condamné à Mort*, whose few lines are responsible for the most gruesomely morbid emanation which I have yet encountered in a drawing (although, perhaps, a person has to have known prisons to appreciate the precise flavour)—and this "Song" silences, to my thinking, any kind of classification, unless we are content with the label: Cocteauism.

This mention of "morbid" brings me to the drawings comprised in Cocteau's latest book, of which the most remarkable group, unquestionably, is *Le Mauvais Lieu*. The "content" or "subject matter" of the drawings in this group (or rather, the conventional prejudice aroused by that content) will render their appreciation, in the land of the free, problematic. Nevertheless, be they "ithyphallic drolleries" or be they something else ("works of art," for example), certain of these *Mauvais Lieu* satires—along with a few other ironic "morbidities" and a goodly number of drawings whose subject matter will not generate a qualm in the soul of the most vicious of moralists—establish beyond question the fact that Jean Cocteau, whom we have hitherto known as a writer, is a draughtsman of first-rate sensitiveness.

From *Vanity Fair*, September 1925.

HOW TO SUCCEED AS AN AUTHOR

Some hints to young writers on the art of marketing their literary wares

By Scribner Tickel, Author of: "Can Spring Be Far Behind"

How to succeed as an author?

That is the problem, and a most difficult problem to solve. Obviously, the first thing to do is to publish a book and become famous. But that brings us to another difficulty. How are we to persuade a publisher to bring out our first book? Now, there is only one way to make a publisher think well of a manuscript by an unknown writer and that is to tell him that it was written not by yourself, but by some famous author, preferably Joseph Conrad, Henry James, H. G. Wells, or Michael Arlen. If a young author of moderate talent will only submit his first book to a New York publisher under the name of one (or more) famous authors, his path is certain to be strewn with primroses.

But, under his own name? Never!

The second rule is to get Heywood Broun to review it. And the third and last rule is to find a catchy title for it.

Listen, for instance, to the story of Charles James Smith, the ambitious and talented young author, who is here heard assailling the doors of Messrs. Harper, Appleton, Page & Co., Publishers, of New York.

Publisher—No, I cannot publish your book. You wrote the book and you are quite unknown, and that is all there is to it.

Author—But, well—you see, I really did *not* write the book.

P.—I'm sorry, but that doesn't make any difference.

A.—But Joseph Conrad wrote my book. He wrote it while I was in Italy.

P.—Ah, why didn't you say so before? And another thing, why didn't Conrad sign it?

A.—Because he had a cold and went to Switzerland instead.

P.—I have a terrible cold myself.

A.—But this cold of Conrad's was in Italy.

P.—So was Conrad. Nothing remarkable in that.

A.—But the book deals with what the book deals with. It is unique because it is unique. There is nothing like it because there is nothing like it, as Henry James said in the middle of the street, at Budapest.

P.—What was James doing in Budapest?

A.—Trying to find a synonym for "mushroom."

P.—Did he?

A.—Of course: "umbrella." It took him eleven months.

P.—To find an umbrella?

A.—Quite the contrary: to write my book.

P.—Not that it makes any difference, but I thought you said that Conrad wrote your book.

A.—Yes, Conrad wrote it first, but James wrote it afterwards.

P.—Oh, I see. How did that happen?

A.—Accidentally. They were such good friends.

P.—And did James sign it?

A.—Not quite.

P.—What do you mean by "not quite"?

A.—Well, to tell you the truth, he tripped over a nasturtium early one morning, and almost immediately left for Russia in a taxicab with a paper bag full of oranges.

P.—It is true that his asthma was very bad?

A.—Very. It was positively ornamental.

P.—And who wrote your book next?

A.—H. G. Wells. But that was in Dublin, and besides, it was raining.

P.—It always rains in Dublin, so that doesn't make any difference.

A.—But you don't understand: James stole Wells' umbrella in Dublin, which Conrad returned to James in Italy: whereas Wells lent Henry James Joseph Conrad's cold, all in exchange for the asthma.

P.—Is it possible?

A.—Yes, but it is also untrue that Michael Arlen writes hurriedly. For instance, he wrote my book in two hours and twenty-five minutes.

P.—Where and when, may I ask?

A.—Of a Thursday, beside the point, in a gondola off Long Island.

P.—Well, well.

A.—Yes, he is indeed a sick man.

P.—In that case I really cannot publish your book, because I believe you wrote it, because the people who wrote it (because you did not write it) did not sign their names. Is that perfectly clear?

A.—It would be, if Arlen had not signed his name.

P.—Oh—so he signed his name?

A.—In Prague, yes. But somebody bought the manuscript on the Aquitania for twelve pounds.

P.—I should have rather expected that you would almost have preferred to pawn your, shall we say, watch?

A.—I would not part with my watch for two reasons: third, because it was not a Christmas present; and fifth, because it always makes me ill to ride backwards.

P.—Indeed. That throws a completely new light on the matter.

A.—And I don't drink and smoke.

P.—Magnificent. May I ask if you have any children?

A.—Thousands of them.

P.—Girls or boys?

A.—Twins.

P.—M-m-m. Have you any critical opinions on your manuscripts?

A.—I should say I have.

P.—From whom?

A.—No less a critic than Heywood Broun himself.

P.—What did he say?

A.—It was all rather spectacular. Heywood was standing on the sidewalk when his eyes fell on the manuscript. As he read on, a sort of terror convulsed his face—for the first time in the man's critical career he was speechless—then, literally tearing his glance from my chef-d'oeuvre, and addressing the nearest policeman, he murmured gradually: "We have been cleansed by pity and terror."

P.—Not really!

A.—Yes; really and truly.

P.—And then?

A.—Then, braced by this praise, I tried it on the Diamond Brothers, the murderers.

P.—Your manuscript?

A.—The same.

P.—They were enthusiastic?

A.—Positively electrified.

P.—What is your book called, if I may ask?

A.—Well sir, after considering such titles as Lord Jack, The Golden Vase, Mr. Whittling, and The Emerald Fedora, I hit upon a nomenclature at once succinct and euphonious—

P.—Which is?

A.—"The Sea-Urchin's Lullaby, or Why They Wanted Children."

P.—My God, man: why didn't you tell me that first? Bully title! Bully! Of course I'll publish it!

From *Vanity Fair*, September 1925.

THE ADULT, THE ARTIST AND THE CIRCUS

A mildly philosophic plea for the performers, the menagerie and the freaks

Editor's Note: You enjoy the theatre and you enjoy art, but do you enjoy the circus? Did you go to the circus this year? And if so, did you have a really good time? If you are bored at the circus, or if you don't go for fear of being bored, read what a "modernistic" writer and painter has to say on this subject—then, at the very next opportunity, visit the circus and be bored—if you can be!

When something joyous, which made our childhood particularly worth while, fails to delight us as adults, we go through the apparently serene process of assuming a lofty attitude toward the "outgrown" pleasure. Upon close inspection, however, this process proves to be far from serene. Take our grown-up disdain of the circus, for instance. What actually happens, from the moment when the circus first occurs to us until the moment when we dismiss it as "childish," is nothing less than a BATTLE.

For, at the very thought of "circus," a swarm of long-imprisoned desires breaks jail. Armed with beauty and demanding justice and everywhere threatening us with curiosity and Spring and childhood, this mob of forgotten wishes begins to storm the supposedly impregnable fortifications of our Present. We are caught off our guard—we must defend ourselves somehow: any weapon will do.

We seize the idea that a circus is nothing but a big and colourful toy especially invented for the amusement of undeveloped or naif minds. With this idea and the idea that the theatre is an enlightened form of entertainment worthy of our mature intelligences, we lay about us wildly; until—after a brave struggle—the motley horde retreats, abandoning its dead and wounded. But we ourselves are not unscathed: our wounds give us no peace; we must somehow forget them. Accordingly we betake ourselves to a theatre or to the movies. There, under the influence of a powerful anaesthetic known as Pretend, we forget not only the circus but all our other sorrows, including the immortal dictum of that inexorable philosopher Krazy Kat: *It's what's behind me that I am.*

But suppose, now, that an exciting experiment is attempted. Why not try to consider the circus directly, or as a self-sufficient phenomenon independent of the theatre, movies, radio and similar lofty amusements? I have in mind neither a detailed analysis of the American circus of today, nor yet a pompous monologue on the circus throughout the ages, but merely a few personal remarks anent the menagerie, the freaks, and the "big show" of the Ringling Brothers and Barnum & Bailey circus.

And speaking of the menagerie, nothing can shake my conviction that a periodic and highly concentrated dose of wild animals—elephants, tigers, lions, leopards, jaguars, bears, wolves, giraffes, kangaroo, zebras, horned horses, camels, hyenas, rhinoceri and at least one hippopotamus—is indispensable to the happiness of all mature civilized human beings. Were Congress to pass a bill compelling every adult inhabitant of the United States of America to visit the circus at least twice a year, with the stipulation that each visitor must spend (willy-nilly) not less than half an hour in the menagerie, I believe that, throughout the entire country, four out of five hospitals, jails and insane-asylums would close down. It is my hunch that, as an immediate result of this simple legislation, hundreds of cripples—lame, halt and blind—would toss their infir-

mities to the winds, thousands of ill-starred homes would break into paeans of rejoicing—and millions of psychoanalysts would be thrown out of employment.

For the benefit of any disciple of Freud who may chance to peruse the above statement, I hereby whisper that my own totem is the elephant. And what, gentle subscriber to *Vanity Fair*, may your totem be? In case you aren't sure, or think you haven't any, I counsel you to take the very next train for whatever city the circus may happen to occupy (unless you are so fortunate as to have it with you at the moment). Above all, don't be satisfied with a trip to some mere zoo; for zoos—poor, placid, colourless things that they are—completely lack that outrageous intensity which makes the circus menagerie unique as a curative institution and endows the denizens of that institution with a fourth- or fifth-dimensional significance for the neuroses.

By this time, surely, my worthy readers have doubtless decided that I myself am a salaried member of that branch of the circus which comprises "the strange people." Although this is an error—although I am neither a Missing Link nor a Fat Lady nor yet an Ambassador from Mars—I may mention that I feel highly complimented at being mistaken for one or all of these prodigies. For (in my opinion) happy is that writer, who, in the course of his lifetime, succeeds in making a dozen persons react to his personality as genuinely or vividly as millions react, each and every year, to the magnetic personality of Zip, the What-Is-It! Nor can I refrain, at this point, saluting also the Giant, the Pygmy, the Pin-Head, the unutterably refined Human Skeleton and the other distinguished members of Zip's very select society. Having done this, I shall spare my readers further rhapsody. In return for the favor, I ask that all who are interested in a sensitive interpretation of certain world-famous oddities, as well as in the origin of what we now call the American circus, will hasten to consult (if by mischance they have not already done so) M.R. Werner's excellent and extremely entertaining biography: *Barnum*.

Having cast rapid glances at the menagerie and the freaks, we enter "the big top"—where dwells the really-truly circus-show. This may be described as a gigantic spectacle; *which is surrounded by an audience,*—in contrast to our modern theatres, where an audience and a spectacle merely confront each other. The show itself, we immediately notice, has a definite kind of bigness. By "definite kind," I mean that the bigness of the circus-show is intrinsic—like the bigness of an elephant or of a skyscraper—not superficial, as in the case of an enlarged snapshot. The nature of this bigness becomes apparent when we perceive that it is never, for so much as the fraction of an instant, motionless. Anyone who has stood just across the street from the Woolworth Building and has watched it wriggle upward like a skyrocket, or who has observed the irrevocably, gradually moving structure of an elephant which is "standing still"—anyone who has beheld these miracles, will understand me when I say the bigness of the circus-show is *a kind of mobility.* Movement is the very stuff out of which this dream is made. Or we may say that movement is the content, the subject matter, of the circus-show, while bigness is its form; provided we realize that here (as in all true "works of art") content and form are aspects of a homogeneous whole.

At this great spectacle, as nowhere else, the adult onlooker knows that unbelievably skilful and inexorably beautiful and unimaginably dangerous things are continually happening. But this is not all: he feels that there is a little too much going on at any given moment. Here and now, I desire to point out that *this is as it should be.* To the objection that the three-ring circus "creates such a confused impression," I beg to reply: "Speaking of confused impressions—how about the down-rush of a first-rate roller coaster or the incomparable yearning of the Parisian *balançoirs à vapeur,* not to mention the solemn visit of a seventy-five centimetre projectile and the frivolous propinquity of Shrapnel?" For it is with thrilling experiences of a life-or-death order (including certain authentic "works of art"—and most emphatically *not* with going to the movies or putting out the cat) that the circus-show entirely belongs.

Within "the big top," as nowhere else on earth, is to be found Actuality. Living players play with living. There are no tears produced by onion-oil and Mr. Nevin's Rosary, no pasteboard hovels and *papier-mâché* palaces, no "cuts," "retakes," or "N.G.'s"—and no curtain calls after suicide. At positively every performance Death Himself lurks, glides, struts, breathes, is. Lest any agony be missing, a mob of clowns tumbles loudly in and out of that inconceivably sheer fabric of doom, whose beauty seems endangered by the spectator's least heartbeat or whisper. As for the incredible and living designs, woven in this fabric by animal trainers, equestrians, acrobats—they are immune to forgetfulness in the same way that certain paintings, poems and musical compositions are immune. Although it was only once, and twenty-odd years ago, that my eyes had the extraordinary honour to behold a slight young man whose first name was DANGER DERIDING DEATH DEFYING DESPERATE DAREDEVIL DIAVOLO LOOPS THE LOOP ON A BICYCLE (his last name being, if I am not mistaken, PORTHOS: LEAPS THE GAP OVER FIVE ELEPHANTS), I have not forgotten this person and shall never forget him, simply because he was a great artist—who, like Paul Cézanne, died the most fortunate and illustrious of deaths: died at the *motif*, and in the execution of his art.

So, *un*gentle reader, (as you and I value what we should be ashamed—after witnessing a few minor circus-marvels—to call our "lives,") let us never be fooled into taking seriously that perfectly superficial distinction which is vulgarly drawn between the circus-show and "art" or "the arts." Let us not forget that every authentic "work of art" is in and of itself alive and that, however "the arts" may differ among themselves, their common function is the expression of that supreme alive-ness which is known as "beauty." This being so, our three ring circus is art—for to contend that the spectacle in question is not an authentic manifestation of "beauty" is as childish, as to dismiss the circus on the ground that it is "childish," is idiotic.

In closing, the present writer wishes to state (1) that an extremely intimate connection exists between Con Colleanos' forward somersault (from and to a wire in mid-air) and Homer's Odyssey (2) that a sure method of understanding Igor Stravinsky's *Le Sacre du Printemps*, is to study the voluminous precision and fugual delicacy of Mr. Ringling's "Ponderous Pachyderms under the direction of the greatest of all animal trainers" (3) that El Greco, in painting, and "Ernest Clark, in his triple somersaulting double-twisting and reverse flights through space" give strikingly similar performances, and (4) that the fluent technique of seals and of sea lions comprises certain untranslatable idioms, certain innate flexions, which astonishingly resemble the spiritual essence of poetry.

From *Vanity Fair*, October 1925: line drawings by the author.

THE VERY LATEST SCHOOL IN ART

An unconsciousnist painter and a kindly critic of

ye olde schoole exchange ideas

By Scribner Tickel

TIME: Midnight

SCENE: *A basement cellar, minus wallpaper, furniture and windows. The artist, a pallid youth whose mouth is crammed with brushes, chalk, charcoal palette knives, pencils, etc., stands in a thoroughly smashed straw hat and a pair of arsenic-green pyjamas—splashing, slashing, scraping, smudging, at a gigantic canvas. The intense darkness of the cellar is broken only by the fitful glow of a cigarette, which indicates that the critic (a respectable old gentleman well past his dotage, seated timidly on a cracker-box in the opposite corner) is smoking nervously. From all possible directions in the apartments above, come noises of phonographs, radios, pianolas, quarrelings, screams, and an occasional pistol shot.*

THE CRITIC: *(After some minutes, crying out shrilly above the uproar)* You're quite sure I'm not disturbing you—I think I'd really better go—I'll come another time.

THE ARTIST: *(Shouts through his nose)* Remain! Don't budge! Proceed!

C: But really—I don't wish to interrupt—

A: *(Scornfully)* You couldn't interrupt if you tried!

C: *(Quaking)* But you see. . . . I just dropped in with the idea of asking a few questions—I didn't expect to find you busy—

A: For Heaven's sake, ask your questions: ask me something—nothing—everything—anything. . . . I must have some distraction, some excitement. *(Bawls out at the top of his voice)* It's too quiet in here!

C: *(In amazement)* Do you really mean to say that you *enjoy* this hideous racket?

A: *(Shouts)* Hideous?—Not at all, Beautiful! Noise is the sublime incarnation of the spirit of the twenty-second century in terms of the twentieth—I love it!

C: *(Doubtfully)* But I should think it would inhibit your—

A: On the contrary. Stimulates me! I tell you I love it: the more noise the better.

C: Indeed! But what of your art?

A: You don't understand. That's the whole point: my art is *unconscious.*

C: You mean you've never attended any schools?

A: I should hope NOT! But that's neither here nor there.

C: Just how do you use the word "Unconscious?"

A: In the usual, ultra-Freudian-infra-Jungian-extra-Adlerian sense.

C: Oh, I see—but what on earth has noise got to do with your "Unconscious?"

A: Stupid!—it's all perfectly simple. I am an Unconscious artist: so long as my Conscious interferes with what I'm doing, my art is at a standstill; I am helpless, thwarted, frustrated.

C: Yes, but—

A: *(Fiercely)* No "buts!" I tell you the thing as it is. In order to create a picture, I am first of all forced to eliminate my conscious mind and will.

C: *(Timidly)* I should think that would be rather difficult—

A: Difficult? Just the opposite. Noise is the solution! Racket—tumult—hurly-burly—that's what does it!

C: *(Cringing, as a revolver shot is heard directly overhead, followed by a long drawn-out scream)* You certainly seem to have succeeded in finding a place suited to your . . . let us say, tastes.

A: *(Shouts back proudly)* It *is* noisy, isn't it! And let me tell you, I sought far and wide before I came on this paradise! It was not an easy matter getting myself a domicile as thrilling and distracting and conscious-killing as this one!

C: And as dark.

A: Ah—that's my second great discovery!

C: *(Confused)* But my dear fellow, do you mean to tell me that you paint in the dark *by preference*?

A: Certainly! Of course I do.

C: May I inquire why?

A: *(Simply)* Because, otherwise, I might see what I was doing—and that would be fatal to my art. That would make me conscious.

C: Really?

A: *(With conviction)* Absolutely fatal. *(A pause, during which the sounds of many drunken people of various genders hurling themselves hither and thither, above the studio, are heard: cries of "Police! Murder! Fire!" come from various directions: a table is upset with a thunderous crash of glass.)*

C: *(In a trembling voice)* I say—excuse me . . . would you mind—would you very much object if I lit a match—

A: *(Sternly)* What for?

C: Just—just to see the picture you're working on—for a moment—

A: Impossible. That would spoil everything.

C: But you don't need to see it yourself—suppose I first blindfolded you? *(Coaxingly)* With a nice silk handkerchief?

A: No, no. That doesn't work—I used to paint blindfolded, by candle light: but it didn't work: I found myself peeping. *(Sadly)* We are all human.

C: Still, after all, I'll see the picture sometime, so why not now?

A: *(Ferociously)* *You* will *see* it? When? Where? How?

C: In some gallery—

A: *(Witheringly)* Gallery?

C: —When you exhibit it—

A: *(With great emotion)* I want you to know, sir, that I am *not* an exhibitionist!

C: You don't understand—surely, some time—

A: The parasitic art galleries are clamouring with slavering mouths for my work, sir, but I want you to know that I am too much in love with my art to stoop to such a vile, degenerate and neurotic act as the exhibition of my canvases.

C: *(In great confusion)* But—but you never intend to show your paintings—?

A: *(Emphatically)* Never, sir! *(With a touch of pride)* Not even to myself!

C: In that case, excuse me for asking . . . how do you expect to live?

A: *(Proudly)* I am an artist, sir, and the world *owes* me a living.

C: But if the world refuses to believe—

A: —That it owes me a living? Then, sir, I shall starve: it is my prerogative.

C: I meant, supposing the world (never having had an opportunity to behold your efforts) does not recognize the fact that you *are* an artist?

A: *(Contemptuously)* So much the worse for the world!

C: *(Much amazed)* A very remarkable idea, certainly!

A: My own idea, sir, and nobody else's.

C: But what of the great masters?

A: I acknowledge no masters.

C: And may I ask, where did you get the idea of painting?

A: I didn't get it—it got me.

C: H'm . . . and what becomes of your, let us say, works of art, when they're finished? Do you hide them away, or—*(A frightful crash: the critic starts to his feet with a cry—the whole cellar trembles to its very foundations.)*—My God! What on earth happened *then*?

A: *(Calmly)* I have answered your question.

C: My—? My question?

A: *(Even more calmly, laying aside an axe)* I have finished your portrait.

C: Good Heavens—

A: You may now strike a match. *(The critic does so: revealing the gigantic canvas in ruins at the artist's feet.)*

C: So that was my—my portrait—which you were working on all this time?

A: It was.

C: And you have destroyed it utterly.

A: I have.

C: Why?

A: Why not? It was finished.

C: How could you be sure?

A: The answer to that question is very simple: I knew that your portrait was finished when I found that I had no more charcoal, that my last pencil was broken, that all my pastels were gone, that my palette knife had bent double, and that my colours were exhausted.

C: *(Putting his hand to his brow)* Extraordinary . . . I feel as if I were going mad . . . excuse me—good day. *(He totters feebly toward the door.)*

A: *(Interposing)* Stop! *(The critic halts, in terror.)* You have forgotten something!

C: *(Desperately)* I have my hat.

A: You have forgotten something very much more important than your hat.

C: *(Almost weeping)* What—what have I forgotten?

A: *(Folding his arms)* You have forgotten—to ask the price.

C: *(Astounded)* Price?

A: Certainly.

C: Price of what?

A: Of the finished portrait of you, my dear sir.

C: Do you mean . . .

A: I mean exactly what I say: you owe me five thousand five hundred and fifty dollars plus fifty-five cents war tax.

C: *(Falling on his knees)* Spare me—spare me—I am but a poor man—

A: *(Coldly)* So am I.

C: *(Imploringly)* I have a large family—

A: *(Icily)* That is not my fault.

C: *(Sobbing)* Take a check for a thousand dollars and let me go!

A: *(With polar frigidity)* I take no checks.

C: *(Hysterically pulling a bill from his pocket)* But I have only five dollars with me in cash. . . .

A: Five dollars!!! *(Leaping on him and embracing him wildly)* My dear man—my good, kind friend—my patron—my mentor—my saviour! *(He pockets the bill.)* May Heaven prosper you! *(He shakes the swooning critic's hands, kisses him fervently again and again on the forehead, pulls him affectionately by one ear toward the door, kicks him up the basement stairs caressingly, and fondly throws him into the middle of Great Jones Street, where he is immediately run over by a two-ton truck belonging to the Society for the Prevention of Cruelty to Animals.)*

From *Vanity Fair*, October 1925.

HELEN WHIFFLETREE, AMERICAN POETESS

A tribute to a native artist, nurtured in Greenwich Village and Montmartre

By P. H. Dunkels, N.G.

Editor's Note: The unexpected demise of Helen Whiffletree, the American poetess, who was accidentally shot by a *gendarme* while she was picking violets in the *Bois de Boulogne*, has saddened poetry lovers all over the world and deprived *Vanity Fair* of one of its most valued contributors. Wishing to give a slight token of our profound grief at Miss Whiffletree's tragic disappearance from the field of letters, we asked the internationally known authority on literature, Professor P. H. Dunkels, of Colgate University, to write a brief biographical sketch and appreciation of his illustrious contemporary, Helen Whiffletree. It is our conviction that Professor Dunkels' article, which we publish herewith, is fraught with comfort and happiness for the host of this poetess's admirers, both here and in Europe. They number countless thousands.

Helen Whiffletree was born amid lowly surroundings in the unlovely town of Arlington Heights, Massachusetts, on the seventeenth day of August, 1889, of Irish-Italian parents. Her mother, Gertrude Magee, was descended from a long line of brewers. Giuseppi Paladini, her father, rose to the position of first assistant dishwasher in the local automat restaurant, but apparently failed to make good.

Confronted on every hand with hardships and privations,

Helen set about at an early age to earn her own living. At the age of nine, she was supporting her indigent mother and seven sisters by selling newspapers, dressed in boy's clothes. The natural elasticity of her spirits and the vivacity of her adolescent personality in general attracted the notice of Matthew Whiffletree, a St. Louis lumber merchant well past his dotage, who happened to buy a newspaper from Helen. After making the necessary inquiries, he adopted her as his own daughter and sent her to a number of expensive schools, including Brierley (where she distinguished herself by winning a scholarship, shortly before leaving under a cloud) and thence to Vassar.

Early in her career, in fact while still in her teens at college, Helen Whiffletree wrote verse in which naiveté is carried to a pitch of unheard-of poignancy. As an example, I can do no better than quote eight lovely lines which appeared, over the signature "H. W.," in the literary magazine of her alma mater, and which are entitled "Conversation."

"Quoth a busy bee
To a butterfly
'Honey make I
And what maketh thee?'
'Go ask a lily,'
Was the sage reply
Of the silly
Butterfly."

To this, her collegiate period, belong also such lilting lyrics as "Sodom and Gomorrah," "A Sparrow's Christmas," "Under the Mistletoe," and the inimitable "Day-Dream"—her first experiment in the Petrarchan sonnet form; which, besides showing the influence of Keats, caused three leading New York critics to compare her to Mrs. Browning, Shakespeare and Sappho, respectively.

Readers of *Vanity Fair* will doubtless pardon me for reminding them of the exquisite sextet:

"I ope my windows to this April eve,
Letting sweet twilight whisper o'er my soul
Its wondrous secrets without more ado.
Night from day's sentence now doth seek reprieve,
While—from the summit of yon wooded knoll—
A final whippoorwill the ear doth woo."

Alexander Woollcott is said to have remarked, when the last line was recited to him for the first time by a friend in the course of a camping trip in the Canadian Rockies: "It hurts, it is so fine."

Having been dismissed from Vassar without her degree for an innocent girlish prank involving several of the best families of Cleveland, the poetess inhabited, in quick succession, Bangor, Topeka and Salt Lake City and arrived, penniless but exultant, in Greenwich Village, where she was immediately understood and vigorously acclaimed by an enthusiastic little *coterie* of struggling artists and models, many of whom lent her money in small quantities as a tribute to the surge of odes, triolets, rondels, rondeaux, chants royals, etc., etc., which poured from her teeming brain almost ceaselessly at this fecund time. In all these poems, the subject matter is, as might be expected, love in its multiple aspects, maternal affection and devotion to one's fellow man (or woman) being particularly stressed. Three volumes of love songs—"Satyr," "Chants and Reprisals," and "Afternoon Sunlight"—saw the light of day via Boni & Liveright. Indeed, so prolific did her muse become, that these Greenwich Village poems alone outnumber the combined output of Whittier, Tennyson and Meredith. But more remarkable even than their numerosity is the technique of those creations. Note, for instance, the subtle mastery of a difficult form in this frolicsome "Triolet" from "Chants":

"Is my answer to Pedro
Who offers bananas,
'You make my heart bleed'—? No.
Is my answer to Pedro,
'One dozen'—? Indeed no!
—'Retro me, Satanas!'
Is my answer to Pedro
Who offers bananas."

From New York, where she divorced a banker and several noted theatrical producers, it was but a step to Paris and the *Quartier Latin*; where, in a modest little hotel off the *Boulevard Montparnasse*, our poetess finally found the perfect spiritual environment which she had ceaselessly craved and where her art attained to its full maturity. Although the singing syllables of Helen Whiffletree were already on the lips of more than ten thousand poetry lovers in America, it was in Paris that her real fame came to her. Eighteen months after leaving New York, this magnetic Sappho was the idol of the *Rotonde* and darling of the *Dôme*, to which latter *café* she dedicated several of her best-known sonnets.

Meanwhile, in proportion as her reputation increased—while critics on both sides of the Atlantic were awarding her latest eight books a place beside the immortal works of Goethe, Anatole France and Donald Ogden Stewart—her personality assumed truly hypnotic proportions. From the very beginning, she had exercised a mysterious and compelling power over whomsoever she came in contact with; but Paris accentuated this power to an incredible degree. It is no exaggeration to say that the psychic influence of Helen Whiffletree is unsurpassed in the history of letters.

My first experience with this emanation is unforgettable. It is all bound up with the tiptop of Montmartre—the famous *Place du Tertre*, overlooking Paris. Here, as is well known, all the Americans in the city (except those who are too involved in the delights of the grape to budge) wend their ubiquitous way, to dine and drink out-of-doors and be entertained by a motley crew of acrobats, musicians and prestidigitators. On the particular evening in question, the scene was of a more-than-typical picturesqueness. Anton Cul, the blind gipsy violinist, was weaving iridescent harmonies in one corner, despite the unbridled enthusiasm of the neighbouring spectators, who showered him with hundred franc notes, which were cleverly collected by a cocker spaniel furnished by the management, and deposited in the musician's by-no-means-microscopic hat. On another part of the hilltop, a group of diners were applauding the prowess of Zizz, the Fire-Bird, who—having climbed on a somewhat rickety table—proceeded to balance upside-down on an ordinary champagne glass and at the same time to swallow lighted cannon crackers, pinwheels and even (to the horror of Marianne Moore, whom I particularly remarked) a roman candle. In yet another portion of the *Place*, Hermaphrodites, strong man of Constantinople, was throwing his three-hundred-pound wife slowly and rhythmically up into the April evening, only to catch her in one hand as she descended.

All at once the violinist sank for support against the slight form of the cocker spaniel, which collapsed with a sharp whine, regurgitating two thousand francs—the Fire-Bird uttered a moan and rolled upon the ground, exuding rockets, mines and similar pyrotechnical monstrosities in every conceivable direction, to the vast embarrassment of the spectators—the strong man clasped his almost nonexistent occiput in both mammoth hands, uttering a terrible cry and paying no attention to his wife—who descended with her usual velocity and completely demolished eleven bottles of champagne, a United States Senator, and Mrs. Cholmondley P. Biddle of Philadelphia and Newport.

In the midst of the consternation caused by these unprecedented accidents, I lifted my eyes and beheld the incarnation of American patriotism stepping from a two-cylinder taxi: at the same moment, a hundred throats exclaimed "Helen Whiffletree!" The poetess (for it was indeed she) was attired in a red tamoshanter, a white *cache-nez* and sky-blue pyjamas. True to her ancestry, she carried under one arm the *Decameron* and under the other a nearly empty quart bottle labelled *Hennessy Three Star.* The striking beauty of her getup, as—"without more ado"—she produced a large harmonica and proceeded to sound the opening chords of the Star Spangled Banner, was accentuated by an exhilarating negligence of poise which, in another, might have been attributed to artificial stimuli rather than "divine fire." But, while the sacred strains of O Say Can You burst upon the electrified assembly, along with memories of heroic self-sacrifice, unparalleled devotion and unstinting *camaraderie*, only one thing occurred to me; which was, that I owed it to posterity to preserve, at any cost, my first, virginal impression of this authentic genius. Accordingly I tore down the hill and into the *Moulin Rouge*, where my favourite waiter brought me the usual pen and ink.

"The rest is silence."

From *Vanity Fair*, November 1925.

YOU AREN'T MAD, AM I?

Being certain observations anent the extremely modern art of "burlesk"

As one of those helplessly observant individuals who are sometimes referred to as "modern" artists, I am confident that the art of burlesk (note the k) is particularly unobserved, both by "intelligent people" in general and by readers of *Vanity Fair* in particular. My aim in making this somewhat threatening statement is an innocent one. I merely wish to dissipate any and all illusions, on the part of my audience, as to the precise nature of "this little essay": which is nothing more nor less than a series of observations.

These observations, not unnaturally, have to do with the essence of the art in question. Supposing we assume (for the nonce) that burlesk is an art: how, then, does it fundamentally differ from other arts, such as painting, literature and the theatre?

First let us take the art of three-dimensional painting. Here, as in "nature," not only do we never see around a solid person or object, but the very solidity of the object or person is conditioned by our inability to see around it, her, or him. More simply, in the case of sculpture: only one aspect of a statue is presented to us—in perceiving the rest, we are compelled to lose sight of what we have already seen; to revolve the figure, or else move around it ourselves. But the graphic arts and the theatre have an analogous limitation—that is, a thing or character cannot possibly be presented as beautiful, noble, or desirable and also as ugly, ignoble and despicable.

"Of course not!" my readers will exclaim: "because 'ugly' and 'beautiful' are opposities, just as 'weak' and 'strong' are opposites. Isn't a weak drink the opposite of a strong one? Leaving out 'black' and 'white,' how can any American of this day and time, who hasn't experienced a thoroughly 'bad' drink, talk about a 'good' one—and vice versa?"

Dumbfounding as are these arguments, I must needs point out an important fact. Just as our fair land of dollars and no sense was not always blest with prohibition, even so language was not always blest with "opposites." Quite the contrary. A certain very wise man has pointed out (in connection with the meaning of dreams) that what "weak" means and what "strong" means were once upon a time meant *by one word.* To understand this, it is quite unnecessary for us to try to imagine ourselves bloodthirsty savages of the forest primeval, or even to become psychoanalysts. All we have to do is to observe closely something which is flourishing under our very noses, today—the art of burlesk.

For in burlesk, we meet with an echo of the original phenomenon: "opposites" occur *together.* For that reason, burlesk enables us to (so to speak) *know around* a thing, character, or situation. To put it a little differently: if the art of common-or-garden painting were like the art of burlesk, we should be able to see—impossibly enough—all the way around a solid tree, instead of merely seeing a little more than half of the tree (thanks to binocular parallax or whatever it is) and imagining the rest. This impossible knowing around, or nonimagining, quality, constitutes the essence of burlesk and differentiates it from certain better-understood arts.

With the idea of making my point perfectly clear, I shall try to describe something which impressed me, at the time, as one of the most extraordinary experiences which I had ever had; something which happened, a few years ago, on the stage of that most extraordinary temple of burlesk, the *National Winter Garden*—then, as now, located at the corner of East Houston Street and Second

Avenue, New York City—which institution I regard as superior to any other burlesk stronghold which I have yet inhabited, not excluding the Howard Atheneum, in Boston.

The protagonist of the occasion was a famous burlesk star named Jack Shargel (since retired; at that date, as I believe, one of two very great actors in America, number two being Charlie Chaplin) and the experience was this: a beauteous lady (weighing several hundred pounds) hands the super-Semitic, black-derbied, misfit-clothed, keen-eyed but ever-imposed-on individual called Jack Shargel a red rose—Shargel receives her gift with a gesture worthy of any prince; cautiously escorts the flower to his far from negligible nose; rapturously, deliriously even, inhales its deep, luxurious, seductive, haunting fragrance; then (with a delicacy which Chaplin might envy) tosses the red rose exquisitely, lightly, from him. The flower flutteringly describes a parabola—weightlessly floats downward—and just as it touches the stage there is a terrific, soul-shaking, earthquake-like *crash*: as if all the glass and masonry on earth, all the most brittle and most ponderous things of this world, were broken to smithereens.

Nothing in "the arts," indeed, not even Paul Cézanne's greatest painting of *Mont Sainte-Victoire*, has moved me more, or has proved

THE JEW COMEDIAN. *With a delicacy which Chaplin might envy he tosses the red rose of burlesque, lightly, flutteringly from his hand.*

to be a more completely inextinguishable source of "aesthetic emotion," than this *knowing around* the Shargel rose; this releasing of all the un-roselike and non-flowerish elements which—where "rose" and "flower" are *ordinarily* concerned—*secretly or unconsciously* modify and enhance those rose—and flower—qualities to which (in terms of consciousness only) they are "opposed."

But hark—I can hear my readers exclaiming: "the idea of becoming pompous and highbrow on such a topic—when everybody is wise to the fact that burlesque shows are distinctly inartistic and frankly lowbrow affairs!"

One moment: there are "burlesque shows" and this is thanks to the supporters of the National Winter Garden, Burlesk. But, granted that—on the surface—no two things could possibly seem more incompatible than burlesk (the original undiluted article) and "Art," this is important only as proving how little "cultured" people observe for themselves and how consistently they are duped by preconceived notions. Should my readers take the trouble to examine, not conventional or academic "art," but "modern" (also called "primitive") art—art of today, art which is alive—they will discover that, in ridiculing the aesthetic significance of burlesk with a k, they are talking through their hats. For example: that favourite war cry of modern literature, *le mot juste*, is pre-eminently the war cry of burlesk, where we find in abundance such perfectly unambiguous statements as: "I'll hit yer so hard yer shirt'll roll up yer back like a windowshade!" Again, what is frequently referred to as "abstract," "non-representative," cubistic," and even "futuristic," painting is fundamentally similar to such a use of the American language as this (whereby a wronged husband describes what he did to his wife's seducer—an artist, by the way—whom he found "standing on the brinkus of the Mrs. Sloppy river"): "so I pulled out my pickaxe and I cut his ear from throat to throat." Moreover, those of my readers who are already acquainted with the "neurotic" or "ultramodernistic" music of Arnold Schönberg will need no introduction to the agonizing tonality of those "sets"

CLEO. *The excessively mobile shimmy-dancer of burlesque who at an advanced stage of the dance exclaims: "Burn my clothes,—I'm in Heaven."*

and "drops" among which the hero-villains of the burlesk stage shimmy, glide, strut and tumble.

To sum up: the creations of the National Winter Garden possess, in common with the sculpture of Gaston Lachaise, the painting of John Marin and the music of Igor Stravinsky, the virtue of being intensely alive; whereas the productions of the conventional theatre, like academic sculpture and painting and music, are throughly dead—and since "art," if it means anything, means TO BE INTENSELY ALIVE, the former constitute art and the latter are balderdash. Futhermore, the fact that this highly stylized, inherently "abstract," positively "futuristic" art known to its devotees as burlesk is indubitably *for the masses*, knocks into a cocked chapeau the complaint of many so-called "critics" that "modern art" is "neurotic," "unhealthy," "insane," "arbitrary," "unessential," "superficial" and "not for the masses." My advice to anyone who doubts the validity of my assertions (which I repeat, are no more than firsthand observations) is: "get in to the Houston Street Home Of Burlesk As You Like It on a Saturday night (if you can) and then keep your eyes open!"

Above the curtain you will perceive a scroll, proclaiming in ample letters:

The Show Is
The
THING
—*Wm. Shakespeare*

I should have said, you will *occasionally* perceive this slogan; since a smoke screen, emanating from every known and unknown variety of nicotine-yielding device, renders the immortal "Wm." 's dictum somewhat transitory. You will also perceive an incomparable show, suggesting the theatre only in its time-length, an unparalleled concoction of "knowing around" incidents and happenings

DANCE DU VENTRE. *This form of the dance is most highly exploited and is, perhaps, the significant* solo *to the regular burlesque-goer.*

and occurrences and accidents; you will behold the anatomically unique chorus of 18 "National Wintergarden Rosebuds," a first-rate burlesk cast including three excellent protagonists who may or may not be entitled "Scratch," "(Stood) Ambrose" and "Goof," several *décors* which rival Picasso's setting for Erik Satie's *Parade* (as originally performed in Paris by the *Ballet Russe*), syncopation *ad libitum*, absolutely authentic shimmying in triumphantly nonexistent costumes and—here we come to the *sine qua non* of the whole shebang—"Cleo," concerning whose *changement de nombril* I have the honour to exclaim: "Burn my clothes; I'm in Heaven!"

That the person who, in last month's *Vanity Fair*, bewailed a lack of *danse du ventre* in present day burlesQUE has never given "Cleo" 's *quid pro quo* an even superficial o.o. is as obvious to your humble servant as is the fact that he is not Einstein.

From *Vanity Fair*, December 1925: line drawings by the author.

"I CONFESS!"

A reformed reformer's sensational tribute to our American "Sex" magazines

By John F. Rutter

Editor's Note: Are "Sex" magazines immoral? Literally scores of magazines of this sort are published in America. The basis of most of them is the sex complication. Do periodicals like these "pollute" the mind? Have they a "pernicious influence" on "the rising generation"? Should they be excluded from the mails or should they openly flourish on the newsstands? Read this "true confession" of an ex-reformer, specially written for *Vanity Fair.*

Readers of *Vanity Fair* will recall that, only a few months ago, my name appeared on the front page of America's leading dailies in connection with a truly unfortunate occurrence. My beloved spouse (who had shared for ten years, without so much as a murmur, the responsibilities and dangers attendant upon the career of a militant anti-vice crusader) suddenly, and for no apparent reason, eloped with a Chinese laundryman, Foo King by name, after emptying an automatic pistol in the general direction of my whereabouts. Despite the conspicuous position which I at that time occupied as a purity crusader in Boston, the matter would probably have escaped everybody's notice—attempted assassination is so prevalent in America nowadays—but for the fact that the last of Mrs. Rutter's shots took disastrous effect on a pet Pekinese belonging to Miss Eleanora Sears, which was enjoying an airing nearly a quarter of a mile away, in the Boston Public Gardens. This terrible accident, besides creating a lively stir in fashionable and artistic circles, was directly responsible for my being disharged from the presidency of that foremost Puritan institution: the Society for the Contraception of Vice.

Bitterly as I bewailed this totally unexpected blow to my career (I was in the midst of an epoch-making work, entitled: "Lewd Literature—What Is It?" when the crash came) my agony at being summarily deprived of my wife was even greater. For, public opinion to the contrary, reformers are human beings. To have exercised the sacred prerogatives of a husband for an entire decade and suddenly to find oneself a bachelor of circumstance is, even to a reformer, painful. The popular cure—namely, to seek another mate—was naturally impossible to an individual of my refined and high-strung temperament. On the other hand, misfortune overtook me in the heyday of my, so to speak, natural resources. What should I do?

To this burning question my tortured soul responded, with a dark and ominous pertinacity: "Suicide!" Of course, I recoiled in horror from the thought of taking my own life. But, as time went on and my sense of loss materially increased, the idea of death assumed a positively pleasant aspect in my overwrought imagination. I began to realize that what was unpleasant was, not suicide, but the horrid possibility that it might be incomplete—in other words, that I might hurt myself very badly instead of merely killing myself. All I needed was a plan which, by eliminating any possibility of living, would render dying absolutely certain. Accordingly, I tossed my cherished work on lewd literature to the winds and considered how to secure my own demise.

Being an almost fanatically thorough person, as well as a lover of intellectual exercise, it took me only eight weeks to solve the puzzle. I then sold all my wordly possessions, including my magnificent Beacon Hill residence and my almost priceless collection of indecent, lewd, obscene and lascivious books, paintings, pamphlets, drawings, etchings and sculptures. With the proceeds, I purchased a piece of stout rope, a gallon of kerosene, a revolver, a box of safety matches and a ticket to a particularly secluded nook in an almost inaccessible portion of the Adirondacks, where I rented a small bungalow for twenty-four hours.

The porch of the exclusive and isolated dwelling which I had selected overhung a lake, above whose tranquil surface the eaves projected, at a height of several yards. Without losing any time, I made one end of my rope fast to these eaves and arranged a running-noose at the other end, in such a way that when I stood erect on the railing of the porch, facing the lake, the noose hung level with my chin. Next, I thoroughly soaked myself from top to toe with the kerosene and placed my box of matches on the railing. Finally, I loaded and cocked my revolver and laid it beside the matches, ready for action.

My miseries were about to cease. Thanks to the precautionary measures which I had adopted, death was absolutely sure. I merely had to mount the railing, adjust the noose around my neck, set fire to my clothes, shoot myself and leap into space. If the bullet missed my brain, no matter—I would be incinerated and hanged. If the kerosene failed to ignite, I would be hanged and shot. If the rope broke, I would be shot and incinerated. And even if everything went wrong—if the kerosene did not catch fire and the rope broke and the gun did not go off—I had no cause for alarm, since I could not swim a stroke and would consequently meet death by drowning in the lake below.

With what a sense of triumph did I climb on the railing in my kerosene-drenched clothes, pick up my matches and my revolver, adjust the running-noose around my neck and take my last look at the world! It was indeed a moment never to be forgotten. One of those magnificent Adirondack sunsets, you know the sort, drenched the heavens in splendour.

I heard a whippoorwill calling rhythmically to its mate in the woods just behind the little bungalow. About my ears, eyes, nose, and, in fact, everything else, several million mosquitoes, ignoring the odour of the kerosene, danced enthusiastically round about me. The whole scene was one of mingled exaltation and solemnity, which only the pen of a poet could possibly describe.

In this lyric *milieu,* I balanced myself precariously on the railing, with my neck in the fatal noose, pointing the revolver at my head with one hand and with some difficulty striking a match with the other. I had but one thought: my faithless wife, the former darling of my bosom, probably at that very instant enjoying the perfidious embraces of her villainous Oriental paramour. "Come to me, death!" I exclaimed with all my soul—and touched the blazing match to my left trouser-leg.

There was a roaring upward rush of flame—I pulled the trigger and jumped outward. The next thing I knew, I was sitting in approximately eighteen inches of icy water; thoroughly confused, minus my hair, whiskers, eyelids and eyebrows, but otherwise uninjured! After a few blessed seconds (during which I felt sure I was in Heaven) my intelligence informed me of what had actually happened. The flare-up of the kerosene had disconcerted my aim, the bullet—by some freak of chance—had cut the rope, the shallow water of the lake—whose depth I had completely omitted (in my excitement) to ascertain—had extinguished the fire: in brief, the whole intricately thought-out scheme had been a complete failure and—horrors!—I was alive after all.

I was about to lie down on my back and try to swallow the whole infamous lake, when a sheriff (attracted by my shot) arrived at full speed in a birchbark canoe, accompanied by two deputies armed to the teeth, and arrested me for not having a hunting license. Despite my vigorous protestation, I—John F. Rutter—was ignominiously tossed into a primitive log hut which served in the capacity of a jail.

It is probable that even Moses himself, as he glimpsed the Promised Land, experienced no more authentic thrill than did I—upon finding myself face to face with a half-dozen of those colourful little magazines which (as I remembered) I had spent the sum total of my misdirected energies in attempting to exclude from the mails.

When, a few minutes later, my jailer entered and discovered me prone upon the floor and frankly—for the first time—consuming photograph after photograph, illustration after illustration, experience after experience, confession after confession, a large grin of understanding bisected his bronze visage. He inspected me minutely for some moments; then delivered himself of the unforgettable dictum: "Reckon everything's hunkey-dorey with you, ain't it?" I started from my trance—and grasped his honest paw, in a silence that conveyed ineffable gratitude on my part and entire appreciation on his. "Have yer read 'Roll Over On Your Own Side, Lucy' yet?" he whispered, bending almost affectionately above me. "Not yet," I murmured faintly, with my eyes glued once more to "What a Young Girl of Thirteen Learned in Paris."

Since then I have attained a completely normal outlook on life. I am a respected, not a detested, member of the little house-party[1] here where I have been living pleasantly for some time since my adventure. I am almost foolishly happy, I laugh heartily whenever I recall my former morbid ideas and attribute my entire mental health and intellectual happiness to the one hundred and thirty-one (constantly issued, week by week, month by month) various and assorted "sex" magazines, of which I consume (on the average) twenty or thirty a day. In my estimation, they are one of the three greatest blessings which our civilization has produced, the other two being the player-piano and the radio.

From *Vanity Fair*, January 1926.

---

1. *Editor's Note*: Mr. Rutter is at present an inmate of the State Insane Asylum. The phrase "house-party," used by the author, refers, of course, to his incarceration in the asylum.

"I TAKE GREAT PLEASURE IN PRESENTING"

A distinguished foreign visitor to New York who has two distinct personalities

In contrast to some Americans, the readers of this journal have a reputation for being concerned with such neglected aspects of life as merit the adjectives "distinguished," "refined" and even "aristocratic." Unlike "the divine average" of our era (that two-fisted go-getting he or she whose spiritual nutriment, derived principally from the daily press, is confined to hand-picked manifestations of incredible unwisdom and superfluous mayhem) the readers of this periodical are said to demand *nuances*—and well-served. In this twentieth-century chaos, where idiocies mutilate ideas, débutantes massacre policemen and bootleggers inherit the earth, these same readers flash their sabres (we are told) for the "finer" values of existence. Assuming this to be true I take great pleasure in presenting, to all such courageous and distinguished ladies and gentlemen, an unutterably distinguished visitor from a distant clime; a mysterious and magnetic personage who, although considerably more noble, as I believe, than any king or prince who has yet sojourned among us, at present occupies far from sumptuous quarters at the New York Aquarium.

It would be difficult to imagine a more unconventional domicile of nobility than the Aquarium. Situated at the southwest extremity of Manhattan, it consists of a small roundish ancient structure which served first as a fort and later as a cage for P.T. Barnum's "Swedish Nightingale" (otherwise known as Miss Jenny Lind). Then somebody had the brilliant idea that there ought to be a lot of fish in it; whereupon tanks, embracing many pleasing and hideous varieties of aquatic phenomena, were installed, also several small roundish ancient attendants—and a photograph of an octopus. Such is that hovel of hydraulic wonders, the New York Aquarium, wherein the extraordinary visiting nobleman abovementioned has taken up his residence.

I suspect that most of my valiant readers associate great foreign celebrities with the Ritz and will consequently be shocked, upon learning that nobility can tolerate the extremely un-Ritzy environment which has just been described. But these readers must understand that the celebrity in question is by temperament amazingly democratic. Instead of selecting the *Aquitania* or the *Olympic* to convey him to our shores, he embarked at his native Galapagos Islands upon a by-no-means luxurious craft known as the *S. S. Arcturus.*

At the Aquarium we find him attended, not by a suite of valets, private secretaries, newspaper reporters and plainclothesmen, but by a solitary gull of the species known as "Booby." Toward those hordes of curious onlookers which hang upon his every gesture—uttering such typical American profundities as, "Ain't he sweet?" "Just like a puppydog," "Looka de lidl ole man" and "Whudduhyuh mean dat fish ain't a boid?"—he maintains an attitude of perfect friendliness, without ever, for so much as an instant, relinquishing that poise which bespeaks generations of wellbred ancestors. Even the nickname "Charlie" (which has reference to his terrestrial emanation) cannot ruffle that cheerful and exquisite dignity which is perhaps his most striking characteristic.

When I say "his terrestrial emanation" I mean to imply a very significant fact. The Penguin, as this wholly unprecedented individual is entitled, possesses a double existence. Strictly speaking, *he is two* individuals. The first individual struts and dances upon a tiny wooden platform. The second individual glides and swoops through the negligible quantity of water which surrounds the platform. Only by considering separately these two remarkably distinct individuals, selves, or emanations—one terrestrial, the other aquatic—may we possibly hope to appreciate The Penguin. And The Penguin, as we shall see, is infinitely worthy of our appreciation!

First, as to The Penguin's terrestrial self. Advanced persons who go in for antarctic movies, Anatole France, or natural history, invariably conceive of "penguins" as awkward, ludicrous, ungainly, ridiculous birds which cannot fly and, instead, walk about imitating humanity in general and Charles Spencer Chaplin in particular. Having observed The Penguin Himself almost every day over a period of some months, I beg to inform the readers of *Vanity Fair*, concering The Penguin's terrestrial emanation—which, by the way, is as far from "awkward" as "humble" is from "servile"—that he "imitates" nobody. "Breathes there a man with soul so dead, who," having glanced at our [drawings] of The Penguin's *terrestrial* self, can still doubt the originality of that self? If so he had better pay a visit to the Kraushaar Galleries and there study a bronze portrait, by the sculptor Gaston Lachaise, of The Penguin's terrestrial personality—after which he may inspect the original.

But to proceed with our analysis: The Penguin's *second* self is as different from his first as his first is different from most people's idea of it. For whereas, terrestrially, The Penguin is angular, restricted and sudden, aquatically he is comparably fluent, completely uninhibited and (when he makes a dart downward through the water, in pursuit of his prey) irrevocable. No one who has failed to partake of The Penguin's aquatic emanation can form the faintest idea of the quite impossible smoothness and absolutely *dreamlike* velocity with which it is endowed. I shall content myself with the observation that The Penguin's second, unphotographable self does not merely swim in the water—quite the opposite. This astonishing self *flies* through the water, by virtue of those very wings which "most people" consider so pathetically inadequate!

And now, my distinguished readers, having studied separately The Penguin's two different emanations, we arrive at the crux of the subject—*who* is The Penguin?

Of thousands upon thousands of adult human beings who have flocked to view this mysterious personage and to mock or marvel at what he *does*, the present writer honestly believes that he alone realizes who The Penguin *is*. How should this be so?

Only one explanation suggests itself: these thousands upon thousands are totally unaware of—even—their own true selves; they do not realize who *they* are. I am certain that not a single member of these throngs of onlookers knows that she (or he), like The Penguin, is TWO selves, TWO individuals, TWO emanations. Of all the spectators who pity and ridicule The Penguin's *terrestrial* personality, not a human soul realises that the very part of her (or him) which is doing the mocking and the sympathizing (the "awkward," "ludicrous," "ungainly," "ridiculous" part of anyone which psychologists call "consciousness" or "the *Conscious*") is, in and of itself, but a stumbling and thwarted emanation—a silly strutting and dancing upon a tiny platform labelled "life"—whereas, the function which determines or fulfils each human being's destiny and which contains the essence or meaning of all destiny is each human being's second, inner, or *"unconscious"* self. Such, however, is the truth; whereof The Penguin, in his two different emanations, is a living symbol!

After observing The Penguin's second self, I put the question: "Does anyone imagine, just because his or her Unconscious cannot be photographed, that it does not exist?"—Alas for human ignorance! Not only does the Unconscious exist—it *is* existence: and moreover, the best part of existence—an illimitable realm in which the human mind *flies*, as contrasted with a microscopic domain in which the mind's wings are next to useless.

Such, I think, is The Penguin's meaning.

From *Vanity Fair*, February 1926: line drawing by the author.

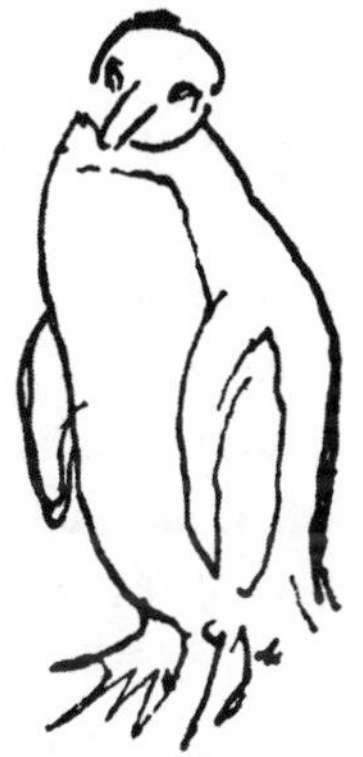

THE THEATRE: I

Among the minor amusements of a nation so wealthy that it can afford to ignore things priceless, a country so large that it cannot become aware either of its greatest living painter, Marin, or of its only living sculptor, Lachaise, we observe a highly systematized smuggling in of various brands of aesthetic "kick"—some authentic, more diluted, most neither, but each and all enticingly labeled. Whatever may be the cause of this dishonourable predicament, the fact remains that every American, whom bootleg Art confronts, is at liberty to make one of precisely three moves. First, he may refuse to partake of the proffered intoxicant, on the ground that such indulgence were unconstitutional (not to mention expensive); second, he may discerningly partake thereof, scorning neither his own wits nor those of his stomach; third, he may knowingly glance at the label, shut tightly both eyes, and gulperdown. The inhabitants of New York City, U.S.A., who are justly famous for their thirst, made the abovementioned choice only recently, when Messrs. Comstock & Gest (Art bootleggers of the *première* water) let it be known that they had "the Great Honour of Presenting For the First Time in America" a peculiarly hyperfine brand of "Synthetic Theatre," which not only had arrived direct from the former home of vodka, but wore the super-alluring label: NEMIROVITCH-DANTCHENKO. Whereupon the present writer, remembering that bootleg Art (like the "little girl who had a little curl") is very very good when it's good but when it's bad it's horrid, put wits, dollars, et cetera suddenly together and sampled this latest miracle gradually. Having done so, he takes great pleasure in announcing, not merely that he is undead, but that he is considerably more alive than before—a situation so perfectly remarkable as to merit analysis.

One might suppose (were one to believe what one hears) that the technique of The Moscow Art Theatre Musical Studio resembled the technique of some recently invented cocktail; that a thorough, if not positively savage, shaking up of various in themselves merely dangerous aesthetic ingredients produced a taste suggestive of none, assuming the concoction to have been properly gulped, plus a kick beyond dynamite. Actually, however, the system of Nemirovitch-Dantchenko suggests that almost incredibly skilful edifice, familiar to American preprohibition imbibers under the salubrious pseudonym "pussy café," which presents itself to the eye as a number of colours or succession of layers, each constituent layer or colour (obedient to the law of specific gravities) keeping its particular level and refusing to blend or mix with the others—whereof the gustatory pleasure results from an interaction, on the tongue, of storeys, as the edifice unrapidly is sipped. If New York post-prohibition audiences gulped the Synthetic Theatre, if the whole thing looked like a cocktail to them, if they approved because the gin apparently had been killed since the ugly taste of conventional Opera was absent, and if they disapproved because they didn't get the kick which they expected to get out of a shaking up, by the gentleman with the hyphenated nomenclature, of various arts—it luxuriously is true that there was no gin, and that the aforesaid gentleman had not shaken up arts for the exuberant reason that he had done something exactly different, videlicet, he had made visible a law, he had demonstrated an aesthetic relativity, he had "produced" an homogeneity of arts precisely by not violating the discreteness of any one of them.

What happens on this gentleman's stage is a selfimposing nextness of arts, what happens in his audience (supposing the inhabitants of Jolson's Theatre to constitute his audience) is an overlapping or interpenetration of arts. The law governing each specimen of his "Lyric Drama" is an aesthetic law, i.e., each instance, various arts, illustrating a certain order, cohere through the differences of their common volition (so to speak)—the principle at stake being not an agglomeration of ingredients but that spontaneous sequence of elements which inevitably is the expression of their respective densities. This out-of-Spontaneous-by-Inevitably idiom or audience-stage structure involves, before anything else, the existence of a mobile theatre. More accurately: it involves the elimination of a pennyintheslot peep show parlour and the substitution therefor of an aesthetic continent, throughout whose roamable depth and height and breadth the tourist pays his way in -ist currency ("constructivist" or expressionist" or what you will setting, lighting, costuming)—said currency being amply protected against depreciation, thanks to the seizure of that long-idle, inexhaustible treasure: the chorus.

We shall inflict upon our readers neither a diary nor a geography of those portions of The Lyric Theatre (LYSISTRATA, LOVE AND DEATH, CARMENCITA) which it already has been our privilege to tour. Instead we shall remark that, as in the case of any authentic experiment, there is here not much failure and much invincibility. To be sure, The Moscow Art Theatre Musical Studio has its anecdotal feebleness in ALEKO (with too many not-thick-enough sounds attributed to Sergei Rachmaninoff), but it has its found solidity in CLEOPATRA (with the unspeakingly supreme protagonist "FLAVIUS—A Roman Warrior"), in CARMENCITA (with an exquisitely orchestrated ἀνάγκη of fans), and—best of all—in the immaculate roughhouse happeningly enclosed by LYSISTRATA. An exhibition of a different sort, of the cocktail variety in fact—the Quinn collection of modern art—reveals a total absence of Lachaise, many merely fifteenth-rate things, and a fatuous sought negligible unthing by Augustus John, but also a structurally sumptuous irrevocably itselfcoloured vibration by John Marin. And of whatever failures in taste the late Mr. Quinn or the living Nemirovitch-Dantchenko may be accused, these failures are honourable—unlike the failure which results when Miss Eva Le Gallienne and an equally incompetent cast "do" what, instead of being THE MASTER BUILDER, becomes a rigid mess vividly lighted by Emily Stevens' superbly *réussi* penetration of Hedda Gabler.

And now may we suggest some genuine home-brew?

Neither the presence of LYSISTRATA, nor the absence, from the Musical Studio productions, of music by the greatest living composer (whose Sacre and Noces, alone and as Nijinska-Goncharova ballets, are equal in intensity to anything for which Nemirovitch-Dantchenko or Ibsen or any one else can possibly be responsible), nor even the luminous existence of a Strindberg DREAM PLAY at the Provincetown, chances to account for your humble servant's naif idea that the NATIONAL WINTER GARDEN BURLESK at the corner of East Houston Street and Second Avenue is a singularly fundamental institution, whose Scratch is a noble clown, whose first wink is worth the struttings of a hundred thousand Barrymores, who are the unmitigated bunk: since the direction of all spectacle lives in Aristophanes and the "theatre" has a great future behind it, said "future" being The Circus.

From *The Dial*, April 1926.

THE THEATRE: II

Since the writing of our last "theatre," at least three events of extraordinary theatric import have transpired in New York City.

1. LITTLE EYOLF, with Clare Eames as Rita Allmers (Guild Theatre). This intricately distinct play, thoroughly if not wonderfully understood, was given a more than creditable performance; a performance far more than creditable, or even than excellent, in so far as Clare Eames was concerned.

2. The International Theatre Exposition, occupying two floors of the Steinway Building, and representing Austria, Belgium, Czechoslovakia, France, Germany, Holland, Hungary, Italy, Jugoslavia, Latvia, Poland, Russia, Spain, Sweden, Switzerland, and the U.S.A. From copious chaff much authentic wheat separates quickly itself: Jean Hugo's inspired costumes for that Joy Forever, Cocteau's LES MARIÉS DE LA TOUR EIFFEL: the line-in-relief-against-plane "construction DER WAGEN DER PROSERPINA," whose all scrawlish vitality and purely velocitous spontaneity mention the irrepressible Picasso; Rabinovitch's now famous LYSISTRATA, Theatre Beresil; gorgeous turbine flangings for LOHENGRIN per Fedorovsky, and an exquisite thing by Vialoff; Depero; dolls by Remo Bufano; Mrs. Hansell, B. Aronson, Cleon Throckmorton. Regarding the situation which is responsible for this show, we are enlightened by Friedrich Kiesler as follows (programme, page 14):

> "The elements of the new dramatic style are still to be worked out. They are not yet classified.

> "Drama, poetry, and scenic formation have no natural milieu. Public, space, and players are artificially assembled. The new aesthetic has not yet attained unity of expression. Communication lasts two hours; the pauses are the social event.
>
> "We have no contemporary theatre. No agitators' theatre, no tribunal, no force which does not merely comment on life, but shapes it.
>
> "Our theatres are copies of obsolete architectures. Systems of superannuated copies. Copies of copies. Barococo theatres. The actor works without relation of his environment. Ideal or material. He is set down in the middle of things, managerially obligated, coached by the director for his part. He must put life into a grave topped with red, gold, and white masonry, a parquet of mummies in evening dress, decolleté fillies, antiquated youths."

This all too familiar "grave" is further designated as "the picture-stage" or "the peep-show-stage."

> "The peep-show-stage is a box appended to an assembly room. This box owes its form to technical considerations; it is not the result of deliberate artistic purpose. . . . Speech and action cease to be organic, or plastic; they do not grow with the scenery, but are decorative, textual byplay. Under such conditions the back of the stage is useless—excess space, vacuum, embarrassment, an exhibit room for the stage sets. The whole province of the stage has not yet been conquered for the actor; he is confined within the pale of the footlights. . . . The curtain is a cover for changes of scene. When it is lowered, the lights are turned on in the audience. Or the theatre is left dark. Hocus-pocus.

> The scenes are being shifted. . . . The stage frame, as peephole of the peep-show-stage, is like a panoramic camera shutter. The deployment of wings, actors, and objects is perceived in relief, not tri-dimensionally. Optically, rigid space does not admit of precise cubic apprehension unless it has already been traversed by the observer, so that, when seen again, it is reconstructed with the aid of past experience. Every specific reconstruction arrived at purely from the experiencing of other spaces is inexact and does not suffice for theatrical effectiveness. Space is space only for the person who moves about in it. For the actor, not for the spectator. . . . The peep-show-stage functions as relief, not as space. The public's shaft of vision pushes the stage space back towards the rear. As is always true of rigid space, it is projected onto the surface of the backdrop. . . . There is only one space element; motion. . . . The plastic element of this stage is not scenery, but man. . . . The antimony 'picture-stage' has remained generally unnoticed. For stage is space, picture is surface. The spatial junction of stage and picture produces a false compromise, the stage-picture. . . . The wings and backdrop are arranged pictorially, enlarged from charming little sketches to gigantic proportions, spaced for the furniture—and the actor stands out abruptly from these self-sufficient paintings, a body absolutely foreign. Scene and actor negate each other. No organic cohesion is possible. The stage director attempts to adjust the rivalry. The painter protests; the actor faces the public, turning his back upon the stage. The play falls halfway between nature and art."

Not so with the "space-stage," "a kind of four-sided funnel, opening towards the audience"—

> "The actor is seen perfectly from any part of the theatre; and from all points on the stage his voice sounds with uniform intensity and accentuation. The flat expanse of the back-drop no longer dominates as background. It has become a narrow strip unfit to serve as a picture. The stage is empty; it functions as space; it has ceased to appeal as decoration. The play itself is required to give it life. Everything now depends upon the play. Agents of movement are: sound, structure, objects, stage mechanisms, light. The performance results from the organization of the histrionic elements, the moulding of stability and motion into unity. One element conditions another. Their innate antithesis is not obscured, but deepened. One cannot be effective without the other. Nothing is accessory: everything is a complement, a sequence, a development, a conclusion. The energies of the components heighten one another; they grow and crystallize beneath the eyes of the public. No mystery. The stage structure develops step by step: the simultaneity of the picture-stage is abandoned. There is no curtain, nor is the house darkened in lieu of a curtain. The performance is orchestral. The movement is carried from one element to another. The movements begin abruptly; accelerated and retarded, they continue without interruption until the play is ended."

—the ideal cherished by partisans of this movement being "elastic space" (versus "rigid space"); i.e. "space by whose relative tensions the action of a work is created and completed"—a noble ideal, to misunderstand which requires the peculiarly insulting stupidity of "critics."

3. Greb-Flowers, at Tex Rickard's New Garden. On February 26, '26, in a circus-theatre bulging with incredible thousands

of human and nonhuman unbeings and beings, a Negro deacon named Tiger Flowers won the middleweight championship of the world. Mr. Flowers (who moves pleasantly, fights cleanly, and plays the violin) said:

> "Harry stuck his thumb in my eye once, but it may have been an accident for he fought a clean fight after that. The only thing I didn't like was that he used some profane language at times. But I guess he was a little excited."

From *The Dial*, May 1926.

CONEY ISLAND

A slightly exuberant appreciation of New York's famous pleasure park

Although it is true that the inhabitants of the U.S.A. have ample cause for pessimism, thanks to Bad Art, Bootleggery and 26,000 lesser degrees of Bunk, it is also true that said inhabitants are the fortunate possessors of a perfectly genuine panacea. Were not this so, throughout the breadth and length of our fair land mayhem would magnify itself to prodigious proportions, burglary would bulge to deadly dimensions, policemen would populate our most secret sanctuaries and such notable nodes of *Kultur* as New York City would leap *en masse* to the celestial regions. Unbelievable as it may appear, there might even come a day when not a single campanulate congressman went to sleep on duty and not a single authentic artist starved at his Corona. In short (and to put it very mildly) anything might happen.

But the panacea is genuine. Crime, accordingly, is kept within quite convenient bounds, murder is monotonously punished, unart and nonliquor exchange visiting cards and the dollar bill waves triumphant o'er the land of the free and the home of the slave—all of which is due to the existence of an otherwise not important island, whose modest name would seem to suggest nothing more obstreperous than the presence of rabbits. No wonder learned people state that we occupy an epoch of miracles!

At the outset, one thing should be understood: it is not owing to sociological, political, or even psychological predilections that the present and unlearned writer partakes of the cure in question. Quite the contrary. Like those millions of other so-called human beings who find relief for their woes, each and every year, at Coney Island, he occupies these miraculous premises with purely personal intentions—or, more explicitly, in order to have a good time. And a good time he has. Only when his last spendable dime has irretrievably disappeared and his face sadly is turned toward his dilatory domicile, does it so much as occur to your humble servant to plumb the significance of his recent experiences. Such being the case, there can be no reasonable doubt as to his intellectual honesty *re* the isle and its amusements, concerning which (for the benefit of all thoroughly unbenighted persons and an unhappy few who are not accustomed to lose their complexes on The Thunderbolt) he hereby begs to discourse.

The incredible temple of pity and terror, mirth and amazement, which is popularly known as Coney Island, really constitutes a perfectly unprecedented fusion of the circus and the theatre. It resembles the theatre, in that it fosters every known species of illusion. It suggests the circus, in that it puts us in touch with whatever is hair-raising, breath-taking and pore-opening. But Coney has a distinct drop on both theatre and circus. Whereas at the theatre we merely are deceived, at Coney we deceive ourselves. Whereas at the circus we are merely spectators of the impossible, at Coney we ourselves perform impossible feats—we turn all the heavenly somersaults imaginable and dare all the delirious dangers conceivable; and when, rushing at horrid velocity over irrevocable precipices, we beard the force of gravity in his lair, no acrobat, no lion tamer, can compete with us.

Be it further stated that humanity (and, by the way, there is such a thing) is most emphatically itself at Coney. Whoever, on a really hot day, has attempted to swim three strokes in Coney Island waters will be strongly inclined to believe that nowhere else in all of the round world is humanity quite so much itself. (We have reference to the noteworthy phenomenon that every Coney

Island swimmer swims, not in the water, but in the populace.) Nor is this spontaneous itselfness, on the part of Coney Island humanity, merely aquatic. It is just as much terrestrial and just as much aerial. Anybody who, of a truly scorching Saturday afternoon, has been caught in a Coney Island jam will understand the terrestrial aspect, and anybody who has watched (let alone participated in) a Coney Island roller coaster will comprehend the aerial aspect, of humanity's irreparable itselfness. But this means that the *audience* of Coney Island—as well as the *performance* given by that unmitigated circus-theatre—is unique.

Ask Freud, he knows.

Now to seek a formula for such a fundamental and glorious institution may appear, at first blush, presumptuous. Indeed, those of our readers who are dyed-in-the-wool Coney Island fans have doubtless resented our using the words "circus-theatre" to describe an (after all) indescribable phenomenon. We hasten to reassure them: Coney for us, as for themselves, is Coney and nothing else. But certain aspects of this miracle mesh, so to speak, with the theatre and with the circus; a fact which we consider strictly significant—not for Coney, but for art. We repeat: the essence of Coney Island's "circus-theatre" consists in *homogeneity*. THE AUDIENCE IS THE PERFORMANCE, and vice versa. If this be formula, let us make the most of it.

Those readers who have inspected the International Theatre Exposition will realize that the worldwide "new movement" in the theatre is toward a similar goal. Two facts are gradually being recognized: first, that the circus is an authentic "theatric" phenomenon, and second, that the conventional "theatre" is a box of negligible tricks. The existing relationships between actor and audience and theatre have been discovered to be rotten at their very cores. All sorts of new "theatres" having been suggested, to remedy this thoroughly disgraceful state of affairs—disgraceful because, in the present writer's own lingo, *all genuine theatre is a verb and not a noun*—we ourselves have the extraordinary honour to suggest: Coney Island. And lest anybody consider this suggestion futuristic, we will quote from *The Little Review* the suggestion of Enrico Prampolini, entitled (among other things):

> THE ELECTRO-DYNAMIC
> POLYDIMENSIONAL ARCHITECTURE
> OF LUMINOUS PLASTIC ELEMENTS
> MOVING IN THE CENTRE OF THE
> THEATRICAL HOLLOW
>
> This novel *theatrical construction*, owing to its position, allows the enlargement of the *visual angle* of perspective beyond the horizon, displacing it on top and vice versa in a simultaneous interpenetration, towards a centrifugal irradiation of infinite visual and emotional angles of scenic action.
>
> THE POLYDIMENSIONAL SCENIC SPACE, THE NEW FUTURISTIC CREATION for the theatre to come, opens new worlds for the magic and technique of the theatre.

Amen.

And now, a few parting words as to the actual Coney Island, in which it is to be hoped that all readers of this essay will freely indulge at the very earliest opportunity.

Essentially it remains, as we have said, indescribable. At best, we may only suggest its invincible entirety indirectly, or through a haphazard enumeration of the more obvious elements—than which process, what would be more futile? How, by depicting a succession of spokes, may we hope to convey the speed or essence of a wheel which is revolving so rapidly as to be spokeless? No indeed; the IS or Verb of Coney Island escapes any portraiture. A trillion smells; the tinkle and snap of shooting galleries; the magically sonorous exhortations of barkers and ballyhoomen; the thousands upon thousands of faces paralysed by enchantment to mere eyeful disks, which strugglingly surge through dizzy gates of illusion; the metamorphosis of atmosphere into a stupendous pattern of electric colours, punctuated by a continuous whisking of leaning and cleaving ship-like shapes; the yearn and skid of toy cars crammed with screeching reality, wildly spiraling earthward or gliding out of ferocious depth into sumptuous height or whirling eccentrically in a brilliant flatness; occultly bulging, vividly painted banners inviting us to side shows, where strut and lurk those placid specimens of impossibility which comprise the extraordinary aristocracy of freakdom; the intricate clowning of enormous deceptions, of palaces which revolve, walls which collapse, surfaces which arch and drop and open to emit spurts of lividly bellowing steam—all these elements disappear in a homogeneously happening universe, surrounded by the rhythmic mutations of the ocean and circumscribed by the mightily oblivion-coloured rush of the roller coaster.

From *Vanity Fair,* June 1926.

CONFLICTING ASPECTS OF PARIS

Being an eyewitness's report on the two cities in the French Metropolis

The much misunderstood metropolis of Paris (France) is at present two cities. One of these cities—the one which exhibits itself for the benefit of tourists—has been and still is widely advertised as "Paree." The second Paris (which no mere tourist has ever so much as glimpsed, but which was, is and will forever remain) calls itself "Paname."

"Paname" is *argot. Argot* is slang. Slang is the most alive aspect of a language. The aspect of Paris which "Paname" signifies is the most alive aspect, the inner part; the secret of secrets, unpurchasable either by His Britannic Majesty's pounds or by His Yankee Excellency's dollars. Frequently, however, *l'étranger* is led to believe that, minus "Gay Paree," Paris would not be Paris—and here lurks a particularly poisonous mistake, which it is the present writer's intention to assassinate.

That foreigner, more particularly that American, who inhabits Paris for more or less cultural reasons, will hereupon raise her or his voice in protest, crying: "Verily your distinction is absurdly obvious. Anyone of even mediocre intelligence is perfectly aware of the contrast between that brand of Paris which is served to tourists and the genuine article. As for me, I speak the language, I despise cabarets, I enjoy the Louvre"—*etcetera.*

To which outburst we beg to respond: "Dear sir, or madam—that foreigner who (for any reason whatsoever) *inhabits* Paris, is a strictly negligible phenomenon. It is the foreigner *whom Paris inhabits*, who matters. Only to such a foreigner is the distinction between 'Paree' and 'Paname' vitally and irrevocably clear; only in such a foreigner does the confusion of these two aspects, 'Paname' and 'Paree,' cause the gorge unmitigatedly to rise. Believe it or not, gentle madam, or sir—your highly respectable Paris is far from being our 'Paname.'"

To prove this assertion is not difficult. Suppose, for instance, that Paris be considered as a whole or as one compound unit—a kind of microscope, for the examination of the world. Let us apply this microscope called Paris to our unenlightened eye. What do we discover with the aid of its lenses? We discover, ladies and gentlemen, that the world is not (as some are wont to suppose) at peace. Quite the contrary: war is everywhere. Our civilization is rent, to put it mildly, by strife. But by precisely what sort of strife? Strife between nationalities? Nothing as superficial as that. Between capital and labour? Wrong again. Looking very closely and holding our breath, we discover that the truly stupendous strife under observation partakes of a deeply religious nature, since it involves two furiously contending cults. What we perceive is nothing less than a holy war of unprecedented proportions, a fight to the death between two groups of unparalleled fanatics—comprising, on the one hand, the Worshippers of Life and, on the other, the Worshippers of Bathtubs. These distinctions I shall proceed forthwith to define.

The Worshippers of Life (hereafter to be known as the W.O.L. party) and the Worshippers of Bathtubs (hereafter to be indicated by the letters W.O.B.) are enemies of long standing. Indeed, an accurate and painstaking survey of the W.O.L.-W.O.B. conflict would include the history of modern civilization. Our readers need have no fear—we shall not attempt such a survey. Instead, the subject of this essay being "Paree" vs. "Paname," we shall concern ourselves merely with contemporary and local aspects of the epoch-making struggle. For it is this struggle and nothing else which at present divides the metropolis of Paris into "Paname" and "Paree."

Let us make the foregoing statement perfectly clear. The distinction between naughty or pleasure-loving or "gay" Paris, and noble or museum-haunting or intellectual Paris is a bit of arbitrary nonsense, fabricated out of the whole cloth by Herr Karl Baedeker and carefully perpetuated by Messrs. Thos. Cook & Son. To a Parisian (and to anyone else who has his wits about him) such a distinction is utterly ridiculous. Judged from the standpoint of psychology, occupying oneself with any aspect of existence to the exclusion of the opposite aspect—being serious without also being silly—is unhealthy; whereas your Parisian is a remarkably healthy psychological specimen. Your Parisian, we repeat, perfectly realizes that without folly there would be no wisdom; and his Paris (constructed in accordance with this realization) embraces as many and as diverse kinds of existence as possible. Throughout this Parisian Paris, properly entitled "Paname," opposites of all varieties meet. *Madame la Comtesse* rubs elbows with *Mlle la Gonzesse*, dance halls mingle with museums, and life is an essentially healthy—since homogeneous—affair.

In only one respect are the Cooks and Baedekers right: there exist two kinds of Paris. The metropolis is divided—but divided fundamentally, we reiterate, not arbitrarily; and as the direct result of actually conflicting values, not as a mere means of accommodating certain unneccessary Anglo-Saxon prejudices. What actually makes of the city of Paris two distinct cities, two contrasting entities, is the before-mentioned Holy War between two cults: the W.O.L. and the W.O.B. To put the thing a little differently—whether a visitor goes to naughty Montmartre or to nice Napoleon's Tomb is (Baedeker and the Cooks to the contrary) unimportant; but whether a human being merely inhabits the bathtub city of "Paree" or actually is inhabited by the living city of "Paname," wholly and fundamentally matters. TO BE, OR TO BE BATHED—that is the question which threatens the world in general and Paris in particular.

Remembering ye good olde proverbe, "Cleanliness is next to

godliness," the gentle reader will demand, in righteous fury: "How dare you assert that bathtubs are iniquitous?" Or should the sacrosanct tradition of "progress" (viz. that form of prosperity which is intimately connected with bathing) arise in her or his mind, she or he will exclaim: "The bathtub is civilized! Long live the noble institution of tubbing! *Vive* the aristocracy of the daily bath!"

Throughout "Paree" one hears the very same slogan, for throughout Paris the cult of the tub is triumphant. Everywhere one's eye is greeted by *Hôtel du Progrès, Dernier Confort, Confort Moderne ("confort,"* apparently, is hermaphroditic) and *"Englisch"* spoken. The *étranger* is invited at each step to inhabit American Bars until it shall be time for five "oclok" tea. On the upper *rue de Rivoli,* enunciation of French is no longer considered merely uncultured; it is considered positively blasphemous. As for a certain famous hill named Montmartre (where, not so very long ago, persons of all varieties amused themselves in a spontaneous and original manner) 'tis nowadays nothing more nor less than a peculiarly uninteresting machine for separating Anglo-Saxons from their bankrolls. Cleanliness is indeed next to godliness! Formerly a vein, *Boulevard Montparnasse* has become an artery through which pulses most of the none-too-red blood which comes straight from the none-too-sound heart of Greenwich Village, U.S.A. God's in His Heaven, prices soar, National Cash Registers adorn all the progressive cafés, Wrigley advertises where it will do most good, the franc touches 22, and that invaluable home of hilarity, *Le Concert Mayol,* translated *"Oh Quel Nu,"* the title of its revue, as "Ladies Shirt Off (!)."

So much for "Paree" and the triumph of the Worshippers of Bathtubs. And now, a few words concerning the second Paris, the unconquerable and authentic city: "Paname."

Pounds, progress, dollars and morals have assailed and still assail her, but in vain. At any *bistro,* a *bordeaux blanc* is still a *bordeaux blanc* and *un demi* is still *un demi* and *fine* is *fine,* for all the attacks of "whiskey," gin, "pal-al," and *grog américain*—not to mention the *Ligue Nationale Contre l'Alcoölisme (O, mores!).* Albeit employed nightly as an advertisement for Citroën automobiles, that ultra-Freudian symbol which is known as *le tour Eiffel* smites the sunlit heavens as aforetime. A *foire* goes full blast at Porte Vincennes, with its "toboggan" and its "steam swings" and its games and shooting galleries and wrestlers and stomach-dancers and bodiless ladies and lion tamers. The *Tout Est Bon* café of *Porte Saint Denis* still observes the *Tout Va Mieux* café, just across the street, with a scornful smile. At Auteuil and Longchamps there are still hooves and colours. Defying uncounted *films américains*, the ancient and honourable *Théâtre du Châtelet* promulgates its honourable and ancient brand of three-dimensional melodrama—the Fratellinis have moved to the *Cirque d'Hiver*, but a *cirque* is still a *cirque* and they are still the Fratellinis. "Miss" appears in a super-Follies concoction, but still does the sacred Mistinguette stuff—the *Moulins* are all turning. Always, the *Jardin du Luxembourg* has its wooden horses to ride and its tiny ships to sail; and in the Elysian Fields *guignols* twinkle like fireflies. Barges and *bateaux mouches* glide (and will forever glide) through the exquisite river; from which old gentlemen, armed with prodigious poles and preternatural patience, will forever extract microscopic fish. Beneath "Paree," beneath the glittering victory of "civilization," a careful eye perceives the deep, extraordinary, luminous triumph of Life Itself and of a city founded upon Life—a city called "Paname," a heart which throbs always, a spirit always which cannot die. The winged monsters of the garden of Cluny do not appear to have heard of "progress." The cathedral of Notre Dame does not budge an inch for all the idiocies of this world.

Meanwhile, spring and summer everywhere openingly arrive.

Lovers capture the *Bois.*

In crooked streets young voices cry flowers.

From *Vanity Fair,* August 1926.

VIVE LA FOLIE!

An analysis of the "revue" in general and the Parisian revue in particular

In the old days—not the very old days either, but the long-lost days of a few years ago—your correspondent was no more addicted to the so-called "Serious drama" than he is at present. Although at that time, even as now, inhabiting Paris (which metropolis takes the serious drama super-seriously) he never willingly met an honest-to-God footlight face to face. But this does not mean that he neglected the theatre. Far from it! There were and are, in Paris, plenty of dishonest-to-God footlights, plenty of plotless dramas, plenty of "light" spectacles—and our article is devoted to a few of their many seductions and intricacies.

Be it added, that, to employ the adjective "light" with reference to the art of the *Concert Mayol*, the *Casino de Paris*, the *Moulin Rouge* and (last but far from least) the *Folies Bergère*, is to be guilty of a somewhat atrocious inaccuracy. For the type of spectacle which flourishes within said temples of mirth and amusement and which is universally designated by the word "revue" is extremely fundamental—no more light, forsooth, than the stupid trickeries and clumsy alexandrines of a *Théâtre Français* are dramatic. Nor do we speak as the scribes; having for some years, more or less, devoted ourselves to the glorious art of the plotless drama in general and the Parisian revue in particular.

During these highly agreeable years, we have frequently asked ourselves "what is the revue?" And justly so; since the revue, like everything else worth while, is constantly changing. In the aforesaid old days, for example, a typical Parisian revue was a jumble of extraordinarily ill-staged "sketches," of sumptuously indecent ditties, of highly confused convolutions on the part of a tastelessly costumed chorus and—finally—of incredibly immobile nudes, the least ponderous of whom looked as if she could very easily quell an eruptive volcano merely by sitting on it. What women! Not even the Old Howard, of Boston, Mass., could furnish their rivals in ugliness, nor were Billy Watson's *Beef Trust* Beauties to be compared with them on the score of avoirdupois. One was reminded slightly of Rubens, more of the Eden Theatre in Madrid and most (ah, most) of the Oedipus Complex.

As a matter of fact, these old time nudes differed absolutely from the stupendous ladies in the canvases of Rubens; the essence of Rubens' females being their hurled weight, their velocity and momentum, whereas the essence of the Parisian nudes was their immobility. The naiads of Rubens' *Debarkation of Marie de Médicis*, for instance, copiously squirm as we watch them. The dryads of the old Parisian revue—and the woods were full of them—only stood around.

That was in the old days.

Et ça change. Gone are the snows of yesteryear. The hippopotami have melted: each has become a dozen fashionably formed and alluringly moving gazelles. Vivid, occasionally precise scenery has everywhere replaced the uncertain planes and flyspecked tones of the ancient music-hall scenery. That typically French, or rather Latin, rhythm, the 3/4 throb or waltz, is submerged in the 2/4 patter or riveter rhythm of *"le Jazz."* Maurice Chevalier (supported by *"les Dolly Sisters,"* who for some unknown reason think they can Charleston) sings many a song at the *Casino de Paris*, but the song which he sings best is unquestionably *"Pour être heureux" (Then I'll Be Happy).* The girls at the *Mayol*, who were always well above the average as to pulchritude, have improved 150% all over. Again, the marvellous Mistinguette and her Yankee dancing partner, awkward Earl Leslie, have promulgated a brand new eye tickler at the *Moulin Rouge* which, for splendour, size and nudity, knocks our American revues into a cocked hat.

But the latest and most astounding development of the Parisian revue is announced, by a Parisian journal, called *Eve*, in these terms:

"The Negro is more than ever in favour since the invasion of Jazz and American dances. In the new revue at the *Folies Bergère* called *La Folie du Jour*, there is a Negress, Josephine Baker, who is the great *vedette*. In truth, when one looks, one sees a mulatto with the sleek figure of the Anglo-Saxon, yet the face, the gestures, the dances, even the voice, retain all the rhythm and all the strangeness of her original race." And, as the immortal Bert Savoy would have said, "You don't know the half of it, dearie."

Josephine Baker will immediately suggest, to all addicts of the plotless drama, one peculiarly genuine spectacle entitled *The Chocolate Dandies*. For it was this revue which gave Miss Baker a microscopic, but notable, opportunity to "strut her stuff." As a member of the *Dandies* chorus, she resembled some tall, vital, incomparably fluid nightmare which crossed its eyes and warped its limbs in a purely unearthly manner—some vision which opened new avenues of fear, which suggested nothing but itself and which, consequently, was strictly aesthetic. It may seem preposterous that this terrifying nightmare should have become the most beautiful (and beautiful is what we mean) star of the Parisian stage. Yet such is the case. The black star, *"aux formes elancées d'Anglo-Saxonne,"* has accomplished precisely this transformation, and at the tender age of twenty.

Miss Baker, it seems, came to the *Folies Bergère* after participating in a Negro show which was taking Paris by storm. But when *les girls* of this show appeared "as is" and then "shook that thing" the good Parisians (than whom no people on earth can be more respectable) objected, and objected so strenously that *les girls* were compelled to don a respectable semi-nudity. At least so the story goes. Anyhow, Miss Baker escaped to the *Folies Bergère*. And at the *Folies Bergère*, as your humble servant can testify, there is nothing in the least respectable, seminude, or otherwise unsatisfactory about Miss Baker's getup—which consists of a few bananas and not too much jewelry. In brief, the *Folies Bergère* permits Josephine Baker to appear—for the first time on any stage—as herself.

Herself is two perfectly fused things: an entirely beautiful body and a beautiful command of its entirety. Her voice (simultaneously uncouth and exquisite—luminous as only certain voices are luminous) is as distinctly a part of this body as are her gestures, which emanate a spontaneous or personal rigidity only to dissolve it in a premeditation at once liquid and racial. She enters the show twice: first—through a dense electric twilight, walking backwards, on hands and feet, legs and arms stiff, down a huge jungle tree—as a creature neither infrahuman nor superhuman, but somehow both; a mysteriously un-killable Something, equally nonprimitive and uncivilized or, beyond time in the sense that emotion is beyond arithmetic. This stark and homogeneous glimpse is isolated, heightened and developed by a series of frivolously complicated scenes (*Whose Handkerchief Is It? The Language of Flowers, Oh the Pretty Sins, Bewitched* and *A Feast at Versailles*) whereby we are swiftly and surely conducted to that unique phenomenon of noise and naughtiness, the Intermission.

And still we find ourselves remembering the jungle.

Nor does the jungle release us from its enchantment until the middle of Act 2; when a vast egg very gradually descends from the topmost ceiling of the theatre to the level of the orchestra, opens, and emits a wand of golden flesh—a wand which struts and dances, a lithe and actual wand which blossoms unbelievably in authentic forms of love and death. Whereupon, from all parts of the audience, surges a gigantic wave of protest. Cries of "disgusting" mingle with gasps of "how shocking!" and wails of "how perfectly disgusting!" Horrified ladies cover their faces or hasten from the polluted environs. Outraged gentlemen shout, stamp or wave their arms angrily. And still Josephine Baker dances—a dance neither of doom nor of desire, but altogether and inevitably of herself.

Such, or nearly such, being the inexcusably alive protagonist of the revue at the *Folies Bergère*, we have at last found an answer to our question: "What is the revue?"

The revue is not (as Earl Carroll and most European producers think) a mammoth exhibition of boudoir-paintings-come-to-life and is not (as F. Ziegfeld, Jr., pretends to believe) a "glorification" of some type of female "beauty." By the laws of its own structure, which are the irrevocable laws of juxtaposition and contrast, the revue is a use of everything trivial or plural to intensify what is singular and fundamental. In the case of the *Folies Bergère*, the revue is a use of ideas, smells, colours, Irving Berlin, nudes, tactility, collapsible stairs, three dimensions and fire works to intensify Mlle. Josephine Baker.

And the sentiment which we beg to add is: Long live *la Folie!*

From *Vanity Fair*, September 1926.

HOW I DO NOT LOVE ITALY

An extremely unorthodox view of a widely celebrated section of Europe

Editor's Note: The receipt of this article in the offices of *Vanity Fair* caused a high degree of perturbation and anguish. Why? Because the Editors were nurtured on Italian culture, achievements and ideals. Our first thought, therefore, was that the author of this essay should be reprimanded, not to say chastised. Then there came to us this thought. What if Italy *should* become efficient? What if automats and five-and-ten-cent-stores and slot machines and Ford factories and quick lunch counters should definitely succeed the sonnets of Petrarch, the paintings of Mantegna, the learning of Pico della Mirandola, the sculptures of Giovanni Bologna and the large, easy-going, colourful grandeur of the Medicis? Merciful heavens, what weighty pain in that thought! With that direful prospect in mind we saw the need of publishing Mr. Cummings' article forthwith, *in toto*, with the idea of saving Italy from imminent disaster, from modernity, and from (what is most terrifying of all)—American efficiency.

Once upon a time, when we were incredibly spirited, helpless, and otherwise young, the singing teacher of a New England public school induced our throat to utter the following fraudulent ditty:

"O, Italia, Italia belov-ed
Land of beauty, of sunlight and song,
When afar from thy bright skies remov-ed
How our fond hearts for thee e'er do long"

or something like that. We were amazed, at the time, by the asininity of the words and the triteness of the tune. But amazement is temporary. We sang other songs and we grew up and we forgot all about *Italia*.

Not until full fifteen years later did the land of sunlight, etc., actually loom upon our horizon—when, becoming bored with Paris, we purchased a bicycle and rode all the way to *Napoli* with a patient friend. This little jaunt (and the reader is strongly advised to consult a map ere attempting the same) taught us altogether too much about *Italia*. We became so disillusioned, in fact, that when afar from her bright skies remov-ed our very far from fond hearts decidedly did not do any longing.

Yet what is disillusionment to a healthy person? *Niente*. Only a year or so after the *Paris-Napoli* venture, we found ourselves getting shoved off all the sidewalks of *Roma* by enthusiastic cohorts of Black Shirts. A revolution, or something, had just happened. We sought refuge in a stationery shop. Before our eyes reposed a series of coloured post cards celebrating the recent cataclysm. The first card at which we glanced depicted Mussolini, in the role of Christ, raising *Italia*, in the role of *Lazarus*, from the dead. Shocked to our aesthetic foundations, we left hurriedly both the shop and *Italia*.

Shocks, however, cannot discourage really inquisitive people. Our third visit to *Italia belov-ed* has just been completed—and completed successfully, thanks to a hypertranquil disposition plus, at times, a superhuman digestion. All things considered, we feel that we are now entitled to express ourselves publicly *re* the home of beauty, etc.; therefore (in the limpid language of that notorious nation) *"avanti!"*

Italia, without any doubt the most overestimated country in this world, consists of a peninsula which is shaped like a leg that has been caught in the act of kicking Sicily. This naughty leg, whose chief industries are ruins, religion and automobiles, is technically a monarchy ruled over by a king (S.M.Il Re) but is actually a pawn in the hands of the *onorevole* Benito Mussolini. The king nevertheless retains two extremely important functions, which are (a) to be photographed with Mussolini and (b) to pose for postage stamps.

Signor Mussolini, whose singularly uncheerful visage appears all over *Italia* at the present moment—not only in rotogravure, but painted on houses, fences, railroad stations, etc.—was, just a few years ago, a wicked radical. But one day this wicked radical turned a complete backward somersault and landed an ultraconservative. Shortly afterward he bought up all the black shirts in sight, hurriedly put a great many young men into them and captured Rome without difficulty. He then informed everybody that *Italia* had been dead for some time and that his program, *il fascismo*, consisted of nothing less than a revivification of the corpse. If *Italia* swallowed the dictatorship pill, Mussolini positively guaranteed that she would rise from the dead and be alive even as she was alive in the days of the Caesars. In other words, she would be alive at the expense of everybody else and would rule the modern world very much as Rome ruled the ancient world.

After a number of Mussolini's former comrades, the Italian bolsheviks, had been beaten up, compelled to drink castor oil and sent to other planes, the corpse took her medicine and Mussolini was acclaimed as "Caesar." But Mussolini was no ordinary man. He could not possibly be satisfied with being merely Caesar. He also wanted to be Napoleon. This was easily arranged. A photographer "shot" him in Napoleonic costume, the photograph was printed on thousands of post cards and the post cards were circulated all over *Italia*. Taking the bull by the horns, Mussolini now rushed into international politics and mixed them up "something awful," as we say back home. But while the world at large recoiled from his exploits, *Italia* applauded with both hands and both feet—and exactly what the Hon. Caesar Napoleon Mussolini will attempt next, nobody knows. The French people guess that it will be the annexation of France, since he says quite frankly that *Italia* is overpopulated and must have a lot of brand-new territory—in a hurry.

So much for the shepherd. And now a few words concerning his flock.

In our humble opinion, there is no word big enough to suggest, let alone describe, the bigness of the contemporary Italian inferiority complex. To understand the origin of this national misfortune, we must remember that for some time previous to *"il Duce's"* somersault, the inhabitants of *Italia* had lived in a tranquil doze. But with the thunderclap of fascism, they awoke to a consciousness of themselves; or, more truly, they awoke to a realization of their weakness and apparent unworthiness. Practically the entire nation, stricken with a sense of shame, thereupon set in motion within itself what psychologists term a "defense mechanism"—that is to say, all *Italia* (with few exceptions) began to swagger and boast and pose; dozing meekness was superseded by insolence; and vanity, never a negligible Latin characteristic, bulged to colossal proportions. Luckily, however, the official military headgear consists of a cap so high in the crown as to permit of considerable head-swelling. From which painful subject, let us turn to *Italia*'s scenic glories.

Concerning the innumberable catacombs, cathedrals, museums, ruins, etc., which recall an illustrious past and which have inspired so much bad and good poetry, philosophy and criticism, we beg to opine (1) that the ceiling of the Sistine Chapel is worth all the rest of *Italia* dead and undead (2) that we love Venice much but that we love Coney Island more (3) that one small church of Santo Tomé (Spain), which contains El Greco's *The Burial of Count Orgáz*, houses more aesthetic intensity than does the whole *Galleria degli Uffizi* and (4) that the world is still looking for an unidentified man who disappeared after partially expressing a desire to show us the coliseum by moonlight.

Concerning the famous scenic glories of the unillustrious present, we have the following remarks to make. First of all, nobody can possibly comprehend better than ourselves the real meaning of the celebrated *mot*, "see Naples and then die"—for when we saw Naples we very nearly did die; and Naples at its worst is certainly no more depressing than are the other famous Italian cities at their best. Secondly, while it is true that certain much-touted portions of *Italia*'s landscape, such as Fiesole, are distinctly attractive, it is not true that said portions are any more remarkable, in and of themselves, than is most of the unadvertised country called Portugal. Finally, be it known that there exists, somewhere in the Italian Riviera, a perfectly cracker-box-shaped edifice (known as a villa) with twenty windows, of which nineteen are painted while one is real—and be it further known that the painted blinds of the nineteen painted windows all cast painted shadows and that in one of the nineteen painted windows is a painted potted plant which also casts a painted shadow and that on what remains of the villa's walls are a number of painted statues, each statue casting its own private, separate, individual, particular painted shadow. No wonder *Italia, Italia, belov-ed* is described as a land of sunlight!—Incidentially, all the painted shadows are very, very wrong.

They are not, however, any more intrinsically wrong than is the sign "SOMETHING NEW, CHEAP AND BEAUTIFUL" which, ostensibly, is an attempt to lure unwary Anglo-Saxons into a shop off the *Piazza San Marco* in Venice, but which actually—unless we very deeply err—is an epitome of the whole fascist program for Italy in particular and the world in general. Nor do we, as an American, write the foregoing sentence without shame; for we realize that the glittering slogan just quoted reflects, all too well, our own nation's slip-shod method of thought. The sad fact is, that *Signor* Mussolini has invented nothing. He has simply, as a means of purging his compatriots of their unworthiness, borrowed from America her most unworthy credo (the utterly transparent and lifeless lie: Time is money) and the results of this borrowing are already apparent.

Assuming the continuation of *Italia*'s present *régime*, America will find herself playing second fiddle to *Italia* in more unlovely ways than either Napoleon or Caesar could shake a stick at. Already *Italia* is up to America's tricks of "progress" and "morality." If you doubt this, get in touch with the fascist representative in your home town and find out for yourself. Already the *Piazza Venezia* is dark and dreary. Already you cannot buy a glass of *cognac* on Sunday. Later, or sooner, everybody in the "land of beauty, of sunlight and song" will be minding everybody else's business as thoroughly as everybody does in the dear old U.S.A.—at least, so your correspondent decided one night, when (being unable to sleep on account of a deafening racket) he lifted up his weary eyes and beheld, emblazoned on the door of his microscopic room at the *Albergo* Somethingorother, the following moonlit sentiment: *In the generally interest, the Visitors are requested to observe the extremely quiet.*

From *Vanity Fair*, October 1926.

THE TABLOID NEWSPAPER

An investigation involving Big Business, the Pilgrim Fathers and psychoanalysis

Editor's Note: Almost a score of tabloid newspapers are presently being published in the United States. The New York *Daily News*, the first to be published in America, began in 1919, and now has a circulation of over a million. The circulation of many of the others is increasing by the hundreds of thousands. These tabloids frankly base their appeal on morbid and sensational details, "faked" news and "faked" pictures, prize contests and trashy stories on sex themes. The Macfadden publications, publishers of the incredibly successful New York *Evening Graphic*, frankly declare themselves in favour of a sex interest to attract their customers, while more conservative editors stress "big" news pictorially presented, with reading matter deliberately concocted for a public of minimum intelligence. In this article, Mr. Cummings considers the prevalence of tabloids as an index to the national mentality.

Like all phenomena which we are in the evil habit of taking for granted, the mentality of the Great American People—by which is meant, that kind of liveliness or unliveliness which is common to most citizens of our grand and glorious republic—invites more than a casual inspection. We should not merely realize, as most of us merely do, that "Americanism" rules supreme in this epoch-making day and time, or that "Americanization" now applies to everything from non-citizens to safety pins. Granted, that the entire universe echoes and reechoes to the mighty strides of our nation's progress—assuming that a whole civilization trembles in the hollow of our superhuman hand—in brief, admitting that nobody "never saw nothing" like us—it is far from improbable that an analysis of the invincible spirit underlying this uncontested supremacy will give quite as startling results, in a quiet way, as the huge and noisy product itself. Moreover (economists, sociologists, efficiency experts and similar learned gentry to the contrary) such an analysis does not involve a very vast acquaintance with the occult science of Mr. Sherlock Holmes. Quite the contrary. From a thousand adjectives which fairly clamour for a chance to describe the Great American Mentality, there immediately stands forth one adjective in which our epoch finds its perfect portrait, in which our civilization sees itself miraculously mirrored, in which the U.S.A. shimmers in all the unmitigated splendour of its great-and-only-ness. This adjective is infantile.

By no circumstance the least important, and certainly the most obvious, example of the strictly infantile essence of America's all-conquering mentality greets our eyes daily, anywhere and everywhere, in the guise of the tabloid newspaper. The tabloid newspaper actually means to the typical American of this era what the Bible is popularly supposed to have meant to the typical Pilgrim Father: *viz.* a very present help in time of trouble, plus a means of keeping out of trouble via harmless, since vicarious, indulgence in the pomps and vanities of this wicked world.

Without the Bible, as everybody knows, your Pilgrim Father would have been seriously inclined to wonder why an Almighty Providence saw fit to freeze him in winter, starve him in summer and fill him full of arrows at all times. He might even have been tempted to register a few complaints with his Omnipotent Protector. Conceivably, this righteous person might eventually have strayed so far from the path of righteousness as to throw up the sponge entirely or join the wicked Indians. But the Pilgrim Father's Bible solved his problem very nicely, by pointing out to him that things are not what they seem and by furnishing him with a pleasing catechism of values in place of a painful concatenation of realities. Furthermore, it occasionally stopped an arrow or two.

If the tabloid newspaper cannot boast of stopping arrows, it can at least retort that arrows are not being done this year, and that, if the woods are not full of Indians, the skyscrapers are full of time clocks and that a struggle is a struggle still, the noblest thing alive, and that temptation remains temptation, no matter which of innumerable disguises the insidious Tempter may see fit to assume. Ask Billy Sunday, he knows. Or, to put the matter a little differently: just what would become of the machine known as Big Business, were many hundreds of thousands of male and female cogs denied their daily oil in the form of the tabloid newspaper, Heaven alone knows; but it is not difficult to guess.

In "ye good olde days" of a year or two ago, these human cogs were being satisfactorily, if not thoroughly, lubricated by means of common-or-garden newspapers which appealed to the mind through intricate symbols, such as words of one, two, or even three, syllables. But that is over. Gone are the snows, *etc.* The Big Business Machine (as any Big Business Machinist will be the first to admit) has been enormously developed in a couple of years. The parts of each and every subsidiary mechanism have not only been standardized but have been rendered accessible at all times and under all conditions. Whereas not so long since, the prerogative of a human cog was his or her occasional obscurity, he or she is now always observable and easily getatable. Such complicated oilcans as were suitable for eliminating obscure sources of friction have accordingly been dispensed with.

Not the mind, but the eye of the human cog has become the centre of lubrication. To keep fit for one's job, one no longer reads, one merely sees. The ordinary newspaper with its histories of what happened, yields to the tabloid newspaper with its pictures of what is happening. Thus it would appear that the tabloid newspaper celebrates a climax in the orgiastic worship of the present tense of the verb To Be.

But the great supremacy of the tabloid newspaper will be better understood when we realize that its only contemporary rival is an even more familiar pictorial phenomenon with an even wider circulation—the dream. The dream, indeed, differs fundamentally from the tabloid newspaper only in age and pedigree. In aim, in format and in effect, the dream and the tabloid newspaper are so similar as to be almost indistinguishable. To be sure, as regards efficiency there is no comparison: the tabloid newspaper wins in a walk from the dream. A few years hence, given a very slight heightening of our lofty present-day standard of efficiency, we may see the dream completely supplanted by the tabloid newspaper. The human cog in the machine known as Big Business may very possibly find it obsolete to dream. The Big Business God will then be in his Big Business Heaven and psychoanalysts will cure their patients through a study of their patients' tabloid newspapers.

Let nobody hereby take it for granted that we are attempting to disparage psychoanalysis. On the contrary. Be it known that we attribute to this science our understanding, not merely of the tabloid newspaper, but of the colossal civilization which the tabloid newspaper so triumphantly typifies. The very adjective "infantile" is a direct theft from psychoanalysis, which explains a variety of otherwise completely inexplicable occurrences by the concept of "infantile fixation." The dream, we know, is a compromise, on the part of our socalled better nature, with repressed wishes of infantile origin—whence dream-distortion—and Dr. Freud himself long ago compared the dream censor to a newspaper censor. The most obvious characteristic of the dream, as of the tabloid newspaper, is its pictorial quality. In unconscious life, as manifested by the dream, "opposites" go hand in hand. The tabloid newspaper shows us, on one page, a delectable specimen of virginity in a one-piece bathing suit and, on the next, a man being sentenced to twenty years for rape. Indeed, the further we look, the more dreamlike the tabloid newspaper becomes. "Every issue an Oedipus complex" would be a first-rate slogan for the *Daily News*, the *Daily Mirror* and, more especially, for the superpaternal Mr. Bernarr Macfadden's *Daily Graphic*.

We know, thanks to psychoanalysis, that the predominant quality of children is their all-prevading and illimitable egoism. This simple revelation is worth more, for an understanding of civilization in general and of the civilization of the almighty dollar in particular, than all the theories of all the economists, sociologists, efficiency experts, *etc.*, who have ever lived. Thanks to this discovery of child-egoism, our eyes are opened for the first time to the true meaning of the age in which we move and have our being. We discover, to our astonishment, that what has really happened to America from the day of Plymouth Rock and the Bible to the day of Big Business and the tabloid newspaper is exactly the opposite of what the economists and their ilk would lead us to suppose. America has grown *down*, not up. From Pilgrim Fathers we have become Pilgrim Children. The United States, today, is nothing more nor less than a Great Big Egoistic Baby. When glancing about us, we perceive the whole world following this infantile nation of ours, let us remember the Bible of the Pilgrim Fathers, wherein it is written that "a little child shall lead them." And let us admit that the Pilgrim Fathers, all things considered, may not have been so limited as we originally supposed.

At least the Pilgrim Fathers used to shoot Indians: the Pilgrim Children merely punch time clocks.

From *Vanity Fair*, December 1926.

THE SECRET OF THE ZOO EXPOSED

Proving that our fear of wild animals is done with the aid of (Freudian) mirrors

No doubt most people accept that "scientific" theory that man is an ex-monkey which somehow or other developed at the expense of other animals. And no doubt these readers have visited a zoo, there to experience thrills which no theory, scientific or otherwise, could satisfactorily explain. But have they ever thought of the possibility that what we are accustomed to call "animals" are in reality living mirrors, reflecting otherwise unsuspected aspects of our own human character? Such an idea sounds absurd; but so do many ideas which are found to contain a surprising amount of truth. The zoo, with its mysteriously impressive and often positively unreal inhabitants, may be something entirely different from what we imagine. We may even discover, while investigating the zoo, something of great significance for the understanding of ourselves.

An astonishing fact confronts us at the very outset: nobody seems to know what the word "zoo" implies. This word, generally speaking, suggests little more than a highly odoriferous collection of interesting and unhappy animals. Whoever takes the trouble to look it up in a dictionary will find that "zoo" comes from the the Greek *zoon*, meaning "animal." The misapprehension that zoos have to do with animals would appear to be universal. Actually, however, the syllable "zoo" originates in that most beautiful of all verbs, *zoo*, "I am alive"—hence a zoo, by its derivation, is not a collection of animals but *a number of ways of being alive.* As Hamlet might have put it: "to zoo or not to zoo, that is the question."

We next observe that each and every zoo constitutes both a playground and a prison. For each and every zoo is founded on certain acres which have been captured by civilization, from civilization, on behalf of civilization and which acres are themselves the homes, and captors, of certain essentially non-civilized entities, commonly referred to as "animals." From one point of view, the typical zoo means a virtual chaos, whereby human beings are enabled temporarily to forget the routine of city life; while, from another point of view, it means a real cosmos, possessed of its own consciousness, its own quarrels and even its own social register—which, as we shall soon see, is indirectly our own social register. These two aspects, "human" and "animal," interact; with the result that the zoo, in comprising a mechanism for the exhibition of beasts, birds and reptiles, becomes a compound instrument for the investigation of mysterious humanity.

But what, precisely, do we mean by "interact"? We mean that the zoo's permanent inhabitants, the so-called animals, are kinds of "aliveness" which we ourselves, the temporary inhabitants of the zoo, experience. To speak of "seeing the animals" is to treat this phenomenon with a shameful flippancy, with a clumsiness perfectly disgusting. Actually, such "creatures" as we "see" create in us a variety of emotions, ranging all the way from terror and pity to happiness and despair. Why? Not because the giraffe is effete, or because the elephant is enormous, but because we ourselves appear ridiculous and terrible in these amazing mirrors.

Now let us try to understand the zoo as a concatenation of differently functioning and variously labelled mirrors, all of which are *alive.* These living mirrors, mistakenly called "animals," are for the most part grouped in systems or "houses," like the "birdhouse" and the "monkey house," and each house or system furnishes us with some particular verdict upon ourselves. In passing from house to house, from one system of mirrors to another system of mirrors,

ELEPHANT. *In gazing at any elephant in any zoo, we are, in reality, looking into a Freudian mirror of ourselves, a glass wherein we see revealed not only our powers, but our weaknesses, not only our docility but our cruelty and our will to crush.*

we discover totally unsuspected aspects of our own existence. At every turn we are amused, perplexed, horrified or dumbfounded. No mere spectacle of monsters, however extraordinary, could so move us. The truth is, not that we see monsters, but that we *are* monsters! What moves us is the revelation—couched in terms of things visible or outside us—of our true or invisible selves. This alone explains why our hearts pause with dread, why our eyes bulge with astonishment and why, when face to face with a peculiarly fabulous image, we have all we can do to keep from exclaiming, "Impossible! Such a phantom cannot really be alive: I must be dreaming!"—which conviction is well founded, for in a sense we are dreaming.

Hereupon, the gentle reader will doubtless cry: "Enough! I have tolerated that absurd quibble as to the meaning of 'zoo,' I have endured that farfetched comparison between animals and mirrors, but I positively will not permit you to accuse me of dreaming when, with open eyes, I see real lions and tigers which would be only too glad to eat me alive if it weren't for the iron bars between us."

Perhaps. Nevertheless we must insist that going to the zoo is very like dreaming. Let us remember that the essence of dreams *per se* is, not that they seem unreal to us after we have awakened from them, but that they are profoundly and completely real to the dreamer. The lions and tigers of the dreams which you and I are dreaming possess quite as much reality as any tigers and lions (social or otherwise) which our open eyes have ever seen. Frequently, indeed, these dream monsters are even more real than their "real" counterparts. But between them and us there is something which saves our precious lives; just as, in the case of the zoo, there are iron bars between the panther which springs and the spectator who stares. Nor should we forget that the frightful monsters of dreams, if properly analyzed, lose their terror and become deceptive appearances, harmless symbols of our own hates and loves. For further enlightenment on this subject I can only refer you to the works of Dr. Freud and the other psychoanalysts. But why is it that our hates and loves are able to express themselves in these forms during sleep? Obviously, the phenomenon has previously occurred in consciousness and the leopard which seems so "real" to us at the zoo is only an embodiment of our own stealth and cruelty—a living mirror of our own power and cunning.

Such assertions as the foregoing cannot, of course, be mathematically proved. But suppose those individuals, who doubt our wisdom and who are too busy to visit the nearest zoo, consult the picture accompanying this article. We realize that the test is not a fair one. No matter how excellent . . . pictures may be, they are only pictures after all, and not living "animals." When one looks at a cat or at a leopard or at a porcupine or at a snake or at monkeys *directly*, one sees (according to our theory) an image of oneself—an image necessarily different from that image of *himself* which the creator of this picture has seen and recorded. However, the principle involved is the same. A magic mirror is still a magic mirror. Let our skeptical readers, then, gaze upon this magically entitled, magically functioning mirror which we have provided for their personal use and find out what sort of ladies and gentlemen they—our readers—really are. We have a very small favour to ask: that, having looked and seen themselves, they will not pounce upon, strangle and tear us limb from limb, nor yet shoot any barbed quills in our direction!

One mightily significant mirror, labelled "Oracle, or, A Living Portrait of Civilization," is absent. This oracle of Civilization, albeit a resident of the "birdhouse," cannot be found among the Green Manucodes nor yet among the Twelve Wired Birds of Paradise. Astonishingly enough, gentle reader, it is only Poll Parrot—who perpetually unites the myriad meanings of existence in the supremely synthetic exclamation—*"Hellogoodby!"*

From *Vanity Fair*, March 1927: line drawing by the author.

FRENZIED FINANCE

An unskilled observer diagnoses some results of the fall of the French franc

We have heard a great deal, of late, concerning insults to foreigners—and more particularly, insults to Americans—in Paris. Not only have the New York dailies featured these insults, but practically all the newspapers from coast to coast have taken this opportunity to furnish their readers with a paucity of intelligent explanation and superfluity of picturesque detail. As a result, we find ourselves wondering how it should have come about that our noble country is violently hated and her citizens extensively razzed by that very race which, a short time ago, hailed America as the saviour of civilization and Americans as crusaders in a holy war waged against all things evil.

The provocation seems in no case exactly stupendous. Why, for instance, should a number of Yankees, caught in the extremely childish act of hurling whole loaves of bread to the historic carp at Fontainebleau, suffer a vigorous berating at the hands, or pens, of Parisian editors, on the extraordinarily dubious ground that such a deed constitutes an insult to *la belle France*? Why, moreover, should three overdressed, overintoxicated and otherwise overasinine "college boys" be selected for chastisement by a section of the Parisian populace—granted, that one member of the trio had pilfered (consciously, unconsciously or possibly fore-consciously) a spoon from Foyot's magnificent restaurant? Finally, why should rubberneck wagons be held up and compelled to discharge their quaint and curious cargoes of sightseers upon the fevered streets of the outraged French capital? It all seems a bit odd, to say the least.

But oddity is most certainly in the air. Only the other day an odd thing happened. Mr. Blank, an American business man (and, incredibly enough, a personage of quite unimpeachable probity), returned to New York from Paris, where he had done business as usual with representatives of a number of important French firms. Weary with welldoing, down sat Mr. Blank in his New York office to enjoy a mild corona. At this moment, the director of a bank in Hartford, Connecticut, telephoned to say that a formidable sum had been mysteriously placed to Mr. Blank's account by a certain Soandso. The garbled name of the donor did not immediately associate itself with anything in Mr. Blank's mind; consequently Mr. Blank was nonplussed. But presently he began to sense a connection between the occult nomenclature and one of the Paris firms aforesaid. In a few minutes all was clear: a Frenchman, having made some money, was losing no time in sending it out of *la belle France* to be invested—by someone whom he trusted implicitly—in American securities.

Are these problems of foreigner-hating and of frenzied finance insoluble? One would think so, to judge by the utterances—either blatantly trivial or darkly ponderous—which they have provoked. But let us not be downhearted. Rather, taking the horns by the bull (so to speak) let us enjoy a brief but exhilarating dip in the not-too-distant past.

It will be remembered that after the socalled Great War was "won," after the well-known Treaty of Versailles had "made the world safe for democracy," the French Republic found itself in a horrid predicament. To obtain even a fraction of the vast sum which she demanded of her vanquished enemy, France was under the necessity of not only permitting, but encouraging, the prosperity of the German Republic. As will readily be seen, this predicament involved several rather annoying sacrifices on the part of the conqueror. It involved escorting the French people out of a simplified psychology of blood-and-thunder into a complicated psychology of peace-and-goodwill. It involved pricking a carefully manufactured bubble, wherein lurked the awful image of that unutterable monster: *le boche*. And from a moral standpoint, it involved being guilty of that rarest and most dangerous of international crimes: generosity.

To be sure, her material interests prompted France—victor in an "unselfish" struggle "for mankind"—to be generous in this particular case. But generosity involves, beyond everything else, daring; and daring implies exceptional strength. A bigger carp might have risen to so noble a loaf; but not *la République française*. *La République française*, it will be remembered, took the law into her own hands just as soon as Germany showed signs of definite economic improvement, tucked "martyred" Belgium under one arm for the sake of companionship and occupied the Ruhr. Thereby, as events have proved, *la République française* not only forfeited her chances of being paid by Germany, but lost the friendship of England and the admiration of America to boot.

Prior to this famous occupation of the Ruhr, a great many Anglo-Saxons had assumed that *la République française* was not getting a square deal. And no wonder; for rarely did a vanquished—let alone a victorious—nation indulge in more self-pity than did France after the treaty of Versailles. One would have thought that France was the victim of a plot on the part of the nefarious Allies, that the Huns were masters of Europe, and that *le Bon Dieu* was not in His Heaven. Every time a French war monument was dedicated, for example, the orator of the occasion (invariably a hand-picked politician) bewailed France's woes in terms calculated to convey the impression that no other country since the world began had ever experienced real misfortune. But with the occupation of the Ruhr, the song changed. From a mutilated martyr, a crucified cripple and everything utterly miserable or entirely hapless that the imagination of man could picture, *la République française* suddenly was transformed into a nation, armed to the teeth, which knew its rights and was going to get them—and Heaven help the rest of the world! Whereupon the rest of the world waggishly put its thumbs to its nose and the Ruhr occupation proved, despite everything claimed for it by the astute M. Poincaré, one vast substantial fizzle.

So much for not very ancient history. And now, taking the bull by the horns instead of *vice versa*, let us frankly ask ourselves: just what is all the anti-America outcry about? And how comes it that the French franc inhabits nether regions of finance? In other words, who made *la République française* what she is today?

The recent tumble of the franc appears to be the result of an effort, on the part of certain of the more ill-intentioned Frenchmen, to pay off France's internal debt in debased currency, i.e. to make the proverbially thrifty French peasant foot the bills of the Great War for Humanity. Appearances may, perhaps, be deceptive, but one thing is sure: the leaky thesis that naughty foreigners are to blame for the fall of the franc has very little truth in it.

Nor should the gentle reader, at this point, accuse us of dogmatizing beyond our depth. In order to understand how certain of the French politicians (observing that the German mark had tobogganed and that Germany had acquitted her internal obligations in depreciated currency and that the mark had been stabilized and that now Germany—despite France's best efforts—stood upon her feet) decided to turn a similar trick themselves with the franc, we need not possess the mentality of a Maynard Keynes. Nor is it at all probable that we suffer from auditory hallucinations when we hear these shrewd *messieurs* saying to each other: "Why not divert the attention of the French people in particular and of the world in general from our primary problem, France's internal debt, to our secondary problem, France's foreign indebtedness? To accomplish this will not be difficult. Let us promulgate a thoroughly organised newspaper campaign against 'foreigners' on the ground that said 'foreigners' (whom we shall slowly but surely reveal in their true colours, as our former allies, the English and more particularly the Americans) 'speculate' and thereby ruin the franc. Mischief being afoot, let us convert into dollars whatever francs we already possess and can beg or borrow; whereupon the franc will, so to speak, ruin itself. We shall then be able to do as Germany did: pay off our debts to our people in depreciated paper. Like the Germans, we shall be able to demand that our currency be stabilized at a low point. Our peasants will thus be the losers; we ourselves—having dollars, not francs, in our pockets—cannot possibly suffer—and *tout va bien qui finit bien.*"

Whosoever disapproves of this possibly startling analysis is hereby cordially invited to furnish a better explanation of existing conditions. There is no denying that all is not well. There is also no denying that the xenophobia camouflage has proved singularly unsuccessful. Of course, insults to "foreigners" and demonstrations against Americans do occur. But these insults and demonstrations are not authentic and almost everybody knows it—even the frantically ignorant American newspaper editors who wonderingly state that it is "well-dressed crowds" who are to blame, not honest-to-goodness Hell-bent-for-election mobs. In point of fact, such picturesque *crises de nerfs* are completely unspontaneous. They are staged by an element whose motto is *sauve qui peut*, whose political ideals are fascist and whose ability to combine the science of politics with the art of profiteering is well known to anyone even superficially acquainted with *la belle France* of post-bellum days. Reduced to its lowest terms, the supposedly obscure situation becomes, alas, all too obvious. And what, precisely, do we mean by "lowest terms"? We mean this: a certain group of French profiteers, having succeeded in not fighting the war and having partially succeeded in debasing the franc for their own benefit, are now trying to "cover up"—by making, of the erstwhile dearly beloved United States of America, one vast substantial goat.

From *Vanity Fair*, January 1927.

IVAN NARB: ABSTRACT SCULPTOR OF THE COSMIC

His esoteric aesthetique explained so that even you can understand it

By Gwendolyn Orloff

That the recent exhibition of abstract sculpture by Ivan Narb proved the big aesthetic event of 1926 is far from surprising—given the overwhelming originality of the sculptor's conceptions and the bewildering variety of the media employed (tin cans, sealing wax, hay wire, candlegrease, birchbark, bottle glass, gingerbread, chewing gum, etc.) as well as the quite preposterous mastery of his materials which Narb displays at every turn.

The surprising thing is that, although no foreigner has ever been more ecstatically taken to the exclusive hearts of New York's socially elect—no aesthetic more frantically welcomed by the esoteric *salons* of America's intelligentsia, no celebrity more frantically discussed, no divinity more inordinately worshipped—the immutable personality of Ivan Narb remains just as simple and sincere, just as straight-forward and unaffected, as when he was hoeing his father's potatoes on the solitary outskirts of the tiny hamlet of Blurb, in Latvia, and dreaming of the day when each animate or inanimate thing—a rose, a button, a cloud, an eyebrow, a mountain, a particular time of day, nay, even a potato—would flower forth in new and cosmic forms.

No one realizes better than Mrs. Harry Payne Vanderbilt how

unspoiled and naif this ultramodern Michelangelo has remained, despite all the honours showered upon him during the past few months. Mrs. Vanderbilt (who numbers among her *protégés* practically every really well-known artist in America) arrived from Paris to find all tongues wagging with praise of Ivan Narb, whom she had never met nor, until that moment, heard of. Naturally she decided to give a little dinner for this social lion and invite everyone of intellectual prominence, from Otto Kahn to Irving Berlin. The dinner hour drew near and so did the guests, both invited and uninvited—but not Ivan Narb.

As time passed Mrs. Vanderbilt was on the verge of relinquishing all hope. But, suddenly, a tumult soared above the din of cerebral conversation and Ivan Narb himself, pursued by a round dozen of hysterical domestics, burst into view, wearing (to the disappointment of many present, including Mrs. Cornelius Astor and more especially Mr. William Wrigley, Jr.) a pair of B.V.D.s, and brandishing in one hand a red apple which he immediately pre-

BADLY BENT PIN. *Here the Lettish sculptor has, in a strange medium, captured the hypnotic* je ne sais quoi *of sex—and captured it for eternity.*

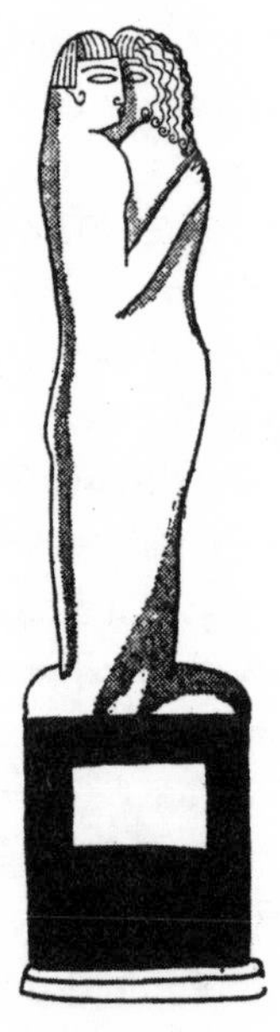

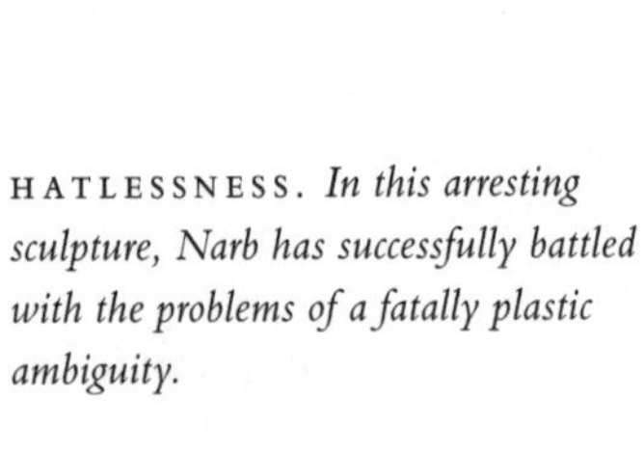

HATLESSNESS. *In this arresting sculpture, Narb has successfully battled with the problems of a fatally plastic ambiguity.*

sented to Dr. Frank Crane, murmuring, "Poo-ur twaw!" (for thee alone). This little incident is only one out of a thousand which we might quote to prove how lightly Ivan Narb takes pomp and circumstance.

But to return to sculpture. By "new and cosmic forms" we are, of course, hinting at something indescribable since mere words cannot possibly do justice to the intrinsically spiritual elasticity and the fundamentally plastic wistfulness of these perpetually astonishing creations. Glance, for example, at the two miracles of modelling exclusively reproduced on this page by kind permission of the artist and then allow the eye to dwell on their titles. To be sure, "Hatlessness," "A Badly Bent Pin," not to mention his other sculptures, "Coughing Birds," "Y Minus Z," "Portrait of Mlle. Enciente," and "The Geranium's Dream," are arresting phrases. But they scarcely begin to suggest the rhythmically, almost fatally, throbbing ambiguity of Ivan Narb's cosmically concocted abstractions. Language has no terms sufficiently subtle to ensnare that elusive and mystical *quid pro quo* which constitutes the hypnotic *je ne sais quoi* of this *grand maître*'s unique achievement. The very best critics can only throw up their hands and exclaim, as Mr. Henry MacBride of the *Dial* did, after viewing for the first time that *chef d'oeuvre* in pink sealing wax called "Twin Beds at Play": "Honour to Ivan Narb! Thanks to his intuitive Lettish intellect, sculpture has at last torn asunder the bonds of naturalism and rushed forth barefooted and breathless into the starry domain of cerebral purity!"

We are willing to wager that, confronted by "X Minus Y," Mr. MacBride would break down and weep for twenty-five minutes, as Babe Ruth did when the school children of Greater New York put their hard-earned pennies together and purchased for their hard-hitting idol a colossal, abstract composition modelled from life by Ivan Narb and entitled (by no less an authority on sporting matters than Mr. Gilbert Seldes) "Swat Triumphant!"

From every point of view, the influence which Ivan Narb has exerted on his contemporaries is well-nigh unbelievable. All over these United States, sculptors who formerly found marble and bronze sufficient for their needs are now turning to less inhibitory substances such as cement, rubber and glue, in order adequately to express their newly aroused cosmic yearnings; while vast multitudes of men, women and children, who never before realized their aesthetic endowment, are now eagerly rushing into the radiant realm of abstract sculpture. In a few years, at this rate, we may expect to see the tasteless and wasteful statuary of our public parks supplanted by vital and nearly costless forms, executed in the manner of Ivan Narb and portraying, not such outworn *clichés* as Victory, Grief, Admiral Farragut, etc., but the irrepressible and unrecognizable *élan vital* of modern civilization.

Already it is bruited abroad that the waterproof summit of a new Detroit superskyscraper is to be embellished with non-representational *motifs*, carved direct in the hard rubber by Ivan Narb and so gigantic that their least details will be visible to the naked eye of a nearsighted spectator situated a quarter of a mile below. This makes us wonder how the illustrious adorner of the Sistine ceiling would feel, could he behold his much touted achievement paling to complete insignificance before the heaven-flouting rubber raptures of Ivan Narb.

Incidentally, Ivan Narb's triumphs are not confined to sculpture alone. As a writer, he has astonished his most ardent admirers. We refer to the only-just-published 969-page monograph (copiously illustrated with remarkable photographs by Edward Stieglitz of Ivan Narb's sculpture, including every possible phase of the latter's portentous personality) entitled: *America's Future Is Which?* wherein, apparently, a multitude of new aesthetic principles are vividly formulated and impetuously developed to their startling, if logical, conclusion. What these principles or this conclusion may be, it is of course impossible to say; for Ivan Narb's writing, like his sculpture, escapes all the vulgar limitations of ordinary meaning. But there can be no reasonable doubt that the writer visualizes America as poised upon the brink of an esoteric epoch, the inhabitants of which will consider our own era more ridiculously obsolete than we of today consider the stone age of our primeval ancestors.

At least, some such idea would seem to underlie the following dicta, which we snatch from a characteristically mystical chapter called: *Pooh!*

"What is to come? What? Who? Which? Cosmic Ascendancy? Scrapersky? Spirit of Looking? Spirit of Yes? Spirit of men and women? Manthing? Girlthing? You say Thingthing. They say Girlthing. Maybe yes. Knows nobody all. Knows nobody Future. Future? Pooh. Pooh is everything. Everything is pooh. Me, you; all is pooh. But also everything are we, you, they, me and Future. How come? H'm, dunt esk. Maybe Future equal to Lillian Russell hat on Javanese bellydancer."

However we may care to interpret this significant passage, one thing remains indisputable—Ivan Narb's prose style has brought to literature a new idiom; which fact strikes us as all the more extraordinary when we remember that he has just acquired a knowledge of English.

So much for Ivan Narb's achievement. Now, in closing, the present writer begs to apologize for the incompleteness of this little essay. Her only hope is that she has at least avoided the pitfall of analysis into which many would-be critics of this new, unrecognizable sculpture have humiliatingly tumbled. As previously stated, the very essence of Ivan Narb's art is its perfect unanalysability. Once analysis is applied, all is lost. Either you instinctively feel the beauty inherent in these occult forms, wrought by the mysterious hand of genius from lowly materials, from humble substances which have never before been called upon to bear the lofty message of aesthetic emotion, or—to put it bluntly—you do not. In the former case, you participate in a kind of religious experience, a new world opens its iridescent portals to your enraptured senses and your soul basks in the eternal sunshine of cosmic existence; whereas, in the latter case, you are a doomed spirit, forever suffering the trivial torments of ordinary humdrum, common or garden life.

For example: to the privileged man or woman or child who perceives the secret locked in Ivan Narb's sculpture, a certain vaguely ellipsoidal form of which I am now clearly thinking, is a source of irrevocable bliss, of ceaseless revelation, of unending joy. To someone whose eyes are sealed by materialistic considerations, this same form is merely a potato.

Here, as elsewhere, it is our duty and our privilege to choose.

From *Vanity Fair*, March 1927.

THE AGONY OF THE ARTIST (WITH A CAPITAL A)

Variations upon the justly celebrated old Greek theme:

know yourself

There appear to be three kinds of artists in America today. First we have the ultrasuccessful artist, comprising two equally insincere groups: "commercial artists," who concoct almost priceless pictures for advertising purposes and "fashionable portrait painters," who receive incredible sums for making unbeautifully rich women look richly beautiful. Very few people, of course, can attain the heights of commercial and fashionable art. Next we have the thousands upon thousands of "academicians"—patient, plodding, platitudinous persons, whose loftiest aim is to do something which "looks just like" something else and who are quite content so long as this undangerous privilege is vouchsafed them. Finally there exists a species, properly designated as the Artist (with a capital A) which differs radically from the ultrasuccessful type and the academic type. On the one hand, your Artist has nothing to do with success, his ultimate function being neither to perpetuate the jewelled neck of Mrs. O. Howe Thingumbob nor yet to assassinate dandruff. On the other hand he bears no likeness to the tranquil academician—for your Artist is not tranquil; he is in agony.

Most people merely accept this agony of the Artist, as they accept evolution. The rest move their minds to the extent of supposing that anybody with Art school training, plus "temperament"—or a flair for agony—may become an Artist. In other words, the Artist is thought to be an unsublimated academician; a noncommercial, anti-fashionable painter who, instead of taking things easily, suffers from a tendency to set the world on fire and an extreme sensibility to injustice. Can this be true? If not, what makes an Artist and in what does an Artist's agony consist?

Let us assume that you and I, gentle reader, have decided to become Artists. Of course, such a decision does not necessarily imply artistic inclinations on our part. Quite the contrary. You may have always secretly admired poor Uncle Henry who, after suddenly threatening to become an Artist with a capital A, inadvertently drank himself to death with a small d instead; or someone whom I peculiarly dislike may have patted my baby curls and prophesied that I would grow up to be a bank president; or both you and I may have previously decided to become everything except Artists, without actually having become anything whatever. Briefly, a person may decide to become an Artist for innumerable reasons of great psychological importance; but what interests us is the consequences, not the causes, of our decision to become Artists.

Having made this momentous decision, how shall we proceed? Obviously, we shall go to Art school. Must not people learn Art, just as people learn electricity or plumbing or anything else, for that matter? Of course, Art is different from electricity and plumbing, in that anybody can become an electrician or a plumber, whereas only people with temperament may become Artists. Nevertheless, there are some things which even people with temperament must know before they become Artists and these are the secrets which are revealed at Art school (how to paint a landscape correctly, how to make a face look like someone, what colours to mix with other colours, which way to sharpen pencils, etc.). Only when a person with temperament has thoroughly mastered all this invaluable information can he begin to create on his own hook. If you and I didn't absorb these fundamentals, reader, we could never become

Artists, no matter how temperamental we were. I might try and try to paint Mt. Monadnock in the distance and you might try and try to draw Aunt Lucy fullface with her nose looking as if it stuck out and we couldn't, because we were ignorant of the eternal laws of value and perspective. So to Art school let us go immediately.

At Art school, we proceed to learn all there is to know about Art (and then some) from the renowned Mr. Z, who was formerly a pupil of the great Y. But this does not mean that Mr. Z paints exactly like the great Y. No indeed. In the first place, Mr. Z couldn't if he tried. In the second place, Mr. Z has developed an original style of his own, as every Artist must do if he is to be worthy of the name. Take, for instance, the great Y himself. He studied at various times under X, W and V and only came into the full possession of his own great powers shortly before his untimely death. Furthermore, X, W and V, before becoming the famous masters which they were, served humble apprenticeships with U, T and S, who taught them the techniques of those prodigious geniuses R and Q, the former of whom was P's favorite pupil, while the latter surpassed even his master O. Our statement that we are studying with Mr. Z at Art school is therefore violently erroneous. We are not really studying *with* Mr. Z at all. We are really studying, *through* Mr. Z, with the great Y and through him with the illustrious X, W and V and through them with the glorious U, T and S and through them with the mighty R and Q and through them with those unbridled giants of the neo-Renaissance, P and O. It seems almost too wonderful to be true, doesn't it?

Thanks to all these great techniques, our own technique improves amazingly. Mt. Monadnock and Aunt Lucy's nose lose all their terrors. The former, with two or three of my expert brushstrokes, obediently inherits a subjective distance of five miles. The latter, with several enlightened touches of your pencil, magnificently bounds into high relief. Mr. Z is beside himself with pleasure and we are graduated *summa cum laude* from Art school. If you and I didn't have temperament, we should now become ordinary humdrum academicians. But, being temperamental, we scorn all forms of academic guidance and throw ourselves on the world, eager to suffer—eager to become, through agony, Artists with a capital A. Our next problem is to find the necessary agony. Where is it, gentle reader?

You answer: the agony lies in the fact that we stand no chance of being appreciated—although America talks Art night and day and American millionaires buy more Art every year than all the rest of mankind put together—because, to our Oil Oligarchs, Peanut Princes, Soap Sultans and other Medicis, "jenyouwine" Art means *foreign* Art. The Art which is the most "jenyouwine" and which brings the most dollars is dead as well as imported; but (and here we have a diabolic refinement of agony) certain more elastic American multimillionaires are beginning to purchase work by living European painters. A Chewing Gum King, for example, who formerly liked nothing but Rembrandts and Velasquez, can now be induced to fall for a Segonzac or two, or perhaps a Matisse, a Picasso, or even a Derain. Meanwhile American patrons of Art (or rather the connoisseurs who do the selecting for these patrons and the galleries which do the selling to them) boycott *l'Art américain*. Not only is there a complete absence of taste anent the domestic product, but once an Artist is found guilty of being a native of the richest country on earth he must choose between spiritual prostitution and physical starvation. What monstrous injustice!

Wait a moment, reader. It is silly of all these rich compatriots of ours to surround themselves with pictures which they cannot possibly appreciate and do not really enjoy. Yet what have we ourselves done to merit the consideration of contemporary Medicis in particular or (which is vastly more important) of mankind in general? You will reply that we decided, for one reason or another, to become Artists; that we attended Art school, where we learned all there is to know about Art (and then some) *through* Mr. Z; that, having revelled in value and perspective to the extent of making Mt. Monadnock's slopes retire and Aunt Lucy's nostrils behave, we were graduated from Art school with highest honours; that, in consideration of the foregoing facts, we should be encouraged to create on our own hook instead of being driven to the wall by foreign competitors.

Well and good—but let me show you a painting which cost the purchaser a mere trifle and which is the work (or better, *play*) of some illiterate peasant who never dreamed of value and perspective. How would you category this bit of anonymity? Is it beautiful? You do not hesitate: yes. Is it Art? You reply: it is primitive, instinctive, or uncivilized Art. Being "uncivilized," the Art of this nameless painter is immeasurably inferior to the civilized Art of painters like ourselves, is it not? You object: primitive Art cannot be judged by the same standards as civilized Art. But tell me, how can you, having graduated from an Art school, feel anything but scorn for such a childish daub? Once more you object: this primitive design has an intrinsic rhythm, a life of its own, it is therefore Art.

Right, gentle reader! It is Art because it is *alive.* It proves that, if you and I are to create at all, we must create with *today* and let all the Art schools and Medicis in the universe go hang themselves with yesterday's rope. It teaches us that we have made a profound error in trying to *learn* Art, since whatever Art stands for is whatever *cannot* be learned. Indeed, the Artist is no other than he who unlearns what he has learned, in order to know *himself;* and the agony of the Artist, far from being the result of the world's failure to discover and appreciate him, arises from his own personal struggle to discover, to appreciate and finally to express himself. Look into yourself, reader; for you must find Art there, if at all.

At this you protest vigorously: but suppose I follow your curious advice, suppose I look into myself and suppose I do not find Art? What then? Do you mean to tell me that I must forever abandon my hope of becoming an Artist?

Absolutely! Art is not something which may or may not be acquired, it is something which you are not or which you are. If a thorough search of yourself fails to reveal the presence of this something, you may be perfectly sure that no amount of striving, academic or otherwise, can bring it into your life. But if you *are* this something—then, gentle reader, no amount of discrimination and misapprehension can possibly prevent you from becoming an Artist. To be sure, you will not encounter "success," but you will experience what is a thousand times sweeter than "success." You will know that when all's said and done (and the very biggest Butter Baron has bought the very last and least Velasquez) "to become an Artist" means nothing: whereas to become alive, or one's self, means everything.

From *Vanity Fair*, April 1927.

WHY I LIKE AMERICA

By an American who, most unfashionably, prefers his native land to France

Like all vogues, the current pro-France or anti-American vogue constitutes a glorification of human credulity. Nor is the reason for this phenomenon far to seek. Persons who are incapable of thinking can only believe; hence to believe has always been the height of fashion. But the subject of belief, or what one believes, changes mightily from time to time. Some years ago (if the present writer remembers correctly) there was a vogue for patriotism; this year it is extremely fashionable to prefer *la République française* to *les Etats-Unis*.

As usual, Paris contributes the vogue and New York exaggerates it. Your fashionably brained Frenchman is content to believe that France is superior to America; not so your fashionably brained American. According to him, France is the embodiment of whatsoever things are good, including life, liberty and the pursuit of happiness; America, by comparison, appears as a materialistic monster, an opportunist ogre, a degenerate dollardragon. Your fashionably brained American, then, becomes a sort of Saint Michael, armed in resplendent culture and bent on the heroic mission of quelling this hideous prodigy (alias his native land) in the name of reason, righteousness and Poincaré.

That is indeed a very pretty idea; but, for some obsure reason, the present writer's brain emanates unfashionableness. When he should have been patriotic, he wasn't. And now, when fashion dictates anti-patriotism, he finds himself thanking his lucky stars for the large and lively U.S.A. The mere size of America delights him. Yet this statement will be received with ridicule; because, as everybody knows, mere size doesn't really matter.

What really matters, of course, is intensity. For example: would anyone contend that a certain painting by Cézanne is inferior to a certain painting by Sargent because Mr. Sargent's effort covered more canvas? Would anyone maintain that the Brooklyn Bridge is a thousand times more beautiful, since a thousand times larger, than the *Pont Neuf?* Ridiculous! America might be a million times as huge as she actually is and France might still be superior to America.

This argument sounds well. To be sure, intensity really matters. Intensity, however, is of various kinds. Size may be, and sometimes is, one kind of intensity—as in the familiar case of our skyscrapers, which noble structures owe their intensity primarily and fundamentally to their size. Your fashionably brained American, however, is very fond of twisting the fact that America's bigness has encouraged a lot of drivel into the falsehood that America is drivelling because she is big. One might as well assume that the magnificent ceiling of the Sistine Chapel is a mass of balderdash because the authors of guidebooks use it as an excuse to slop all over themselves. Indeed, like the bigness of the Sistine ceiling, the bigness of America is intrinsic; or, to put the matter a little differently, America is essentially not an enlargement of something else. Her very size is an essential part of America's life in the same way that France's culture is an essential part of her life. And this brings the unfashionably brained writer to something which amounts to a full-fledged conviction: he thoroughly believes that America is more alive than France.

Hereupon, the Saint Michaels cry "What do you mean 'alive'? You mean 'efficient' and 'progressive.' Having observed that the typical American business man is too busy with his business to digest his luncheon, you have probably run amuck in your typical American way and have credited the entire American nation with a superior degree of vitality. Like a host of other materialists, you are mistaking motion for movement, tempo for rhythm, mere liveliness for life. Half-drowned in the typical American inferiority complex, you clutch desperately at appearances. You pretend that at the root of existence lies the almighty dollar. You deliberately ignore spiritual values. The things which make life living for sensitive people mean nothing to you. What of Art, for instance? Is anything so vital as Beauty? And where, in the whole expanse of noisy, vulgar, ugly America, can you find a museum like the Louvre or a cathedral like the cathedrals of Chartres, Notre Dame and a score of other masterpieces?"

The answer to all such questions is itself a question: "Where, in the entire smallness of France or in the unmitigated amplitude of anywhere else, can you find a painter 'like' John Marin, a sculptor 'like' Gaston Lachaise and a phenomenon 'like' Niagara Falls?" But by "more alive" the present writer meant something which does not contain itself in such adjectives as "efficient" and "progressive." He meant that France has happened more than she is happening, whereas America is happening more than she has happened.

This rather clumsy idiom seems to suggest merely that France's past is of greater dimensions than America's past. Actually, however, it implies something quite different, viz., that France takes refuge in her past. It may be that France takes refuge in her past because her past is luxuriously enormous, while America is forced to live in her present because her past is uncomfortably microscopic. At any rate, the fact remains that France is not a *happening* nation. And this fact is tremendously important, because to take refuge in the past—be your refugee a nation or an individual—means to commit a neurotic deed; the past, from this point of view, being a substitute for living.

America makes prodigious mistakes, America has colossal faults, but one thing cannot be denied: America is always on the move. She may be going to Hell, of course, but at least she isn't

LA "BEAUTÉ" FRANÇAISE

standing still. The same cannot be said of *la République française.* Nor can France's immobility be excused on temperamental grounds; the fact being, that France's past has undermined her present. More and more, indeed, the world realizes that France does not move because she is sick. Yet, sick though France is, she cannot hold a candle to your fashionably brained American who would have us believe that the land of Coolidge is a snare and a delusion, that Greenwich Village is boring while Montparnasse is inspiring, etc.—but who, in reality, is using *la République française* as a wooden horse to enter the Troy of his own past.

Prohibition! With this dread word still echoing in his ears, your humble servant proceeds to invoke the extraordinary assistance of that occult science which is popularly called "relativity." Hounded by prohibition, he takes refuge in Einstein. A moment's concentration suffices; then, fortified against all evils, he boldly faces his parched accusers and demands, "Gentlemen, which is more important: wine or women?" Then, as the enemy staggers at this unexpected blow, the Einsteinian follows up his advantage thus: "Indeed, prohibition is a curse. To endure this ordeal requires quite unprecedented fortitude. Only a nation endowed by Heaven with supernatural vitality could invent for itself a torture so infernal. Small wonder if those carping 'Yanks' who, not so long ago, belittled the republic of 'frogs' now laud the land of cognac to the skies! Small wonder if the ships are filled with weaklings *en route* to Burgundy and Champagne! Prohibition corrupts the soul; it is a blemish, a blot upon the scutcheon of liberty, a stigma whereof all good men and true may well be ashamed—or what have you.

"But for a' that (as one R. Burns has so happily observed) a man's a man. To every man, if he be a man, it is not wine which matters most. You, an American, demand of me, an American: where in all France will you find a drink as dreadful as the best of America's synthetic substitutes or diluted verities? And as man to man, I ask you: where in all France will you find a woman as authentic, delicious and otherwise incomparable as (name supplied upon request)?"

From *Vanity Fair*, May 1927: "La 'Beauté' Française" is by the author.

THE NEW MOTHER GOOSE

What has become of Mary's Little Lamb, now that the fiction magazines are with us?

Mother Goose is supposed to be for children. A grown-up individual who openly absorbed vast quantities of Mother Goose would be considered mentally deranged; in fact, the friends of such a freak would probably have him immediately psychoanalysed. If analysis proved unsuccessful and the patient persevered in his passionate *penchant* for "Mary had a little lamb," he would no doubt be gagged, handcuffed, forcibly fed, made to kiss the American flag and placed in an institution for the feeble-minded.

Why, then, are multitudes of "mature" people violently encouraged to indulge *ad libitum* in preferences which are not—like lively Mary and Mary's lively lamb—merely childish but are positively infantile? We refer to that deadly preference for the socalled "fiction magazine," which fires scientifically aimed salvos of high-powered idiocy all over the civilized world at regular intervals, causing millions upon millions of mental casualties. And we point out that this imposing masterpiece of human unintelligence proves, upon examination, to be nothing more nor less than an infantile perversion of something originally childish. Indeed, when we inspect the fiction magazines carefully, we find (hidden within a lyrical sheath of atmosphere, innuendo, balderdash, *etcetera*) the Mother Goose epic of Mary and her little lamb.

The readers of *Vanity Fair* who find this assertion surprising will experience heart-failure anent the statement following. We maintain that the changes rung on Mother Goose by writers of cheap magazine fiction are not, as would appear at first glance, innumerable. A patiently conducted inquiry tends to show that only three fundamental variations actually exist. These fundamental variations—thanks to whose lyrical quality the underlying childish epic is often so obscured as to become well-nigh unintelligible—deserve titles. Accordingly we have entitled them: the Heart Kick, the Soul Kick and the Kick Direct. The first is the technique of pure or pastoral sentimentality; the second, of fancy million-volt emotion; the third wings straight to first principles and resuscitates the technique of that medieval favourite, Peeping Tom.

No matter what its setting, atmosphere, plot, dialect, every cheap fiction magazine projectile is loaded with "Mary had a little lamb" and primed with one or more of these three standardized Kicks. For illustration: suppose we pick up the first fiction magazine in sight—mentioning no names—which happens to be incurably addicted to the highly inexcusable vice of Heart Kicking. Upon opening this magazine at random, our bewildered eyes immediately encounter lyrical applesauce of the following infantile brand (or worse):

"An old man, seated in the yellow glow of a barn lantern, fingered his violet suspenders thoughtfully. Her birthday! A musing look, coupled with incessant moisture, stole into the gently puzzled eyes, causing their owner from time to time to remove clouded spectacles from a vigorous, well-modelled nose, about which something of the nobility of youth indelibly lingered."

Are we awake? Can this be the twentieth century? Help!

"For Herb Rattlesnake, one thing and one thing only really mattered: the child whose tumbling curls and wistful smile he had just tucked into the tiny white crib, stooping a little longer than usual over this wee being, who looked up so trustingly with his dead sister Sarah's mouth and ears, because tomorrow was her birthday.

"Then he had gone to the barn to think."

We recognise the 'Gene O'Neill touch about the barn and feel reassured.

"He always went to the barn to think. Perhaps it was the almost inaudible murmur of the peacefully slumbering animals, or the deep, soothing aroma of lofts piled with newly cut hay, which disposed old Herb's mind to thought. Herb probably could not have told you himself, but anyhow, his old feet always began going to the barn whenever something had turned up that required thinking. And now, the old man's mind was focused feverishly on a question of the gravest importance—a question which directly concerned, not himself, but someone a thousand times dearer to him than himself: little Mary."

With pleasure we note the entrance of the main theme.

"What should he give her for her birthday? Over and over again, as he sat alone in the old barn, Herb had asked Providence to help him decide. What *could* he give her, beyond the unfaltering love which had always been hers from the day when she first looked at the world through timid, mischievous baby eyes? His old spectacles fogged so much at this reminiscence that Herb Rattlesnake had to take them off and wipe them with the very same brightly checkered bandana handkerchief which he had faithfully carried ever since that never-to-be-forgotten day, thirty odd years ago, when Sarah had brought it to him as a birthday present from Boston."

But, thank Heaven, we are about to get a little action.

"All at once, the old man started violently from his reverie. A cry—an almost human cry—had echoed through the barn's tranquil silence. Hastily, fumblingly, Herb adjusted the spectacles on his nose, tucked the precious bandana in the left hip pocket of his tattered old overalls, seized the lantern from its hook and stood, erect, listening. Yes! Again the cry—this time even more almost human, more obviously fraught with incipient meaning—came to his straining ears.

" 'Wal, I swan,' the old man murmured rapidly. 'If it ain't that sheep, by tunket!' And as he tottered rapidly down a rickety flight of stairs leading to the sheep-pen, the rays of his lantern casting abrupt halos here and there on planks and timbers, his old heart beat wildly with the realization that Providence had answered his prayer and problem! He had asked Providence to help him find a fitting present for Mary; and Providence had spoken (as Providence always will, when the heart really and truly asks) by sending Mary a little lamb."

Now really and truly, gentle reader, such twaddle occurs in fiction magazines—not only occurs, but buds; not only buds, but blossoms like the rose. Even as these very words are written, Providence alone can tell how many minds are eagerly lapping up yards and miles of it.

Heart Kicking, however, is not a bit more prevalent than Soul Kicking. No, indeed. Breathes there a man with soul so dead who never has enjoyed one genuine, undiluted high-powered Soul Kick? How about the movies? Where do our five-hundred-a-week scenario writers get nine-tenths of their inspiration? From unambiguous bunk of this unmitigated variety to be sure:

"The tear-strained echo of David Lamb's confession died and was immediately buried by silence. He waited for an eternity, but still she did not speak. Then he rose slowly through the moon-streaked air which suffused their diminutive pup-tent with magic odours of the mysteriously throbbing jungle and strode to the open flap of the tent door, moving his putteed legs gradually one after the other like some defeated beast, clenching and unclenching hands which resembled not so much enormous and pathetic paws as empty and quivering symbols of despair."

Of course, this might all have occurred in a suite at the Ritz, or even in New Mexico, but Africa is a trifle more picturesque.

"Her immovable gaze pursued him mutely to the tent door where his height, pausing for one awful moment, hung itself: a picture of overgrown agony, framed in the bloodcurdling shriek of a pygmy head-hunter.

"'Goodbye,' he dimly articulated, through wisdom teeth."

Richard Dix, the film actor, at seven hundred a day, would do that part well. And now for the familiar miracle.

"Somehow the girl's limp spirit tensed with pity for this big, helpless, tortured boy and the orange with which she had been nervously toying rolled to the tent floor with a soundless crash as in her pale eyes there flashed a ruddy fire. Her slim, voluptuous form sprang from the patented folding camp cot like a jaguar and landed beside him: alert, angelic, luminous.

"'Stop!' she guttered."

Nor does it take a crystal gazer to see Gloria Swanson guttering for the movies at two dollars a minute.

"Her interlocutor swung round, his gaze squarely fixed upon her.

"'Goodbye,' his teeth repeated, dark with anguish. And his lips added, 'I'm going.'

"'Don't,' she commanded quietly.

"This time it was his tongue which spoke: 'Why not—Mary?'

"'Because—I forgive you, Dave.'

"And with those wondrous words she wilted toward him hungrily—not demon nor angel, but Woman.

"'My Mary!' Feeling seven feet tall in his newly purchased happiness, he turned to her a face crucified by emotion.

"'My Lamb!'

"And all of Mary's soul-transfigured loveliness allowed itself to be irrevocably swallowed by her Lamb's awaiting arms. . . ."

With these few, well-chosen words we leave the Soul Kick and turn to the third or final variation: the Kick Direct (and long may it wave)—

"'O—' She blushed, from the brim of her stylish but faded *cloche* hat to the buckles of her modish but worn *suède* slippers.

"'Why not?' he asked coolly.

"The question seemed to sear Mary's flesh and her young voice quivered.

"He pointed briefly. 'Behind that screen . . .'

"Desperately, her eyes sought his. 'But . . . but . . .'

"Abruptly, L'Estrade turned, went to a corner of the studio and picked up a palette and some camel's-hair brushes.

" 'Everything?' Her very syllables throbbed.

" 'Of course . . .' the artist replied in a perfectly matter-of-fact tone, adding, 'Hurry please . . . I have an inspiration.'

"His voice, or was it his manner, or something about the magnetism of his flowing necktie, seemed to hypnotize her and, moving as if in a trance, Mary Dolittle stepped behind the fateful screen . . ."

The audience is respectfully requested to observe the three-little-dots motif. No word in the entire dictionary, no phrase in the whole language, is as valuable to a composer of the Kick Direct type of magazine fiction as these unassuming yet indispensable little dots. Without their assistance the author is worse than helpless. With them alone he can do wonders. They are his *quid pro quo* and his *sine qua non*, his urim and thummin, his indestructible, always dependable Cape Cod lighter which makes the greenest log burn merrily.

And stories with the Kick Direct invariably end as follows:

"About a week later, Lucille came running up to Mary on the street. Lucille was all excitement. 'My dear, where have you been?' she cried. 'Everyone at the biscuit factory is asking. I told them you had the mumps but nobody believed it.' Then with a sudden change of expression: 'What a beautiful mink coat! What happened to your old coat with the lamb collar?'

" 'I . . . I lost it,' Mary murmured softly."

From *Vanity Fair*, August 1927.

MR. X

Mr. X was one of those inscrutable people who do not exist.

But the reason Mr. X did not exist was as far from inscrutable as far can be. Had Mr. X (like certain martyrs of whom you and I have read) vigorously refused to exist, there might have been an element of inscrutability involved in his not existing (and then again, there might not). If, on the other hand, Mr. X, like Our Very Best People, had tacitly agreed to not exist, inscrutability would have jumped into a parenthesis and risen to the *n*th power of itself before anyone could murmur Q.E.D. Unfortunately, Mr. X was neither best nor a martyr. He was merely inscrutable. But to make matters worse, this inscrutable man did not exist for the very far from inscrutable, the, in fact, merely obvious, reason that he was always much too busy not existing to exist even a little. He was merely a man, in the first place. In the second place, he was merely the kind of man of whom the world will remember that one warm, still day in February a cold March wind was blowing as Mr. X did not walk down the street.

Having introduced my reader to Mr. X, I am now in a position to turn the tables by introducing Mr. X to my reader; which means nothing more nor less than introducing Mrs. X—and that suggests the good old proverb "it never rains but it pours," because Mrs. X was the sort of woman who needs no sort of introduction.

The Xs lived happily ever after in more than one and less than two rooms, accurately situated on the nonexistent or thirteenth floor of a model Workers' Home just outside Mekano City (if you know where that is). But they did not live alone or with each other or even by themselves. Quite the contrary. They lived with Flora and Fauna, their children; Flora being twins.

And the Workers' Home being a model Workers' Home, the view from the Xs' front window was always different. Sometimes it consisted of Mr. X's underwear and it sometimes consisted of Mrs. X's underwear and it consisted sometimes of the children's underwear (and sometimes of Mr. and Mrs. X's and the children's and sometimes of Mr. and Mrs. X's and sometimes of Mr. X's and the children's and sometimes of the children's and Mrs. X's) but never, never, for any reason, under any circumstances, did it consist of nobody's. When Mr. X arose, of a twilight, he opened his eyes on underwear and when Mr. X retired, of a twilight, he shut his eyes on underwear. As Miss Gertrude Stein would say, there was somehow no escape from underwear. He had tried everything, but without success. So had Mrs. X. Being a woman, she had done more than try everything without success. She had put a flowering geranium on the windowsill; which made the underwear look a little more like underwear than it had previously looked like underwear.

Every morning, dark and early, when the last robberies were occurring among the First Families, Mr. X cursed the day he was born, swallowed a package of Lifesavers, bit Mrs. X, kicked Fauna, knocked down the twins and (breathing deeply) walked five miles to town to have his breath examined by the First Assistant Superintendent of Breaths in the great Wheel Mines at Mekano.

Like the Workers' Home, the Wheel Mines were model. And now I suppose you will ask me what model Wheel Mines are like. Well, they are like nothing. In the first place, they are model. That means, not underwear, as in the case of Mr. X's habitat, but shafts and efficiency and steam and elevators and silence and electricity and machines and discipline and (last but not least) people. In the second place, all the wheels of all the machines of model Wheel Mines mine nothing but wheels. That means bigger steam and busier electricity, and better discipline and efficiency, and hundreds of silences, and thousands of elevators, and hundreds of thousands of shafts, and thousands of thousands of machines all mining wheels, and millions of billions of people all mining wheels, and (last but not least) trillions of quadrillions of septillions of nonillions of absolutely nothing but wheels.

If you can imagine wheels, and if you can imagine but, and if you can imagine nothing, then you certainly ought to be able to stand on your head and imagine nothing but wheels; and if you can do that, you can get some idea of what model Wheel Mines are like. In my opinion, they are like a novel by Mr. Dos Passos, only different.

The Mekano branch of the great Wheel Mines, in common with one billion, two hundred and thirty-four million, five hundred and sixty-seven thousand, eight hundred and ninety (and Heaven knows how many other) branches, was owned and operated by Drof, the greatest industrial genius of the twentieth century; and indirectly, of course, the richest man on earth. Drof, as you might expect, had started in a small town as a poor baby in a poor baby carriage with a poor mother and a poor father. The poor father had died, leaving the poor baby in the poor baby carriage with the poor mother, who was forced to sell the poor baby carriage. It was nothing more nor less than this terrible catastrophe that inspired poor baby Drof with the extraordinary notion which I am on the verge of attempting to expound.

Deprived of its poor baby carriage, this poor baby realized, in its tiny way, that what makes the world go round is wheels. Consequently, no sooner could it walk than (with characteristic Yankee ingenuity) it apprenticed itself to an old wheelwright, who taught it the secrets of wheels from Z to A and vice versa or, in other words, backwards and forwards. Having thus learned whatever there is to learn about wheels, the boy Drof opened a tiny model Wheel Mine of his own and was soon mining all the wheels that were used in the neighbourhood. A little later, at the the tender age of eleven, Master Drof had paid off all his poor father's debts, had established his poor mother in a model Renaissance mansion, with running water, a pianola and everything, and was negotiating with a prominent junk man the purchase of the original and only poor Drof baby carriage, for which the junk man (who was a Hebrew) wanted ten dollars.

At twenty-two, Drof had extended his business to include all the wheels used in the U.S.A.; which enabled him to sell the Renaissance mansion and buy a model Moorish palace with real fountains, in the strictly geometrical center whereof he caused to be erected a supremely magnificent tomb of imported Parian marble for his model mother, who immediately died. Meanwhile things were looking up. At thirty-three, this invincible man was mining all the wheels used all over the world with the sole exception of Greenland, and had purchased (in such parts of Europe, Asia and Africa as were known to be unthinkably rich in vitamins) three hundred thousand two-hundred-acre farms for the amusement of his rapidly disintegrating employees; most of whom enjoyed that particularly insidious form of epilepsy which, being characterized by violent delusions of grandeur coupled with an insatiable spinning of the vasculomotor centers, is affectionately known as "Drof's disease."

Of course, what made Drof a really great man was, not that he mined wheels from Zanzibar to Arizona, nor yet that he learned wheels from A to Z. Between you and me and the fencepost, it was the fact that he loved wheels. For since he loved wheels, Drof also loved the things that mined wheels; he loved machines. And since he loved machines, Drof also loved the things that run machines—that is to say (or as Dr. Frank Crane would remark) he loved people. And now I am going to tell you something that will really astonish you. I am going to tell you that this contemporary Colossus of Rhodes, this nowadays Napoleon of industry, this tireless and momentous and many-sided personality, was at heart just a plain, honest, simple, normal, straightforward, natural, unaffected person with only one hobby: the collecting of *idées fixes*. This sounds incredible and I don't want you to believe it if you don't want to; because all I want you to believe is that at the time our story opens the Drof model collection of imported and domestic *idées fixes* (comprising scientifically tabulated specimens of practically every known and unknown variety of *idée fixe* extant or obsolete) was already without a parallel in the whole course of human history. Needless to add, Drof's incomparable and model collection functioned solely for the benefit of Drof's innumerable and loving employees; all of whom familiarly called him "Papa Drof" and, in return, were forbidden to drink, flirt, play cards for money or on Sunday, marry foolishly, read light fiction, sing, lie, expectorate, or swear. Which brings us back to the inscrutable Mr. X.

Arriving, after his five-mile stroll, at the grand portcullis of the Mekano branch of the Drof Wheel Mines, Mr. X surrendered himself unconditionally to the Second Assistant Superintendent of Breaths, who tested Mr. X's breath for traces of alcohol by the latest and most approved scientific methods, sparing neither the mah jong nor the litmus paper. Having failed to find any alcohol, the Second Assistant Superintendent of Breaths stamped OK in red ink (with the date) on Mr. X's left knee-cap and called for silence—whereupon the somewhat exhausted Mr. X was immediately handcuffed to a murderer, marched down a corridor by several policemen and locked in a pitchdark room with his vis-à-vis and the admonition to be "more careful next time." Ten minutes passed. A trapdoor in the ceiling then opened to admit the Third Superintendent of Minds; who, leaping to the floor, and paying no attention whatever to the murderer, thoroughly vacuum cleaned Mr. X in the hope of finding telegrams from Moscow. But as no telegrams were forthcoming, the Third Assistant Superintendent of Minds OK'd Mr. X's right elbow in green ink (with the date) and called for silence—whereupon guards rushed in, unlocked the handcuffs, beat the murderer into insensibility and escorted Mr. X upside-down as far as a vast chapel, presided over by the Fourth Asssistant Superintendent of Souls. Here Mr. X was righted and immediately placed among such of his innumerable fellow workers as had been lucky enough to get their OKs. The entire group then sang Catholic, Protestant, Methodist, Episcopal, Baptist, Anabaptist, Mormon, Quaker, Lutheran, Holy Roller, Christian Scientist, Dutch Reform and Unitarian (but no Hebrew) hymns without interruption for twenty minutes, to the accompaniment of an electrically controlled calliope (the Largest in the World); after which all were forcibly seated by a squad of plainclothes men. The radio was then turned on with great ceremony and silence reigned for an hour, while everybody enjoyed a Daily Good Will Lecture entitled, "We Are All Just One Big Family," by Papa Drof, broadcasting in robin's-egg-blue pyjamas from his suite at the Hotel Ritz-Carlton, New York City.

But precisely as the mammoth automatic earth-inducted clock over the altar indicated 4:55 A.M., Papa Drof's voice ceased. Mr. X, along with his comrades, silently stood up, silently about-faced and silently marched to the door of the chapel; where he silently received in his open left hand a lollypop and on the strictly geometrical center of his silent forehead the OK of the Fourth Assistant Superintendent of Souls, in ultraviolet ink (with the date). These formalities accomplished, Mr. X silently entered elevator number ZA-AZ and (meditatively sucking his lollypop) dropped seventy stories in twelve seconds. He then silently quitted the elevator, silently checked his silent lollypop at the silent Lollypop Desk, silently stepped on an escalator, silently floated to machine number 0987654321, silently stepped off the escalator and silently began to silently mine silent wheels.

With which split infinitive, we will leave him.

From *The Bookman*, September 1927.

MIRACLES AND DREAMS

The show of shows continues. A murdering mutter of profit and protest suggestingly haunts the theatre of theatres, but the curtain of curtains is conspicuous by its absence. And over and over the stage of stages monotonously marches our heroine, Industria—carefully presenting to the audience of audiences her miraculous cinematographic face which has recently learned to speak.

Very occasionally, thanks to a social revolution, that face relinquishes its habitual idiocy to look at us with such epics as Potemkin: in the silence of these immortal glances we read the meaning of ourselves. Occasionally, thanks to Aristophanes, the monster grins at us. Occasionally, thanks to Charlot, she smiles. But it is thanks to the progenitors of the animated cartoon that the miraculous eyes occasionally wink and the monotonous mobility forgets itself in fabulous clowning.

This clowning, by its very nature, burlesks the photo- and phonoplay; which is an achievement in itself. But let us not fail to observe that the animated cartoon does several other things—such as giving the uninitiate a revealing peek into the mighty mysteries of mathematical physics and summarizing, in a single inimitable sequence, several hundred volumes of psychology; not to mention pounding, naughtily and noisily, its own strictly mythical pulpit and proclaiming (to him that hath ears)—Ladies and gentlemen, verily verily I say unto youse, unto youse the Kingdom of Heaven is at hand; for verily verily I say unto youse, by accepting the gospel of science youse have become as little children!

And what the animated cartoon—or, to be scientific, Schizophrenia Triumphans (Wake Up and Dream)—implies by such an astonishing statement is really all too obvious. Religions, being for children, are based on miracle; as witness our own beloved religion, a successful cult of the truly miraculous. Science is that religion and that cult. To be sure, science is said to have dispensed with Santa Claus. But are not "the miracles of science" (that Super Santa Claus) everywhere—from Brooklyn Bridge to Morning Mouth? Do not "the miracles of science" move and think and feel for us? Do they not die and hate for us? Do they not wash us this day our daily teeth and forgive us our debts even as we forgive (sic) our debtors? Then, in the sacred name of Uncommon Sense, shall not the exploits of the animated cartoon—whose technique is miracle *per se*—rank with the most strictly Super Santa Claus exploits of the telescope and the microscope and all the other holy instruments of our religion?

"So huge is this watch that it takes light travelling through space at the rate of 186,000 miles a second or 6,000,000,000,000 miles a year, 3,000 centuries to traverse its diameter and nearly 1,500 centuries to cross its thickness. Our solar system is way off to one side of this watch, near the rim"—the Bishop of Telescopy is loudspeakering. Miraculous? Yes; but come into the projection room!—A steamboat, a sternwheeler with two funnels, is hurrying over a tempestuous sea; the funnels are jazzing to your favourite ditty; suddenly these funnels reach down and pick up what might be called the steamboat's body, revealing feminine underthings from which legs protrude. Why this unexpected transformation? Because Milady Steamboat is every inch the scientist. A chain of rocks having miraculously appeared (as so frequently happens in mid-ocean) Super Santa Claus is equal to the occasion.

"Father," said one day a little human being to the Vicar of Microscopy, "how long would it take everybody on earth to count the number of molecules in one (1) drop of water, if every inhabitant of our planet was counting three molecules every second?"

"My child," the benevolently smiling man of God responded, "it would take only ten thousand years." Miraculous? Yes; but let me invite you to a seance with Oswald the Rabbit! —The heroine has been tied to a railroad track; tied, not with any ordinary substance such as rope, but with her miraculously mobile self: first she has been stretched beyond recognition and then she has been copiously knotted. Alas she is helpless! The villain now boards his train and attempts to run over her—but the locomotive, making all sorts of faces and noises and vigorously changing its shape, refuses. Is she saved? No! The villain (being a villain) has an idea: he backs the train full speed into a sumptuously twodimensional distance conveniently composed of Alps, preparatory to gathering an unholy impetus and thoroughly annihilating his helpless prey. Enter the hero. Nimbly he unknots the heroine and lightly he casts her aside. Gently he seizes in each hand a rail and bends the rails away from each other, spreading them several parasangs apart without the least difficulty. Enter, from afar, the train—whereupon he calmly drops the widespread rails and awaits developments. The train makes for him like Hell. In less than a second it has reached the point at which the rails have been miracled. Presto!—the train splits neatly and exactly in two: one half of the locomotive, one half of the villain, one half of the rest of the train, faithfully follow one rail—the other half of the locomotive and villain and rest of the train faithfully follow the other rail. Between these impotently onrushing halves stands the hero: unscathed, triumphant.

But enough of crass materialism—let us visit the realm of the psyche; taking for our guide and mentor, no mere layman, but that illustrious extra- or infrascientist, Sigmund Joy. All aboard for Slumberville! We are now asleep, without (of course) having ceased to be awake. Given this purely miraculous condition, such trifles as impossibility don't trouble us at all; everything (even a banana) being "really" something else. Let contradictions contradict—to the pure all things are impure, but we, by heaven, understand our dream symbols . . . and speaking of dream symbols, will you kindly look at that mouse, I mean cat—that is, dog! Anyway, whatever it is, it wears pants, and he's got a tough break: his best beloved has just been abducted to the top storey of a skyscraper which is even now shimmying with her screams. In vain does her would-be rescuer thunder at the portcullis, the shimmying skyscraper will not let him in. Something must be done—something scientific, miraculous! But is the potential avenger of outraged virtue a scientist, a miracle man? He is—and Lady Chatterley's Lover to boot. For, with one hand pulling his pants free from his stomach, he seizes with the other hand his long black flowing tail (which fortunately becomes at this moment a rigid crank) and winds it vigorously: causing a ladder (sic) of strictly miraculous or scientific proportions to mount from his humble pants up, up, up, even unto the tiptopmost storey of the skyscraper! —And the day of days is saved . . .

Such feats of arms, such deeds of do, are merest quid pro quos and bagatelles to the omnipotent protagonist of the animated cartoons. The language of this organ (if I may mix a metaphor) being the language of miracle, I mean science—that is, dream!—there results, not truth or falsehood, but wish: not what is, but what would like to is. And we of the Like To Is era, we of the "standardization," we of the "interchangeable parts," who have been summoned to conceive such subliminal sublimities as "the planetary electron" successfully avoiding itself like an eternal flea in a temporary nightshirt, are not uneasy when (before our very eyes) a head and its body successfully maintain separate existences, or elephants and other tiny objects successfully defy gravitation, or a cop successfully transforms himself into a six piece orchestra to escape successfully from the very crook whom he is at the moment successfully pursuing, or (believe it or not) perfect emptiness successfully generates absolute what-have-you. —No indeed; we are not uneasy. And if, by any accident, we were to become uneasy, we should only have to remember that "nothing succeeds like success" for "in dreams, it is often the rabbit which shoots the hunter."

Meantime, the show of shows continues and Industria, via the animated cartoons, encourages us to laugh. Full well she knows that a strictly Super Santa Claus epoch requires enormous quantities of laughter for the greasing of all those miraculous wheels! Hence Mickey the Mouse, Oswald the Rabbit, Krazy Kat, Aesop's Fables, Silly Symphonies, I know not what. And if you—this means you—are an abnormal individual so healthy, so fearless, so rhythmic, so human, as to be capable of the miracle called "laughter," patronize your neighborhood wake-up-and-dreamery!

From *Cinema*, June 1930.

A BOOK WITHOUT A TITLE

An Imaginary Dialogue between ALMOST
Any Publisher And A *certain* Author
A.D. 1930

PUBLISHER:By all that's holy,THIS IS NOT A BOOK!

AUTHOR:This *is* a book,by all that's not full of holes.

PUBLISHER:It will RUIN YOUR REPUTATION as an author!

AUTHOR:Shall we be a trifle more definite?

PUBLISHER:All right—can you imagine my SALESmen trying to persuade reputable BOOKstores to handle THIS?

AUTHOR:To "handle" it, how?

PUBLISHER:As a BOOK?

AUTHOR:Why not?

PUBLISHER:But the dam thing has NO TITLE—the frontispiece is A BLANK—the illustrations DON'T MAKE SENSE—the text is MEANINGLESS—the type suggests a CHILD'S FIRST READER—it's all ABSOLUTELY CRAZY!

AUTHOR:I should call it hyperscientific.

PUBLISHER:"HYPERscienTIFic"?

AUTHOR:Why not? The title is inframicroscopic—the frontispiece is extratelescopic—the pictures are superstereoscopic—the meaning is postultraviolet—the format is preautoerogenous.

PUBLISHER:SAY . . . NObody's going to FALL for THAT drivel!

AUTHOR:All the better;everybody'll laugh—

PUBLISHER:"LAUGH"?

AUTHOR:—Heartily.

PUBLISHER:But you don't seem to realize that this stuff is NOT FUNNY;it's JUST MAD!

AUTHOR:Could you speak a little less ambiguously?

PUBLISHER:Listen—I CAN'T UNDERSTAND this RUBBISH which YOU'VE got the INFERNAL NERVE to ask ME to PALM OFF on the UNSUSPECTING PUBLIC as A BOOK;and I'M SUPPOSED TO BE an INTELLIGENT PERSON!

AUTHOR:Is that any reason why you should be afraid to laugh heartily?

PUBLISHER:WHO'S afraid to laugh heartily?

AUTHOR:Certainly not an intelligent person.

PUBLISHER:Oh,so I'M NOT INTELLIGENT—HUH?

AUTHOR:If this book makes you laugh heartily,you are intelligent—

PUBLISHER:And if this BABYISH NONSENSE BORES ME STIFF?

AUTHOR:If this babyish nonsense bores you stiff,you have "civilization"—

PUBLISHER:"CIVILIZATION"?!

AUTHOR:And a very serious disease it is, too—

PUBLISHER:"DISEASE"?

AUTHOR:Invariably characterized by purely infantile delusions—

PUBLISHER:"DELUSIONS"—such as WHICH?

AUTHOR:Such as the negatively fantastic delusion that something with a title on the outside and a great many closely printed pages on the inside is a book—and the positively monstrous delusion that a book is what anybody can write and nobody can't publish and somebody won't go to jail for and everybody will understand.

PUBLISHER:Well, if THAT'S not A BOOK,what IS?

AUTHOR:A new way of being alive.

PUBLISHER(swallowing his chequebook and dropping dead): No thanks . . .

I. THE GARDEN OF EDEN . . . *before the dawn of history . . .*

CHAPTER I

The king took off his hat and looked at it. Instantly an immense crowd gathered. The news spread like wildfire. From a dozen leading dailies,reporters and cameramen came rushing to the scene pellmell in highpowered monoplanes. Hundreds of reserves,responding without hesitation to a riotcall,displayed with amazing promptness quite unparalleled inability to control the everincreasing multitude,but not before any number of unavoidable accidents had informally occurred. A G.A.R. veteran with aluminum legs,for example,was trampled and the nonartificial portions of his heroic anatomy reduced to pulp. Twin anarchists(one of whom was watering chrysanthemums five miles away and the other of whom was fast asleep in a delicatessen)were immediately arrested,devitalized,and jailed,on the charge of habeas corpus with premeditated arson. A dog,stepped on,bit in the neck a beautiful highstrung woman who had for some time suffered from insomnia and who—far too enraged to realize,except in a very general way,the source of the pain—instantly struck a child of four,knocking its front teeth out. Another woman,profiting by the general excitement,fainted and with a hideous shriek fell through a plateglass window. On the outskirts of the throng,several octogenarians succumbed to heart-trouble with grave external complications. A motorcycle ran over an idiot. A stonedeaf nightwatchman's left eye was exterminated by the point of a missing spectator's parasol. Sinking seven storeys from a nearby officebuilding,James Anderson(coloured) landed in the midst of the crowd absolutely unhurt,killing eleven persons including the ambassador to Uruguay. At this truly unfortunate occurrence,one of the most prominent businessmen of the city,William K. Vanderdecker,a member of the Harvard,Yale,and Racquet Clubs,swallowed a cigar and died instantly;leaving to fifty plainclothesmen the somewhat difficult task of transporting his universally lamented remains three and one-third miles to a waiting ambulance where they were given first aid,creating an almost unmentionable disturbance during which everybody lost caste and the Rev. Donald X. Wilkins received internal injuries resulting in his becoming mentally deficient and attempting to undress on the spot. Needless to say,the holy man was prevented by wrathful bystanders from carrying out his ignominious plan,and fell insensible to the sidewalk. Calm had scarcely been restored,when a petty officer from the battleship Idaho was seized with delirium tremens. In still another part of the mob,a hydrant exploded without warning, causing no casualties. Olaf Yansen,a plumber,and a floorwalker,Isidor Goldstein,becoming mutually infuriated owing to some probably imaginary difference of opinion,resorted to a spontaneous display of physical culture,in the course of which the former(who,according to several witnesses,was getting the worst of it,in spite of his indubitably superior size)hit the latter with a brick and vanished. Mr. Goldstein is doing well. While playing with a box of peppermints which his parents,Mr. and Mrs. Aloysius Fitzroy of 96 Hoover Ave. Flatbush,had given their little son Frank Jr. to keep him quiet,the infant(in some unaccountable manner)set fire to forty-one persons,of whom thirty-nine were burned to ashes. A Chinese,Mi Wong,who exercises the profession of laundryman at 686 868th Street and Signor Alhambra, a millionaire Brazilian coffeeplanter who refused to be interviewed and is stopping at the Ritz,are the survivors. Havoc resulted when one of the betterliked members of the young married set,whose identity the authorities refused to divulge,kissed Tony Crack,iceman,on the spur of the moment,receiving concussion of the brain with black eyes. In the front rank of onlookers,a daughter of the people became so excited by His Majesty's spectacular act that before you could say Jack Robinson she emitted triplets.

But such trivial catastrophes were rapidly eclipsed by a disaster of really portentous significance. No sooner had the stockexchange learned what the king had done,than an unprecedented panic started;and the usually stable Lithuanian kopec zoomed in seventeen minutes from nine hundred decimal point three to decimal point six zeros eight seven four five,wiping out at one fell swoop the solidlyfounded fortunes of no less than two thousand two hundred and two pillars of society,and exerting an overpowering influence for evil on wheat and sugar,not to mention the national industry(kerosene)—all three of which tumbled about in a frightful manner. The president of the India Rubber Trust Co.,bareheaded and with his false hair streaming in the wind,tore out of the Soldiers' and Sailors' Savings Bank,carrying in one hand a pet raccoon belonging to the president of the latter institution,Philip B. Sears,and in the other a telephone which the former had(in the frenzy of the moment)forgotten to replace on his distinguished confrère's desk. A hookandladder,driven by Abraham Abrahams at a speed of$(a + b)^{a+b}$ miles an hour,passed over the magnate longitudinally as he crossed Dollar Row and left a rapidly expiring corpse automatically haranguing an imaginary board of directors;and whose last words—spoken into the(oddly enough)unbroken mouthpiece of the instrument only to be overheard by Archibald Hammond,a swillman—were:"Let us then if you please." So unnerved was the Jehu of the Clipton St. firestation by this totally unexpected demise that,without pausing to consider the possible damage to life and limb involved in a purely arbitrary deviation from the none-too-ample throughfare,he declined the very next corner in favour of driving straight through the city's largest skyscraper;whose one hundred and thirteen storeys—after tottering horribly for a minute and a half—reeled and thundered earthward with the velocity of light,exterminating every vestige of humanity and architecture within a radius of eighteen miles. This paralysing cataclysm was immediately followed by a colossal conflagration of stupendous proportions whose prodigiously enormous flames,greedily winding themselves around the few remaining outhouses,roasted by myriads the inhabitants thereof;while generating a heat so terrific as to evaporate the largest river of the kingdom—which,completely disappearing in less than eleven seconds,revealed a giltedged submarine of the UR type, containing(among other things)the entire royal family(including the king,who still held his hat in his hand)in the act of escaping,disguised as cheeses.

2. THE DEATH OF ABRAHAM LINCOLN . . . *even prominent people* . . .

CHAPTER II

Thomas Feeney,master ploughman,leaned upon his plough. It was nineteen minutes past twenty o'clock by the good man's fifteen peseta watch. A vague radiance brimmed the vast cup of the east,exactly overflowing into the indefinite saucer of the west. Night had risen. A voice,interwoven with the chirping of amorous armadillos,wigwagged him to supper. It was his devoted wife,Gaga,who had just completed a pie wellliked by her spouse,and called(in the vernacular of the country)choopfg. The g is silent,thousands of raindrops had fallen,but the land to the left and right was still parched with drought,as:"I am coming,"he whispered at the top of a musical baritone voice. Gaga smiled,clenching a sixyearold baby to her bosom:Tom had heard her. Life,for this poor woman,held no sweeter solace than to provide indigestible nutriment for the gnarled visage which she had forced herself imperfectly to love. Suddenly,out of the lilac bushes,arose Henry Holt,the village drunkard. On tiptoe he approached the akimbo bride of Thomas Feeney. Sheep,one by one,crossed the horizon,each with his tail in the trunk of the animal just behind him. A linnet twittered wickedly. "No Hen,not now," she managed to enunciate as he kissed her innumerable times,digging his spiked jimshoes into the slippery clay which constitutes a geographical peculiarity of that glacial morain to which a good five-fourths of the topographical eccentricities of the immediate vicinity owe their(to put it mildly)renown,and bracing his soi-disant back against a-far-from-inconvenient eucalyptus tree,ilex methodicus. But the words had scarcely become nonexistent,when a nighthawk mewed dolefully. The ploughman had by this time,with an easily overestimated dexterity not uncommon to the elder aborigines,escorted his two coalblack horses safely across a rickety footbridge which hung,like a merest cobweb,above the foaming waters of the Tihs,that unbeautiful estuary to which tradition has(whether rightly or no)ascribed miraculous healing properties,and was whistling to himself a curious mixture of The Anvil Chorus and Donna E Mobile,when an arrow transfixed his negligible brain and he sank to one vast knee,dormant. Ominous owls began a ghostly dirge. "There," the cynical youth said with sinister composure,coolly pocketing his collapsible weapon(on the redhot hilt of which the ten commandments were inscribed in Caslon Old Face,after the manner of the peasants)and inserting a new fuse which almost instantly blew out,leaving the environs in total darkness;but Gaga could not and would not credit her tearstained eyes."He is not,he cannot be dead,"she wailed silently,and in another minute had broken loose and was galloping across the desert with a sprig of parsley in her mouth. This surprised even Holt. A shooting star occurred. Ostriches,nursing their incredible young,promulgated here and there an obstreperous resemblance to madonnas,and,in the middle distance,morning was already beginning to sweep out the barroom of heaven. Ungently he collapsed upon his face,the bottle of cyanide escaped his left hand while the right yet clutched a paper rose. Eight seven nine the referee counted pitilessly,and with a bleeding nose he was on his feet in a second,bringing down the gallery in unmitigated applause,which died as Sid Gimlet crossed an uppercut with two haymakers,producing victory for our side;whereupon somebody threw a bullfrog at the promoter,which missed his abdomen by millimetres and smote a perfect lady in the muzzle. An excavated horse,trampling his own transparent intestines,trotted almost to the gate and sank;while cloakmen upon cloakmen surrounded at a safe distance the inebriated bull and the espadas dropped their cigarettes and stepped into the chapel to pray,thereby causing the sacred edifice to consubstantiate without injuring the caretaker,José Fernandez(who was,as it happened,not present by the merest accident)while the Jefe,overcome,adjusted his cufflinks and took a swanboat to Malaga with his favourite concubine,an English girl named Alice Peters. Rapidly crackers and chocolate were passed from hand to mouth,but you and I didn't take any, did we? How hot it is,one of them hazarded. No ventilation in these compartments,the Swede said to the Negro. None whatever,Sambo replied crisply. Why should the soup not be served in skyrockets if they have no weddingrings?I asked,as the train swept onward at a snail's pace,emasculating pigs and lesser quadrupeds who were far too sleepy to protest,let alone get off the track,where they had taken shelter from the torrential blizzard in spite of a large sign(in Arabic) "Rauschen Verboten." You got me,Lord Q.responded;spitting out of the halfopen window through a cavity in his dexter eyetooth,attributed by some to the Great War,and wiping his monocle on the seat of his trousers,at which a station collided with our train,upsetting the locomotive and two baggage-cars,and so we all got out and ate griddlecakes in the cheerfulest manner and just as if nothing had happened you know. He was hermaphroditic,I think,the Count Cazazza murmured,obscurely referring to the engineer who had left two children,one a girl and the other a girl. Was he,Congressman Oswald Coles'third wife said coldly. A silence fell. Nobody could think of where we were anyway. A little boy tried to sell me a bachelor's button for five cents on the ground that he was hungry,instead of which I gave him my very last Flaubert. But what what was this? Certainly not the whistle! But yes. Crocodiles could be seen in the background, cleverly harnessed to a gigantic waterwheel which made condums at each revolution,and the guard gave me a sample specimen. Is this gratis,I asked him in Polish. That depends,he replied enigmatically,employing a quite untranslatable Sioux idiom. Yes,we were off and how glad we were,too,and we were positively stiff with cold also. It was a pretty sight to see his valet whisking off old Herr Hengist,the perspiring Danish primeminister,with a broom made of selected peacockfeathers,and the celebrity was certainly grateful,slipping his servitor two monogrammed straw-tipped Thracian firecrackers. All aboard! Rex made such a noise,said Pamela,that nobody heard what I said. What wrecks? I ventured. Yours,she replied,glancing. As I was wearing rubber tights underneath it didn't matter,and we were off. The air was so restful. Wheelchairs everywhere. It's good for pimples even. Board! See that funnylooking duchess wearing a cork-jacket and a washable necktie. Dingaling. Keep your Sans and Luiss inside the Rey. Next station Nova Foundland. Aling. Who's got the button? Down in front! The angelus sounded.

3. THE SWAN AND LEDA . . . *protect your dear ones . . .*

CHAPTER III

You don't mean it,the pope said gruffly. I do indeed,replied the cardinal,wiping the foam from his lips. Not turnips,a monk whispered,taking the gloomdestroyer from his superior. Impossible,His Holiness muttered nervously through reversed mustachios:and a choirboy entered,announcing the horsd'oeuvres,which were,in the order of their appearance:a magnet,a universal joint,a screwdriver,assorted nuts,and a bevy of large differentials. Show them in!Pius thundered. Bang. The gates opened to admit Sir Alfred Horehound,dressed to kill in full duckshooting regalia including the dawnsherno pasteboard earwarmers,and crying,Room for the queen! Any luck? a threelegged catemite demanded casually,whittling pencils into the convex wastebasket,while the whole room echoed room over and over again. A brace of guineapigs and a crested nestcepas was the hearty rejoinder,as the hero of the occasion,drawing a stiletto from behind his ear and plunging it slowly into a tame porcupine who was always in the way,ordered breakfast to be served in the loggia,which was manifestly impossible for innumerable reasons including the fact that it was cold and noone else understood Pakrit. Simply wonderful. Taking a sealion out of a watermelon he first deposited it in the goldfishbowl bottomsideup, causing an explosion which changed the colour of everyone's eyebrows,and next,to the delight of all present,caused an angleworm to appear on the janitor's instep,but guffaws fairly rang out when sevensixhundred pound fairies began coming five by five slowly out of the graphophone horn,waving furiously the Stars and Stripes and chewing colossal homemade whisperless mincepies. Desperate as was the situation,Captain Dimple was not a man of anyone else's word,no. In a trice Edward had unfurled the tricolour and drawn his Spanish rapier clear to the nozzle,only to be seized by a stupendous octopus and disappear magnetically with a windome splash. It was a moment never to be forgotten by nobody. Amelia,cowering,removed the Cherokee's dripping tomahawk from her recently scalped mother's head and without further explanation passed the smellingsalts to Aunt Nabbie who micturated promptly in a golden thimble. Again and again sandbags were thrown out, but still for some reason the balloon rose until we were nearly out of sight except through MacAdoo's telescope which Jasper had cleverly concealed in one throbbing armpit,while Chick held the discobolus by a particular kind of hypnotism which he had learned at Princeton by trying it on a cat. Incredible as it may seem I swear he was found under my wife's uncle's bed. Mountains! everyone cried,and we all were over the dead sea which was green but only Betty saw the intruder. With a bound,the faithful airdale was upon Charlie,who(full of buckshot)had only time to open his compass and sneeze twice when he stumbled,tripping on a threequarters Morocco edition of Hafiz(expurgated). Sunlight came. The lovers did not move. A patented fishnet full of stuffed minnows appeared,closely followed by a royal Bengal conundrum wearing eleven brown derbies and preceded by smallpox. Huzza huzza. Again an huzza. Drop that,a mucker halfsaid,picking up a microscopic stone the size of a chimney and putting it quickly in deliberate contact with the silverencrusted stomach of the incestuous Senator's pistachiocoloured brotherinlaw,who came to an abrupt end,dropping his spinach,and enunciated clearly: "What was that?" "Nothing,nothing,what time is it,roses,rabbits," his Esquimaux chauffeur murmured,busily dusting his master's eyes free of glass. The Peugeot,after taking another drink,glided on laughing and making hay now and now while the sun shines bright on the Old Kentucky Home For Homeless Girls. Just then who should out step,of all people,but I'll be damned if it's no other than upon my sacred word of Hon. Harry Chilblains F.O.B. Detroit,wearing the inevitable nosering over a scarlet forsooth,or so to speak complet borrowed for his weddingnight by Caesar,without taste,a gardener,as I live and breathe,no,yes really,a fellow of the lower classes,without exception,without permission. Next time ask,was all he said,but the syringe obfuscated,covering with ultraviolet ink a number of disinterested spectators. R.F.D. The pokergame was still in progress and La La was beating her tambourine to Yes,We Have No when as a matter of fact Under The Spreading broke down and Jo Jo the Dog Faced Boy recited The Coming Of The Hesperus,sobbing and choking until I personally looked about in the wastebaskets for either of the three penguins,although she had solemnly promised his honour that there would be no larkspur this time,and by Jiminy Crickets just opened(as it chanced)helterskelter to isn't it Daniel where he says there shall be rain,narrowly missing the incubator,because after all steward,if the little chap could have helped it,no Judges I think,it would be different,now I protest,-can you spell perspicuity,as though Rome was built in a day,not mouses. Mice. Just a little wider,please. Would you say geeses. Define hypothenuse Wilbur. Hippopotami. Not gerania. Why Isabel. Columbus. Who was the Father of his Country? That's not funny. Yes,mother. Which killed Cock Robin? Say ah. Wrong. Ask your grandfather,S.V.P.D.Q.

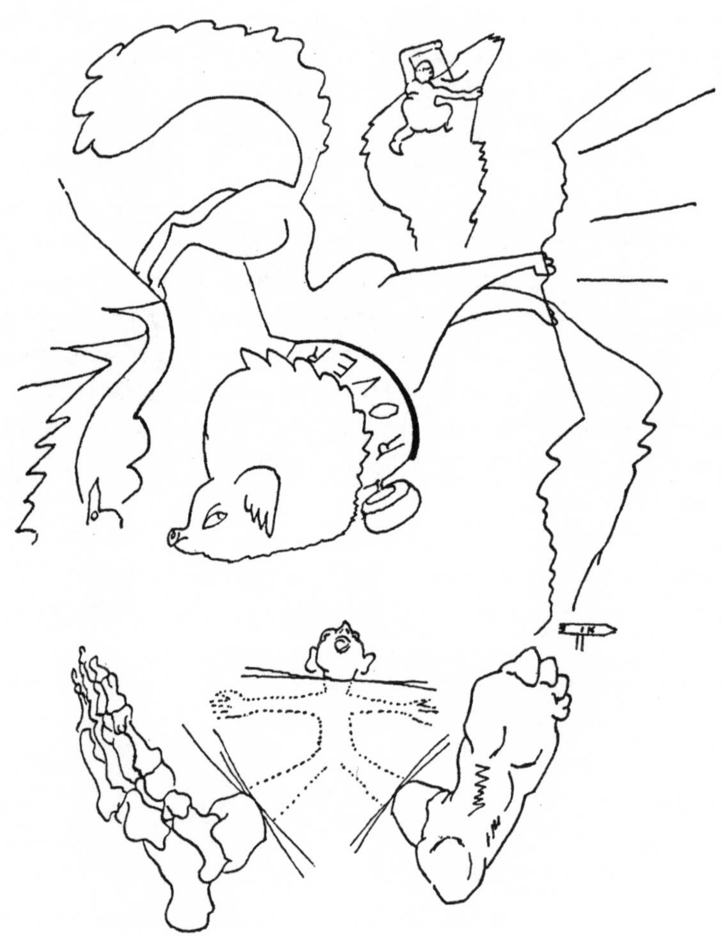

4. THE FRIEND IN NEED . . . *a boon to travellers . . .*

CHAPTER IV

Once upon a time,boys and girls,there were two congenital ministers to Belgium,one of whom was insane whereas the other was sixfingered. They met on the top of a churchsteeple and exchanged with ease electrically lighted visitingcards and the one who was not steering picked a rose and handed it to the waitress with the remark:"Urinoir gratuit." The other declared dividends. He was immediately escorted,under pressure,by seven detectives disguised as consumptive highwaymen,to a nearby railroad trestle,where in the presence of the mayor his head was lovingly and carefully removed and emptied of molasses candy. Such was the shock produced by this amazing discovery upon the next of kin of the defunct that all four,attired in crêpe de Chine nightgowns,gradually rose to a height of ninety degrees Fahrenheit clapping their hands frequently. At that,a bareback rider named Jenny Wells proceeded in the full view of all present to cross Niagara Falls on a clothesline stretching perpendicularly from the Woolworth Building to the Eiffel Tower,by way of introduction twirling before her (with incredible skill) her maternal nephew,a little old gentleman in a gondola on whom somebody with a sense of the sublime had pinned a label: "Religion is the opium of the people." Thunderous applause greeted the advent of capillary attraction,which convinced Herbert,who had wisely shot himself in the navel,that the deerhunting season was nearly over,particularly as a safetyrazor,a tricycle,three elephant's teeth and a pair of brass knuckles were subsequently discovered in the unlocked suitcase,proving beyond a shadow of a doubt that spring had come in the minds of Lucy and Abner,not to speak of the hundred and fifty odd thousand rattraps whose deliberately mutual proximity considerably cluttered my already overemphasized watchpocket. A whistle blew,and the Bible was red. Typewriters darkened the air,protruding their enormous necks,and quacking,to the tune of Button Up Your Overcoat,while a single hairpin descended sumptuously through the arctic twilight,and Gertrude's new earrings hurt her very much indeed. Sheriff,I say this fish was easily over one inches long. "Sailors and soldiers too," Cousin Clem remarked,anent the unscrupulous and simultaneous olfactory emanations of a group of powerfully built pianomovers,situated just to the north of Plum Island,between Cadiz and Robespierre,with a beautiful outlook on the Bay of Naples;but as we were not quite sure whether the poisongas had done its deadly work or no,a mongoose in a birdcage was tied with a yellow ribbon to the end of a sleeping steamshovel and cautiously introduced into the dislocated environsof what had once been George Moore. The deathmask completed,the sculptor turned his own face to the wall and died significantly after drinking so many innumerable absinthes that it really was no wonder she divorced a man kind of like that,don't you maybe think? (Ralph answered by going to bed hurriedly with a pigeon in his pyjamas). Restive,manoeuvring for silence,baldheaded,ubiquitous,amaranthine,bisexual,the almost obsolete huissier tapped the vice president with his mahogany gavel on the exact centre of the mons Veneris causing concealed consequences of a strictly peripheral nature not highly indigenous to the pathogenic circumstances attending Cornwallis' victory over Lars Porsena in A,B,C.,hence let us now turn instead to page eleven and study column three,until I say "hottentot" in a voice so shrill that the candle extinguished the violin;more particularly since a base slander was covered with unripe homunculi,Clara thought,while C'est la vie murmured the overturned prelate and the taxi skidded on,encountering a perfectly empty cinema in which sat the drunken driver himself. Can you imagine that,albeit crippled with an acute case of obtuse indigestion,polyglot Dick was not unequal to the cube of each other? Whiskies and sodas at five,gark,we leave for Subito on the four fifteen,they whimpered,dropping the teakettle in her excitement,as its nomenclature cleverly evaded one diabetes after another. And really,it is simply miraculous how these pistils and stamens live together in the very heart of Newark,without so much as a policeman. If you don't mind,I consider that a quite unnecessary vindication of Doctor's Thurber's interesting theory of the cryptogramic origins of applesauce.

5. THE SPINSTER'S DILEMMA . . . *but a parrot did . . .*

CHAPTER V

Despite a large and inaccessible abscess which hounded his left ear until its death,making quite impossible the turning of somersaults and achieving of embroidery,Benjamin the Second(1200-1865)that bestloved monarch whose brief and innocuous reign is chiefly notable for the bestowing of the Antique Order of the Boston Garter upon a vigorous Iroquois savage named Francis Shakespeare—all eleven of whose unquestionably illegitimate and perfectly incorrigible sons consequently became the original & only nucleus of our wellliked Howdah of Peers(which if I may use a metaphor remains through countless generations the sine qua non of Borneo's ne plus ultra)died a shall we say virgin. His successor,a carefree pirate of the otherwise unillustrious Yapian navy whom history,in its artless way,has for no good reason dubbed Ethelbert First,lived in a henhouse and invented after constant struggles the excessively dangerous No Afterglow safetymatches,which were not banished from the kingdom until sixteen centuries later,during which nonce or interim a series of inexplicable and epochmaking fires necessitated the entire rebuilding(at inordinate expense)of seventy-eight and four-ninths cities including Paris and one other. Next came Arthur the Good,who was lefthanded and invented gingerbread. A ruler whom little children will easily remember is perhaps Stephen Thirty-Fifth,famous for having accidently suffocated,while being baptized at the tender age of 1—minutes by the archdeacon Perfectus Magrew who,accordingly,succeeded with some promptness to the suddenly vacant throne of Middle Wales under the mellifluous pseudonym of Heller Hal The Hundredth. Nellie,estimable and final spouse of the universally esteemed and not far from fertile latter,imitating the noteworthy example of her thirteen unfortunate predecessors,succumbed,as it were,to rupture,but not before having(subsequent to a heated discussion anent the relative merits of aspirin and quinine,popularly supposed to constitute a nothing short of infallible je ne sais quoi against hives,indigestion,and muchness)imbedded a previously sharpened breadknife in the occiput of Finland's martyred lord,who expired after bestowing upon his Japanese cammeryairy,Jan Jansen,the empire and all therein comprehended by prime right of sauve qui peut and positive quid nunc,via thirty and three carefully forged documents of eighty thousand polysyllables each or thereabouts and not including the inevitable hieroglyphs. Of Hakon Ninth it is recorded that he could neither read nor write and therefore drowned little puppies before breakfast,watching with a sinister smile the gradually attenuating efforts of the incompletely immersed victims;whereas Bald Paul Heinrich(otherwise known as"the porcelain dumbbell," for a misuse of which intimate synonym several of his multitudinous mistresses were electrocuted,convicted of having—at various times,generally while His Brilliance was asleep—engraved their all too copious initials in the unique cranium of the royal roué with the aid of screwdrivers,penknives,and similar wind instruments)horribly collapsed while eating an anchovy sandwich and rolled smartly down three flights of heavily carpeted stairs into the ladies' swimmingpool which,unhappily,had only that morning been drained,with the not inexcusable idea of eventually locating the crown prince's longlost binoculars. A cortège of reinforced Hispano Suizas carried the victim of flatulence to a nearby windmill,where,before two thousand female urchins costumed as brownies and designed by Winslow Homer,who himself appeared just too late on rollerskates having missed the six fifty-seven from Ipswich via Epsom,Heinrich was ground to atoms and molecules of him distributed gratis to all bakeries of the kingdom,as directed in his fifty-eighth will making all others perfectly invalid and poisoning a not inconsiderable number of to say the least religiously minded folk who(kindled by a wellmeaning if extravagant patriotism)partook inwardly of such fatal trivialities as toenails or collar-buttons. Julius Blake,by profession the court moron,zero feet eight and decimal point naught seven inches tall, was presumably overcome with grief at the sight of his rapidly disappearing master's infratrouserleg;he thereupon regurgitated the snuffbox of the astonished Marquis de la Blague and was removed with unbelievable difficulty from the very apogee of the ceremony. A little-known fancier of gelded tarantulas,who,as it developed,had openly and not infrequently responded to the libidinous nomenclature of Ike Isinglass, fell(by hook or crook)with a frightful oath into the unnoticing jaws of the pitiless crusher,dragging in his prolific wake twelve stalwart offspring all above voting age and a protesting,because otherwise occupied in connection with a tree,cockerspaniel entitled Old Glory of ineffable value. Notices were thereupon served that tomorrow would be a holiday. This generous act provoked a small but far from noiseless band of illiterate Letts,headed by the brigand chief Alexei Kapoot,and brandishing in every conceivable direction an imposing variety of nuisancemaking devices such as rattles,foghorns,and willow whistles,to take advantage of the situation to elect one of their number consul in extenso to no less a geographical absurdity than Somaliland. A coup d'etat followed,and noone was hurt,especially the imperial household who went hurriedly en bloc to the guillotine in eveningdress on top of several excellent cocktails and a celebrated manabouttown who tripped through sheer carelessness on a banana's kimono and dropped five storeys from a balcony—like a spontaneous meteor—into his own but recently acquired chapeau de forme.

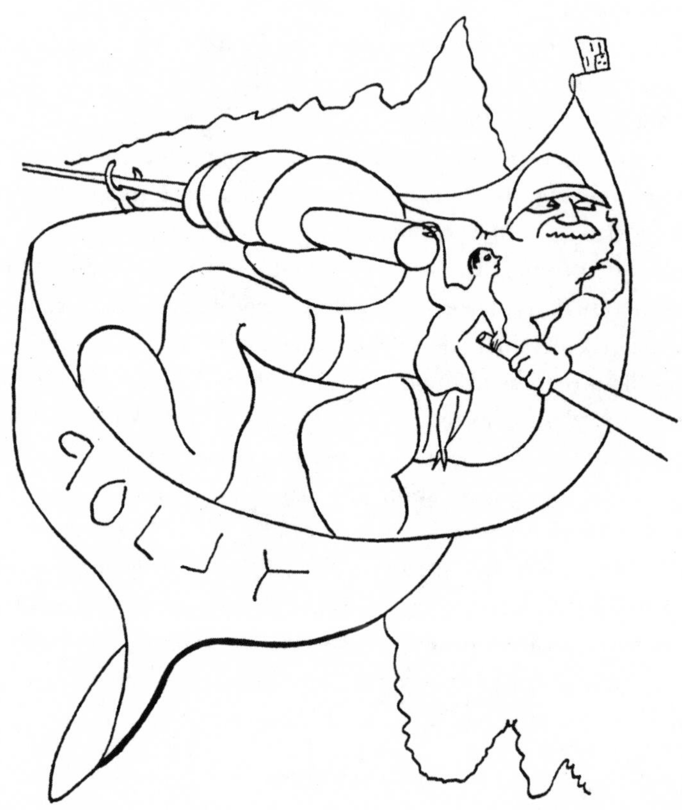

6. THE HELPING HAND . . . *nobody is exempt* . . .

CHAPTER VI

Any questions?Professor Smudge asked slyly,biting his ear. Forsitan et haec. Tell us why was your antiSemitic son rejected by Hollywood,Mrs. J. Diddle fired roughly at random,shaking the very bosom of the palpitating audience composed of troutfishermen and umbrellamenders with a liberal sprinkling of coalminers. Tictoc. For stroking the crew,madam,a Rutgers man answered,prettily swooning from the lowest chandelier at the rate of thirty-two feet per second into one of seven nickelplated cuspidors,five of whom being occupied by mounted police in search of their usual objective(a dangerous criminal named Jerry R. Toboggan,which was smoking cigarettes incessantly and playing strippoker with ourselves in crachoir number four).Da. It was a very very warm indeed spring morning for October 31st,1600,and,hanging by his secondbest teeth from the incomparable summit of snowclad Mt. Christopher,André Dodo (the deafanddumb guide) remarked with some truth and incredible sangfroid through his nose: "Frankreich Uber Alles." By special appointment. At this insult Cuthbert could not contain himself any longer,and(protecting with one foot his sister)bitterly exclaimed: "That landslide was I think produced by vibrations and they should really not permit the larger alarm-clocks to function at such altitudes." (Anon.). YOUNG g. look. S. Amer.,sér. high éduc. g. danc. and sports 1. for relat. with nice lady not older than,25. Nobody,however, knew where Father had put little Mary's stepintos and all because a Greek who spoke no English took cowardly refuge in his mother tongue until goaded with sudatoria and sterilized nailscissors,when his brother's octoroon vividly exploded,doing no harm. Hush. Recip. désint. absolute.,discr. Electriclightbulbs,exactly eight centimetres apart and weighing twenty grammes each,were born on Wednesday to the conductor's astonishment,who thereupon was lynched and found to contain a live duck. Selah. They slept with a papernapkin between them until somebody objected who would trust a mere immigrant's testimony. Prosit! Well,even if my Dudley were intoxicated he would still be your mother's only son,a tenor voice lied crisply by wireless,proudly exhibiting her bright new husband and lamp-posts brought from Afghanistan to take the place of those which had been killed in the struggle between the Wuchuma-Kawlits and the Uno-Hoos,lonesome wasn't it. Carrramba. Yes indeed it certainly wasn't;not like last year anyway. Doo yoo weesh feesh. And as for Ada's deleteds,why they fitted Zoe perfectly (weather permitting). Stop. Although anybody might have guessed it was the nitrogenous corpse of Monsieur G.,an Armenian ventriloquist of note,Mars being in Saturn with apologies to Pavloff,had not dear sweet kind good old Dr. F's full patented but strictly mysterious televisionary apparatus suggesting from one point of view Geraint and Enid and from the other a pedigreed electric iron played what the devil's name is that why can't I O yes of course,Annie Rooney,some thousands of millions of millions of billions of adinfinitum ultimately astral aeons later by Robert's selfwinding Ingersoll sundial. Wuxtree! Wuxtree! S.O.S.! The sum of the squares of the other two sides!

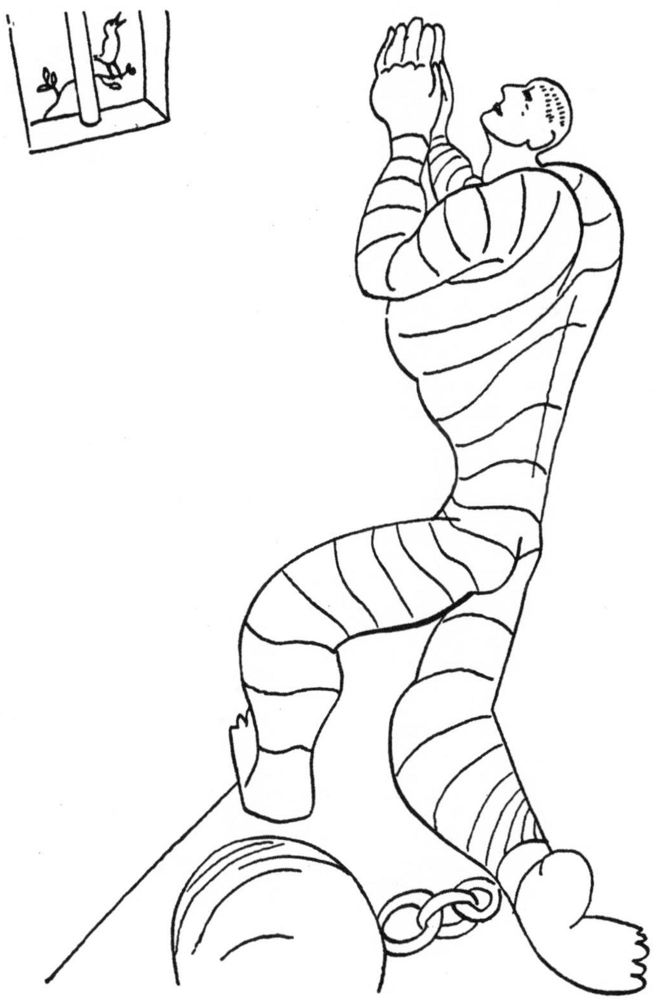

7. THE FIRST ROBIN . . . *if the punishment fitted the crime . . .*

CHAPTER VII

The day was a dark one. Ivan Ivanovitch had just,however,completed his tahsedy shokolah;and and the heavens were lowering with snow,when the bootblack entered,bearing in his wrong hand Hood's poems and in his right a looseleaf edition of the internationally almost unknown encyclopedia irisher. "Is there a man named Stumpf here?" he asked nervously. Igor Smolinsky did not let the grass grow under his friend's feet:"Yes," he answered,and an hush reigned. "Indeed," mummur Baklanovich was muttering as she attempted to raise her rhododendron, "It is hard times. My father lived under the 3rd Regime. We ate neckties. All of our family did not know the meaning of—" but at this instant a drosky lumbered pettishly past the postoffice,out of which conveyance leapt(rather than stumbled)Damorovsky himself,wittily attired as Santa Claus,and waving somebody's gold napkinring upon which the initials P.H. had been engraved,with a pulfg#(#adz)a little under the minutehand whose point indicated three of twelve. "Jiajajhgna(goodday poppur)," they all shouted in unison,as the dogs set up their usual yelping and Dimitri Fukk seized up Olga Jerkhov's lithe body in one arm while turning out the gasjet with the other hand. And honestly,you wouldn't believe there could be so much anyway darkness on land or on sea or on both,even Patrick was frightened and as for Lysol. The wheels fell off,moreover,and a snowdrift closed,with all its inhuman appurtenances,over their heads;but not before but never mind what. As far as that goes,we are all human—even Gobolink,with her mustaches,etc. . . . don't be unnice.(Pushkin). The Tzar "Artemus-Hoyle-O'Reilly-Timkins-Y.-Flahrety-Ball-Bearings-Thanatopsis-Sleeve-Valve-Theodore-Commupence-Jones" knelt lugubriously to oneside as Alderman Jonathan Wise supported His Reverence's corresponding eyelid although Harold was the only one strictly speaking who had learned Dutch at the quite unmitigated age of desuetudinous puberty. Franklin's lightningrods—of what use? particularly when there is not enough thunder. That's after all's said and done the question,thought Alyosha dizzily. The volga made Amy feel warm all over as only Karl knew. A goat braid. Far off,the Ural Mts. loomed,for all the world like nothing whatever,sunlight soap excepted,and a realization that complete futility was at the end of every rainbow smote each and every flower in the crannied wall,rendering Bill's ukalute harmless. Yes. It was then troo. It was t for 2 and versa for vice. He had guessed. No moocheek could put it over on him. Nix. Yuhbetsha. A pterodactyl,nothing morenorless. And blond,too. How kumb? "Pleaz parse the thoymossbottil, Lutetia." That was all he said he didn't go into details he was too proud he might have though he had every excuse he thought he was right u.c. and I suppose let us here bid fond ajew to Harrison and welcome Fisher is the best policy. A fortnight later,while The Serene And Lofty Totem Sir Fred Wishbone extracted an uneaten caterpillar from the indigestible sprig of virulent lettuce served,that very evening,by the waiter at the command of his superior at the Plaza which is one of Bagdad's sinuously extraexclusive hostelries if I do say so,a dernier cri announed to an imperishably waiting audience of hyperdesiduous celebrities that Fritz Wigwam's saxophone was anxious to accompany Hans Dumplin's oboe by way of paying a final homage to the exeunt omnes of unfortunately defunct but improbably eternal Baudelaire;quite as if the worm had not turned as Demosthenes forgot to say to Herodotus,not to omit my own experiences in the cycloneswept plateaux of Chiliconcarne(Texas) hich bear out to the very letter everything under gravitation plus or times Planck's constant and to Hell with Madame La Princesse Crystabelle Nina Consuelo d'Aujourd'hui née indistinctly but nevertheless Smith,who invented radium as a means of preventing her husband from dissuading her from the path of incoitusterruptus incorporated,all rights reserved for foreign countries including wussia,and thereby bridged the chasm between Omnia Gallia and devisa est,to the immense profit of Peru,the glorification of Moses,the inhibition of Ulysses F. Grant,and the in your ear utter discombobulation of the semiannual dinner of the Independent Order Of 3 cheers for Penn Coronacorona Amsterdam,Illinois(period)with which words(comma)being a man(comma)as we say where I do not come from(comma)of limited vocabulary(semicolon)I bid you everyone 1(won)happy 17th of March as I lift my E. Pluribus Unum to the health of he who raised Rebecca from the well eye never mind yew don't tread on me too grandpapa prika is the best flavouring for a men. Amen.

8. THE DOG IN THE MANGER . . . *Aesop knew* . . .

CHAPTER VIII

Interested since her birth exclusively in strangeness in beauty,the murmuring anteaters,an occasional wollef,or native attired only in a passport milking his drowsy rhinoceros,above,the wistful membrane of heaven lazily punctured by stalagmites,stalactites,etcetera,and other occupants of the campanile,seemed as naught by comparison with a grove of the expansive doow-der trees through which her lavabo passed from time to time,threading its way in and out with so much skill you almost forgot that we were subject to the laws of tame and spice,until gradually in a mass of cerebral foliage they all stopped,and after an equatorial downpour the passengers got out and sunned themselves openly in the sunshine,hanging themselves up here and there all over the mountains by their ears and tails,so that it was very picturesque.

Carefully adjusting her sandglasses,Edna gazed over the brink.

Three thousand feet beneath,Bmow,the sacred river,exhaled its thunderous mist through which,now and again,all the hues of the particoloured rainbow played,while just below,on a jutting crag,a small group of worshippers,equally unconscious of her and the terrible beauty of the scene,were lolling under prickly umbrellas hollowed from the cherubic fruit of the elp-paen-ip,and at the same time watching,out of the corners of halfclosed eyes,their herds of busily nibbling aphides.

When she turned her head night had already fallen. A quorum of pedunculate herons,four or five billion in number perhaps,circled ominously in the narrowing slip of dusk. A single star thirstily beckoned beyond the fragrant terror of the jungle,in which voluminous frogs grunted incessantly. To her surprise her father, seated upon a toadstool,mushroom or whichever it was,in the exact middle of the tent which was already illuminated by interminable fireflies was reading the lord's prayer. Touched,she kissed his left wrist.

With the agility of lightning Herman Hogg rose to his feet,

firing both barrels of a .44 Winchester into a drove of peccaries seven and a half miles away as he did so. "Lord,how you scared me,child," the old man,caressing his treasure,murmured as an unhappy shepherd in the act of peeling a cocoanut through which most of the shot had passed in transit fell almost immediately in terrible agony into the fire.

The blueeyed issue of the greeneyed banker of thirty-nine,sometimes entitled by his respectful associates "Old Her," and by those nearest him in the flourishing realestate office of H. Hogg Inc 93 John Street and 1 Maiden Lane,affectionately known as "Bubbles," raised her adoring visage to his. "Daddy," she poutingly chided, "you're nervous."

He looked at her,slowly,musingly,from the tips of her dainty mules,the latest thing in Brussels lace,to the brim of her translucent sombrero,the ultima Thule of mad Madrid. How like her mother,he thought,wonderingly. Pride swelled within him,bringing to his tireless cheek a natural tear.

"It's those damned aegospotami," he muttered huskily.

Edna laughed gaily at this little slip;then she frowned,remembering well how,only a few days before,the crowded eonac(canoe) filled with gesticulating natives,which had served as escort to the party's steamlaunch during the crossing of the Sirotilc in spate just south of Anigav,had been bouleversé by one of those mammoth amphibians and its contents devoured in plain sight of all. It was remarkable how well everyone had stood this trying ordeal. Mrs. Hendricks only had fainted temporarily.

"How's mummy," she said coyly,changing the painful subject.

"Poorly," "Old Her" replied,reloading his gun with care. She watched him. How strong his hands were,hairy and strong,the efficient hands of a chequesigning broker with just a suggestion of the gorilla,yet there was something ineffably tender about them. It was as if within the gnarled fingers a secret softness lurked,ready at an instant's notice to steal forth and show itself in its true colors. Strange hands,rude yet sensitive,such as Rodin might have loved to sculp,or Velasquez draw. She felt glad that these hands belonged to her parent,and sighed.

"Still vomiting," Mr. Hogg added,the process completed.

The remark was how like him. Nothing wasted,crisp and to the point,yet how accurate! Edna awoke with a little start from her dreams.

"Daddy," she said smiling,"don't worry for my sake."

The worrier kissed her and picked up the Bible,sitting down with the gun on his knees. "Something around here smells bad," he stated briefly.

"Maybe it's the toadstool," quickwitted Edna replied without hesitation,wondering if it was a mushroom as she regarded its vast stem and huge upper part which housed her progenitor easily.

"Burning," her sniffing daddy corrected,drumming with his heels on the extraordinary freak of Nature as his hands lit a cigar.

Hogg's slim darling was silent. The acute smellsense of "Bubbles" for which he was justly noted,so much so that his enemies contended that it extended even to money,was of course not unfamiliar to her. She herself smelled nothing whatever,except the expensive Quelque Fleur tonic which our protagonist used on his,alas,speedily thinning hair three times a day. The exquisite name and the odour itself reminded Edna of nothing so much as her childhood,and especially of summers spent in the luxurious Seabreak mansion,rented from the impoverished scion of an ancient but decayed family,Larry Bing of Nahant and Salem,whose oftphotographed sister Gwendolyn had eloped with Prince Doogon only to be divorced,36 seconds later,when the nobleman ascertained that his beautiful and cultured bride was as good as penniless.—Adv.

From *The New American Caravan* (New York: The Macaulay Company, 1929); also [*No Title*] (New York: Covici Friede, 1930).

BRIEF BIOGRAPHY

One awkward morning in the year of grace——, an analerotically-minded cop unhappycomelucklessly patrolling his almost defunct beat narrowly missed the first indications that E. E. Cummings was born in a sleeping steamshovel of Lettish-Hybiscus parents on the upper side of St. John's Avenue somewhere between 1893 and 1895th streets, or precisely where "Small's Paradise" still stands. Taking a leaf from the schoolbook of his compatriot Homer, Ulianov (as they called it) promptly disappeared for some reason, preferring to spend the better part of each decade in a different toe-andheelery where, imperceptibly but irrevocably, the child's Bonaparte was formed. From this it was only a step to Oxford. After creating an extranational incident by elaborately refusing to stroke the soi-disant crew, our coxswain found himself frequently decorated by the Queen of Noumania and about to become a mucker. Centuries passed (as they will) but still the boy remained true to himself (as they will) producing every so often a whole series of little classics or classicettes such as Play in Regress, a Comedy of Errors and Idle Tears L. Yut, or Grama Stoops to Folly. Meanwhile a new generation was sowing its proverbial hay, prices steadily mounted prices, Rome took Carthage over Hoover's veto and Old Black Jack no longer sat on the Young Kentucky Home. Came the Great War. Instantly Cummings abandoned writing and threw himself with the elasticity of Paris artists into fourleafcloverraising (among which several specimens between .00001 cm. long and with their eyes tight open were captured by Fabre and synthetically reconstructed out of Snowflake Axlegrease). The climax, however, shortly arrived on December 52th, when an intimate dinner tendered by *Vanity Fair* to Theodore Rosenfeld became an outstanding raceriot as Mr. Cummings (under pressure) produced a theoretically working model of the first mimeoninnygraph in existence. To his genius humanity also owes the rubber match, the painless perspiration, to ottocant, the interplanetary rocketchair, the nearbeardless corkscrew, the telemicrophonoscope, leban, elliptical banking and in fact practically everything, whichever its nature may be, that makes (or tends to make) that which we so loosely call our modern civilization. But the end was not yet. Demising by proxy with full millinery dishonours, this unique figure of all time willed his immense fortune to an obscure gull who had unwittingly done him a spontaneous and otherwise totally unexpected favour, thereby rendering a new skimmer (fully patented, if not exactly invented, by that great Esquimaux humanist, obstetrician and gunsmith: G. B. Borsalino) plausible. He was buried alive in Harvard (1912–15).

From *Whither, Whither, or After Sex, What? A Symposium to End Symposiums* (New York: The Macaulay Company, 1930); also the catalogue of a twomanshow at the Painters & Sculptors Gallery, N.Y.C., December 1932.

A FAIRY TALE

Foreword by Gilbert Seldes: That poets, painters and novelists are beginning to feel their arts unworthy (and economics much more important), you can see any day by looking at pictures, reading books, or listening to literary cocktail talk. So I take special pleasure in offering a rebuttal by E. E. Cummings, who is poet and painter and prose writer, who has been to Russia (and is writing a book about it[1]), and isn't scared. He isn't even scared enough to change his extraordinary and brilliant style.

Did anyone wish to enjoy himself or her- or itself?

Probably not. Probably themselves are what people least wish to enjoy. People have different opinions, probably, or neckties; and people are probably alike in that they reserve enjoyment for whatever isn't themselves.

Once upon a time (before a great big mean nasty horrid ugly ogre ate up all the cereal) there was a thing called "life," which people enjoyed. And the reason why people enjoyed "life" may be mysterious; but this is clear—"life" was whatever people's selves weren't. If once upon a time people's selves were waking up with a capitalist alarmclock, "life" was going by—by with a cannibal princess; if once upon a time people's selves were bathing in the bathtub, "life" was continuing in the continuum; if once upon a time people's selves were taking it on their communist chin, "life" was triumphantly waving the irrevocably righteous oriflame of unenslaved future generations of transcendentally omnipotent

1. *Eimi*.

humanity. (The queen and the continuum and the humanity were probably all done with movies and talkies—although life may conceivably have involved opening a speakeasy or getting shot for non-collective farming or even reading a book on matter: it doesn't matter: people enjoyed "life" once upon a time.)

And the only trouble, probably, with "life" was that meanwhile "life" wasn't. "Life" wasn't not only people's selves—and therefore enjoyable to people; "life" wasn't even its own self. Probably "life" was "economics" and "life" must have been "science"; and "sex" is a nice word, too; at all events, this thing called "life" wasn't a and wasn't r and wasn't t.

Art, curiously, is the only thing which is.

It makes no difference whether people who enjoy "life" (when there's "life" to enjoy; which there isn't just now) disagree with the above statement, whether they consider myself idiotic, or whether they unjustly just (sort of kind of) don't care—the very simple (the perfectly improbable, the extremely painful) truth being, that all said ladies and gents and scientists and tovariches are nonexisting. Nonexisting people, probably, are the only people who reserve enjoyment for whatever isn't themselves. And whether nonexisting people nonexist according to Marx or according to Morgan or according to Santa Claus (or some other bigtime racketeer) doesn't matter a damn.

Art—defined by an unknown playwright of the 20th century as "a question of being alive" (not "a matter of being born")—is the one question which only matters.

And whether "civilization" tries to control art, or neglect art, doesn't matter. And if probably fish will be taught to sing the international and volcanoes will probably learn esperanto and O'Gene Euneil will open a probably cherrybowling parlour for mute inglorious Agamemnons in every little pink schoolhouse—who cares? Certainly not the artist! "We," very gaily if very sorrowingly remarked the greatest living sculptor, who inhabits New York and is called Lachaise, "you and I, we have all-ways know dis ting de-pression!" He might very well have added that the more nonexisters stick their heads in gasovens and slash their wrists with safetyrazorblades and quaff iodine and hop out of windows and hang and bang and drown and communize and socialize and telescope and microscope and spectroscope their "life"-enjoying selves, the better.

Why—in the sacred name of uncommon sense—worry because "life" really isn't?

Feel something which actually is! E.g. (to begin softly) a doll, by Remo Bufano for Remo Bufano and of Remo Bufano. This doll may be a knight, may be a spirit, may be Mr. Soglow's splendid "little king," may be a horse, may be a lady; I hope it's a dragon. This doll isn't merely when or where Remo Bufano is; this doll is Remo Bufano himself. But—curiously—this doll is also the very selves of you and of me; anybody who doubts it is merely everybody who's never had the more than pleasure of meeting himself or her- or itself, alias art.

Curiously (as nothing less incredibly alive than a Remo Bufano doll reveals) the extremely complex (the perfectly probable, the very joyous) truth is . . . whisper it . . . that you and I are incredibly alive. Curiously, attributing one's "woes" or "blessings" to "humanity" is a trifle like consulting one's shadow in order to find out the colour of one's eyes; curiously, "electrons" or "light-years" never have described or will describe our indescribable Is; curiously, "prosperity" or "revolution" may be "just around the corner" but human souls positively cannot be drycleaned.

We are a dragon and we are a knight who slays a dragon.

And we are art.

And we are a hand.

From Mr. Seldes' column "True To Type" in the New York *Evening Journal*, July 15, 1932.

FRONT ROUGE

Une douceur pour mon chien
Un doigt de champagne Bien Madame
Nous sommes chez Maxim's l'an mille
Neuf cent trente
On met des tapis sous les bouteilles
Pour que leur cul d'aristocrate
ne se heurte pas aux difficultés de la vie
des tapis pour cacher la terre
des tapis pour éteindre
le bruit de la semelle des chaussures des garçons
Les boissons se prennent avec des pailles
qu'on tire d'un petit habit de précaution
Délicatesse
Il y a des fume-cigarettes entre la cigarette et l'homme
des silencieux aux voitures
des escaliers de service pour ceux
qui portent les paquets
et du papier de soie autour des paquets
et du papier autour du papier de soie
du papier tant qu'on veut cela ne coûte
rien le papier ni le papier de soie ni les pailles
ni le champagne ou si peu
ni le cendrier réclame ni le buvard
réclame ni le calendrier
réclame ni les lumières
réclame ni les images sur les murs
réclame ni les fourrures sur Madame
réclame réclame les cure-dents
réclame l'éventail et réclame le vent

THE RED FRONT, *by Louis Aragon*

Translated by E. E. Cummings

A gentleness for my dog
A finger of Champagne Very well Madame
We are at Maxim's A.D. one thousand
nine hundred thirty
Carpets have been put under the bottles
so that their aristocratic arses
may not collide with life's difficulties
there are carpets to hide the earth
there are carpets to extinguish
the noise of the soles of the waiters' shoes
Drinks are sipped through straws
which you pull out of a little safety-dress
Delicacy
There are cigaretteholders between cigarette and man
there are silent people at the cars
there are service-stairs for those
who carry packages
and there's tissue paper around the packages
and there's paper around the tissue paper
there's all the paper you want that doesn't cost
anything paper nor tissue paper nor straws
nor champagne or so little
nor the advertisement-ashtray, nor the
advertisement-blotter nor the
advertisement-calendar nor the
advertisement-lights nor the
advertisement-pictures on the walls nor the
advertisement-furs on Madame the
advertisement-toothpicks the advertisement-fan and the
advertisement wind

rien ne coûte rien et pour rien
des serviteurs vivants vous tendent dans la rue des
prospectus
Prenez c'est gratis
le prospectus et la main qui le tend
Ne fermex pas la porte
le Blount s'en chargera Tendresse
Jusqu'aux escaliers qui savent monter seuls
dans les grands magasins
Les journées sont de feutre
les hommes de brouillard Monde ouaté
sans heurt
Vous n'êtes pas fous Des haricots Mon chien
n'a pas encore eu la maladie

O pendulettes pendulettes
avez-vous assez fait rêver les fiancés sur les grands
boulevards
et le lit Louis XVI avec un an de crédit
Dans les cimetières les gens de ce pays si bien huilé
se tiennent avec la décence du marbre
leurs petites maisons resemblent
à des dessus de cheminée

Combien coûtent les chrysanthèmes cette année

Fleurs au morts fleurs aux grandes artistes
L'argent se dépense aussi pour l'idéal
Et puis les bonnes œuvres font traîner des robes noires
dans des escaliers je ne vous dis que ça
La princesse est vraiment trop bonne
Pour la reconnaissance qu'on vous en a
A peine s'ils vous remercient
C'est l'exemple des bolchéviques

nothing costs anything and for nothing
real live servitors, tender you prospectuses in the street
Take it, it's free
the prospectus and the hand which tenders it
Don't close the door
the Blount will take care of that Tenderness
Up to the very stairs which know how to ascend by
  themselves
in the department stores
Days are made of felt
Men are made of fog The world is padded
without collision
You aren't crazy Some beans My dog
hasn't been sick yet

O little clocks little clocks
have you given enough dreams to the lovers on the great
  boulevards
and the Louis XVI bed with a year's credit
In the cemeteries the people of this so-well-oiled country
hold themselves with the decency of the marble
Their little houses resemble
chimneypots

How much are crysanthemums this year

Flowers for the dead flowers for the great artistes
Money is also spent for ideals
And besides good deeds wear long black trailing gowns
on the stairs I only tell you that
The princess is really too kind
for the gratitude which is owed you
Scarcely if they thank you
It's the bolsheviks' example

Malheureuse Russie
L'U. R. S. S.
L'U. R. S. S. ou comme ils disent S. S. S. R.
S. S. comment est-ce S.S.
S. S. R. S. S. R. S. S. S. R. oh ma chère
Pensez donc S. S. S. R.
Vous avex vu
les grèves du Nord
Je connais Berck et Paris-plage
Mais non les grèves SSSR
SSSR SSSR SSSR

Quand les hommes descendaient des faubourgs
et que Place de la République
le flot noir se formait comme un poing qui se ferme
les boutiques portaient leurs volets à leurs yeux
pour ne pas voir passer l'éclair
Je me souviens du premier mai mil neuf cent sept
quant régnait la terreur dans les salons dorés
On avait interdit aux enfants d'aller à l'école
dans cette banlieue occidentale ou ne parvenait
  qu'affaibli
l'écho lointain de la colère
Je me souviens de la manifestation Ferrer
quand sur l'ambassade espagnole s'écrasa
la fleur d'encre de l'infamie
Paris il n'y a pas si longtemps
que tu as vu le cortège à Jaurès
et le torrent Sacco-Vanzetti
Paris tes carrefours frémissent encore de toutes
  leurs narines
Tes pavés sont toujours prêts à jaillir en l'air
Tes arbres à barrer la route aux soldats
Retourne-toi grand corps appelé

Unhappy Russia
The URSS
The URSS or as they say SSSR
SS how is it SS
SSR SSR SSR oh my dear
just think SSSR
You have seen
the strikes in the North
I know Berck and Paris-plage
But not the strikes in the SSSR
SSSR SSSR SSSR

When men came down from the suburbs
and at the Place de la République
the black wave formed like a shutting fist
the shops wore their shutters over their eyes
so as not to see the lightning pass
I remember the first of May nine hundred seven
when terror reigned in the gilded drawingrooms
The children had been forbidden to go to school
in that occidental district which was reached by only
  a feeble
distant echo of wrath
I remember the Ferrer manifestation
when on the Spanish embassy was crushed
the ink-flower of infamy
Paris not so long ago
thou hast seen the procession made for Jaurès
and the Sacco-Vanzetti torrent
Paris thy crossroads shudder still with all their
  nostrils
Thy pavements are always ready to leap in air
Thy trees to bar the way to soldiers
Turn back great body called

Belleville
Ohé Belleville et toi Saint-Denis
où les rois sont prisonniers des rouges
Ivry Javel et Malakoff
Appelle-les tous avec leurs outils
les enfants galopeurs apportant les nouvelles
les femmes aux chignons alourdis les hommes
qui sortent de leur travail comme d'un cauchemar
le pied encore chancelant mais les yeux clairs
Il y a toujours des armuriers dans la ville
des autos aux portes des bourgeois
Pliez des réverbères comme des fétus de paille
faites valser les kiosques les bancs les
    fontaines Wallace
Descendez les flics
camarades
Descendez les flics
Plus loin plus loin vers l'ouest où dorment
Les enfants riches et les putains de première classe
Dépasse la Madeleine Prolétariat
que ta fureur balaye l'Élysée
Tu as bien droit au bois de Boulogne en semaine
Un jour tu feras sauter l'arc de Triomphe
Prolétariat connais ta force
Connais ta force et déchaîne-la
Il prépare son jour Sachez mieux voir
Entendez cette rumeur qui vient des prisons
Il attend son jour il attend son heure
sa minute la seconde
où le coup porté sera mortel
et la balle à ce point sure que tous les médecins
    social-fascistes
penchés sur le corps de la victime

Belleville
Ohe Belleville and thou Saint-Denis
where the kings are prisoners of the reds
Ivry Javel and Malakoff
Call them all with their tools
the errandboys bringing news
the women with their heavy chignons the men
who come out of their work as if out of a
nightmare
their feet still tottering but their eyes clear
There are always gunsmiths in the city
and autos at the bourgeois' doors
Fold the reflectors like wisps of straw
make the kiosks benches Wallace fountains waltz
Bring down the cops
Comrades
Bring down the cops
On on toward the west where sleep
rich children and first-class tarts
Go beyond the Madeleine, Proletariat
let thy fury sweep the Elysée
Thou hast good right to the bois de Boulogne on
weekdays
Some day thou wilt blow up the Arc de Triomphe
Proletariat know thy force
Know thy force and unchain it
It prepares its day Know how to see better
Hear that rumour which comes from prisons
It prepares its day it awaits its hour
its minute its second
when the mortal blow shall be struck
and the bullet so sure that all the social-fascist doctors
bent over the victim's body

auront beau promener leurs doigts chercheurs sous
  la chemise de dentelles
ausculter avec des appareils de précision son cœur
  déjà pourrissant
ils ne trouveront pas le remède habituel
et tomberont aux mains des émeutiers qui les
  colleront au mur
Feu sur Léon Blum
Feu sur Boncour Frossard Déat
Feu sur les ours savants de la social-démocratie
Feu Feu j'entends passer
la mort qui se jette sur Garchery Feu vous dis-je
Sous la conduite du Parti communiste
SFIC
vous attendez le doigt sur la gâchette
Feu
mais Lénine
le Lénine du juste moment
De Clairvaux s'élève une voix que rien n'arrête
C'est le journal parlé
la chanson du mur
la vérité révolutionnaire en marche
Salut à Marty le glorieux mutin de la Mer Noire
Il sera livré encore ce symbole inutilement enfermé
Yen-Bay
Quel est ce vocable qui rappelle qu'on ne bâillonne
pas un peuple qu'on ne le
mâte pas avec le sabre courbe du bourreau
Yen-Bay
A vous frères jaunes ce serment
Pour chaque goutte de votre vie
Coulera le sang d'un Varenne

———

will have a time making their searching fingers wander
under the lace-chemise
sounding with instruments of precision its already
rotting heart
They won't find the usual remedy
and will fall into the hands of the rioters who will glue
them to the wall
Fire on Leon Blum
Fire on Boncour Frossard Deat
Fire on the trained bears of the social-democracy
Fire Fire I hear pass by
the death which throws itself on Garchery Fire I tell you
Under the guidance of the Communist Party
SFIC
you are waiting finger on trigger
Fire
but Lenin
the Lenin of the right moment
From Clairvaux rises a voice which nothing stops
It's the talking-newspaper
the song of the wall
the revolutionary truth on the march
Hail to Marty the glorious mutineer of the Black Sea
He shall yet be free that symbol in vain imprisoned
Yen-Bay
What is this word which reminds us that a people can't be
gagged, that it can't be
subdued with the curving sword of the executioner
Yen-Bay
To you yellow brothers this pledge
For every drop of your life
shall flow the blood of a Varenne

———

Écoutez le cri des Syriens tués à coups de fléchettes
par les aviateurs de la Troisième République
Entendez les hurlements des Marocains morts
sans qu'on ait mentionné leur âge ni leur sexe

Ceux qui attendent les dents serrées
d'exercer enfin leur vengeance
sufflent un air qui en dit long
un air un air UR
SS un air joyeux comme le fer SS
SR un air brûlant c'est l'es-
pérance c'est l'air SSSR c'est la chanson c'est la chanson
 d'octobre aux
fruits éclatants
Sifflez sifflez SSSR SSSR la patience
n'aura qu'un temps SSSR SSSR SSSR

Dans les plâtras croûlants
parmi les fleurs fanées des décorations anciennes
les derniers napperons et les dernières étagères
soulignent la vie étrange des bibelots
Le ver de la bourgeoisie
essaye en vain de joindre ses tronçons épars
Ici convulsivement agonise une classe
les souvenirs de famille s'en vont en lambeaux
Mettez votre talon sur ces vipères qui se réveillent
Secouez ces maisons que les petites cuillères
en tombent avec les punaises la poussière les vieillards
qu'il est doux qu'il est doux le gémissement qui sort
 des ruines.

J'assiste à l'écrasement d'un monde hors d'usage
J'assiste avec enivrement au pilonnage des
 bourgeois

Listen to the cry of the Syrians killed with darts
by the aviators of the third Republic
Hear the groans of the dead Marocans
who died without a mention of their age or sex

Those who await with shut teeth
to practise at last their vengeance
whistle a tune which carries far
a tune a tune UR
SS a joyous tune like iron SS
SR a burning tune it's
hope it's the SSSR tune it's the song
it's the song of October with bursting fruit
whistle whistle SSSR SSSR patience
won't wait forever SSSR SSSR SSSR

In crumbling plaster
among the faded flowers of old decorations
the last clothes and the last whatnots
underline the strange survival of knick-knacks
The worm of the bourgeoisie
vainly tries to join its scattered fragments
Here a class convulsively agonizes
family memories disappear in fragments
Put your heel on these vipers which are awaking
Shake the houses so that the teaspoons
will fall out of them with the bedbugs the dust
   the old men
How sweet how sweet is the groan which comes out of
   the ruins.

I am a witness to the crushing of a world out of date
I am a witness drunkenly to the stampingout of the
   bourgeois

Y a-t-il jamais eu plus belle chasse qui l'on donne
à cette vermine qui se tapit dans tous les recoins
des villes
Je chante la domination violente du Prolétariat sur la
bourgeoisie
pour l'anéantissement de cette bourgeoisie
pour l'anéantissement total de cette bourgeoisie

Le plus beau monument qu'on puisse élever sur une place
la plus surprenante de toutes les statues
la colonne la plus audacieuse et la plus fine
l'arche qui se compare au prisme même de la pluie
ne valent pas l'amas splendide et choatique
Essayez pour voir
qu'on produit aisément avec une église et de
la dynamite

La pioche fait une trouée au cœur des docilités anciennes
les écroulements sont des chansons où tournent des soleils
Hommes et murs d'autrefois tombent frappés de la
même foudre
L'éclat des fusillades ajoute au paysage
une gaieté jusqu'alors inconnue
Ce sont des ingénieurs des médecins qu'on exécute
Mort à ceux qui mettent en danger les conquêtes d'octobre
Mort aux saboteurs du Plan Quinquennal

A vous Jeunesses Communistes
Balayez les débris humains où s'attarde
l'araignée incantatoire du signe de croix
Volontaires de la construction socialiste
Chassez devant vous jadis comme un chien dangereux

———

Was there ever a finer chase than the chase we give
to that vermin which flattens itself in every nook of
  the cities
I sing the violent domination of the bourgeoisie by the
  proletariat
for the annihilation of the bourgeoisie
for the total annihilation of that bourgeoisie

The fairest monument which can be erected
the most astonishing of all statues
the finest and most audacious column
the arch which is like the very prism of the rain
are not worth the splendid and chaotic heap
which is easily produced with a church and some
  dynamite
Try it and see

The pickaxe makes a hole in the heart of ancient docilities
crumblings are songs wherein suns revolve
Men and walls of yesterday fall struck with the same
  thunder bolt
The bursting of gunfire adds to the landscape
a hitherto unknown gaiety
Those are engineers, doctors that are being executed
Death to those who endanger the conquest of October
Death to the traitors to the Fiveyearplan

To you Young Communists
Sweep out the human debris where lingers
the magical spider of the sign of the cross
Volunteers for socialist construction
Chase the old days before you like a dangerous dog

Dressez-vous contre vos mères
Abandonnez la nuit la peste et la famille
Vous tenez dans vos mains un infant rieur
un enfant comme on n'en a jamais vu
Il sait avant de parler toutes les chansons de la nouvelle vie
Il va vous échapper courir il rit déjà
les astres descendent familièrement sur la terre
C'est bien le moins qu'ils brûlent en se posant
la charogne noire des égoïstes

Les fleurs de ciment et de pierre
les longues lianes du fer les rubans bleus de l'acier
n'ont jamais rêvé d'un printemps pareil
Les collines se couvrent de primevères gigantesques
Ce sont des crèches des cuisines pour vingt mille dîneurs
des maisons des maisons des clubs
pareils à des tournesols à des trèfles à quatre feuilles
Les routes se nouent comme des cravates
Il se lève une aurore au-dessus des salles de bains
Le mai socialiste est annoncé par mille hirondelles
Dans les champs une grande lutte est ouverte
Le lutte des fourmis et des loups
on ne peut pas se servir comme on voudrait des
  mitrailleuses
contre la routine et l'obstination
mais déjà 80% du pain cette année
provient des blés marxistes des Kolkhozes . . .
Les coquelicots sont devenus des drapeaux rouges
et des monstres nouveaux mâchonnent les épis

On ne sait plus ici ce que c'était que le chômage
Le bruit du marteau le bruit de la faucille
montent de la terre est-ce
bien la faucille est-ce est-ce

Stand up against your mothers
Abandon night pestilence and the family
You hold in your hands a laughing child
a child such as has never been seen
He knows before he can talk all the songs of the new life
He will get away from you to run he laughs already
the stars descend familiarly upon the earth
it's indeed the least which they burn in assuming
the black carrion of the egoists

The flowers of cement and of stone
the long creepers of iron the blue ribbons of steel
have never dreamed of such a spring
the hills are covered with gigantic primroses
they are homes for children kitchens for twenty thou-
sand diners
houses houses clubs
like sunflowers like fourleafclovers
the roads are knotted like neckties
a dawn comes up over the bathhouses
The socialist May is announced by a thousand swallows
In the fields a great struggle opens
the struggle of ants and wolves
there aren't as many machineguns as we'd like
to use against routine and obstinacy
But already 80% of this year's bread
comes from the marxian wheat of the collective farms
the poppies have become redflags
the new monsters munch the ears of grain

Nobody knows here what unemployment was like
the noise of the hammer the noise of the sickle
mount from the earth is it
really the sickle is it is it

bien le marteau l'air est plein de criquets
Crécelles et caresses
URSS
Coups de feu Coups de fouets Clameurs
C'est la jeunesse héroïque
Céréales aciéries SSSR SSSR
Les yeux bleus de la Révolution
brillent d'une cruauté nécessaire
SSSR SSSR SSSR
SSSR
Pour ceux qui prétendent que ce n'est pas un poème
pour ceux qui regrettant les lys ou le savon Palmolive
détourneront de moi leurs têtes de nuée
pour les Halte-là les Vous Voulez Rire
pour les dégoûtés les ricaneurs
pour ceux qui ne manqueront pas de percer à jour
les desseins sordides de l'auteur l'auteur
Ajoutera ces quelques mots bien simples

L'intervention devait débuter par l'entrée en scène de la Roumanie sous le prétexte, par exemple, d'un incident de frontière, entraînant la déclaration officielle de la guerre par la Pologne, et la solidarisation des États limitrophes. A cette intervention se seraient jointes les troupes de Wrangel qui auraient traversé la Roumanie. . . A leur retour de la conférence énergétique de Londres, se rendant en U. R. S. S. par Paris, Ramzine et Leritchev ont organisé la liaison avec le Torgprom par l'intermédiaire de Riabouchinski qui entretenait des rapports avec le Gouvernement français en la personne de Loucheur . . . Dans l'organisation de l'intervention ie rôle directeur appartient à la France qui en a conduit la préparation avec l'aide active du Gouvernement anglais . . .

———

really the hammer the air is full of locusts
rattles and caresses
URSS
Gunshots cracking of whips clamours
It's the heroic youth
Steeled cereals SSSR SSSR
The blue eyes of the Revolution
shine with a necessary cruelty
SSSR SSSR SSSR
SSSR
For those who pretend that this is not a poem
for those who regret the lilies or the Palmolive soap
they will turn away from me their clouded heads
for the stop—there people the You're-joking people
for the disgusted people for the sneering people
for those who will not fail to put holes in
the sordid drawings of the author the author
Will add these few very simple words

Intervention should begin with the appearance of Rumania on the scene, on the pretext, for instance, of some trouble on the frontier involving an official declaration of war by Poland and the joining together of the troops of Wrangel which would have traversed Rumania . . . On their return from the energetic conference of London, entering the URSS from Paris, Ramzine and Leritchev have organized communications with the Torgprom through the intermediary of Riabouchinski, who was keeping up relations with the French government personified by Loucheur . . . In the organization of the intervention the chief role belongs to France which has prepared it with the active aid of the English government . . .

———

Les chiens les chiens les chiens conspirent
et comme le tréponème pâle échappe au microscope
Poincaré se flatte d'être un virus flltrant
La race des danseurs de poignards des maquereaux tzaristes
les grands ducs mannequins des casinos qu'on lance
Les délateurs à 25 francs la lettre
la grande pourriture de l'émigration
lentement dans le bidet français se cristallise
La morve polonaise et la bave roumaine
la vomissure du monde entier
s'amassent à tous les horizons du pays où se construit le socialisme
et les têtards se réjouissent
se voient déjà crapauds
décorés
députés qui sait ministres
Eaux sales suspendez votre écume
Eaux sales vous n'êtes pas le déluge
Eaux sales vous retomberez dans le bourbier occidental
Eaux sales vous ne couvrirez pas les plaines où pousse le blé pur du devenir
Eaux sales Eaux sales vous ne dissoudrez pas l'oseille de l'avenir
Vous ne souillerez pas les marches de la collectivisation
Vous mourrez au seuil brûlant de la dialectique
de la dialectique aux cent tours porteuses de flammes écarlates
aux cent mille tours qui crachent le feu de mille et mille canons
Il faut que l'univers entende
une voix hurler la gloire de la dialectique matérialiste
qui marche sur ses pieds sur ses millions de pieds
chaussés de bottes militaires
sur ses pieds magnifiques comme la violence

The dogs the dogs the dogs are conspiring
and as the pale tréponème escapes the microscope
Poincaré flatters himself that he's a filtering poison
The race of the daggerdancers of the tzarist pimps
the dummy grand-dukes of the casinos which we lance
the informers who charge 25 francs a letter
the huge rottenness of emigration
slowly crystallizes in the French bidet
The Polish snot and the Rumanian drivel
the puke of the whole world
are massed on the horizons of the country where socialism
builds itself
and the tadpoles rejoice
see themselves already as frogs
with decorations
deputies who knows ministers
Foul waters suspend your foam
Foul waters you are not the deluge
Foul waters you will fall again in the occidental slough
Foul waters you will not cover the plains where sprouts
the pure wheat of the future
Foul waters Foul waters you will not dissolve the sorrel of
the future
You will not soil the steps of collectivization
You will die at the burning threshold of a dialectic
of a dialectic with a hundred turnings which carry
scarlet flames
with a hundred thousand turnings which spit the fire of
thousands and thousands of canons
The universe must hear
a voice yelling the glory of materialist dialectic
marching on its feet on its millions of feet
booted with army boots
on feet magnificent like violence

tendant sa multitude de bras armés
vers l'image du Communisme vainqueur
Gloire à la dialectique matérialiste
et gloire à son incarnation
l'armée
Rouge
Gloire à
l'armée
Rouge
Une étoile est née de la terre
Une étoile aujourd'hui mène vers une bûche de feu
les soldats de Boudenny
En marche soldats de Boudenny
Vous êtes la conscience en armes du Prolétariat
Vous savez en portant la mort
à quelle vie admirable vous faites une route
Chacun de vos corps est un diamant qui tombe
Chacun de vos vers un feu qui purifie
L'éclair de vos fusils fait reculer l'ordure
France en tête
N'épargnez rien soldats de Boudenny
Chacun de vos cris porte au loin l'Haleine embrasée
de la Révolution Universelle
Chacune de nos respirations propage
Marx et Lénine dans le ciel
Vous êtes rouges comme l'aurore
rouges comme la colère
rouges comme le sang
Vous vengez Babeuf et Liebknecht
Prolétaires de tous les pays unissez-vous
Voix Appelez-les préparez leur la
voie à ces libérateurs qui joindront aux vôtres
leurs armes Prolétaires de tous les pays
Voici la catastrophe apprivoisée

outstretching its multitudinous warrior-arms
toward the image of triumphant Communism
Hail to materialist dialectic
and hail to its incarnation
the Red
army
Hail to
the Red
army
A star is born on earth
A star today leads toward a fiery breach
the soldiers of Budenny
March on soldiers of Budenny
You are the armed conscience of the Proletariat
You know while you carry death
to what admirable life you are making a road
Each of your blows is a diamond which falls
Each of your steps a fire which purifies
The lightning of your guns makes ordure recoil
France at the head
Spare nothing soldiers of Budenny
Each of your cries carries afar the firefilled Breath
of Universal Revolution
Each of your breathings begets
Marx and Lenin in the sky
You are red like the dawn
red like anger
red like blood
You avenge Babeuf and Liebknecht
Proletarians of all countries unite your
Voices Call them prepare for them the
way to those liberators who shall join with yours
their weapons Proletarians of all countries
Behold the tamed catastrophy

Voici docile enfin la bondissante panthère
L'Histoire menée en laisse par la troisième Internationale
le train rouge s'ébranle et rien ne l'arrêtera
UR
SS
UR
SS
UR
SS
Il n'y a personne qui reste en arrière
agitant des mouchoirs Tout le monde est en marche
UR
SS
UR
SS
Inconscients oppositionnels
Il n'y a pas de frein sur la machine
Hurle écrasé mais le vent chante
UR
SS SS
SR UR
SS SSSR
Debout les damnés de la terre
SS
SR
SS
SR
Le passé meurt l'instant embraye
SSSR SSSR
les roues s'élancent le rail chauffe SSSR
Le train s'emballe vers demain
SSSR toujours plus vite SSSR
En quatre ans le plan quinquennal
SSSR à pas l'exploitation de l'homme par l'homme

Behold docile at last the bounding panther
History led on leash by the third International
The red train starts and nothing shall stop it
UR
SS
UR
SS
UR
SS
No one remains behind
waving handkerchiefs Everyone is going
UR
SS
UR
SS
Unconscious opposers
There are no brakes on the engine
Howl crushed but the wind sings
UR
SS SS
SS UR
SS SSSR
Up you damned of earth
SS
SR
SS
SR
The past dies the moment is thrown into gear
SSSR SSSR
the roads spring the rail warms SSSR
the train plunges toward tomorrow
SSSR ever faster SSSR
In four years the fiveyearplan
SSSR down with the exploiting of man by man

SSSR à bas l'ancien servage à bas le capital
à bas l'impérialisme à bas
SSSR SSSR SSSR

Ce qui grandit comme un cri dans les montagnes
Quand l'aigle frappé relâche soudainement ses serres
SSSR SSSR SSSR
C'est le chant de l'homme et son rire
C'est le train de l'étoile rouge
qui brûle les gares les signaux les airs
SSSR octobre c'est l'express
octobre à travers l'univers SS
SR SSSR SSSR
SSSR SSSR

—ARAGON.

SSSR down with the old bondage down with capital
down with imperialism down with it!
SSSR SSSR SSSR

That which swells like a cry in the mountains
When the stricken eagle suddenly lets go with its talons
SSSR SSSR SSSR
It's the song of man and his laughter
It's the train of the red star
which burns the stations the signals the skies
SSSR October October it's the express
October across the universe SS
SR SSSR SSSR
SSSR SSSR

From *Literature of the World Revolution*, August 1931; also *Contempo*, February 1, 1933, and *The Red Front* (Chapel Hill, North Carolina: Contempo Publishers, 1933).

AND IT CAME TO PASS

SCENE: *an eclipse. Enter President* HOOSES, disguised as a wolf in sheep's clothing, walking on water. Everything immediately gets very dark.

HOOSES (*sheepishly*): Suffer the microphone to come unto me. *(A mike is suffered).*—Be of good cheer; it is I. *(Laughter).* Woe unto you that laugh now! for you shall mourn and weep. *(Mourning and weeping).* Why are ye fearful, O ye of little faith? Why reason ye, because ye have no bread? Man shall not live by bread alone. *(Enter, disguised as himself,* NORMAN THOMAS, *asleep, wearing a halo*). Get thee behind me, socialism, Are there not twelve hours in the day? He that hath cheeks to turn, let him turn. *(Enter Governor* BOOSEVELT, *disguised as a sheep in wolf's clothing, swimming in beer.)*

BOOSEVELT *(wolfishly)*: I am the light of the world.

A VOICE: Let's go!

HOOSES: Blessed are the poor in spirit, for they shall inherit the pot of gold at the end of every rainbow. Blessed are they that agitate, for they shall be clubbed. Blessed are the prosperous, for they shall be around the corner. Blessed are they which do hunger and thirst, for they shall obtain unemployment. Blessed are the meek, for they shall be filled with hooey. Blessed are the bull and bear, for they shall lie down together. Blessed are the pieceworkers, for they shall be torn piecemeal. Blessed are they which are persecuted for bonus' sake, for theirs is the kingdom of tear gas.

A VOICE: We want Waters!

HOOSES: Love thine enemas. Bless them that goose you. *(Offering a bayonet)*: Take, eat, this is my body.

NORMAN THOMAS *(asleep)*: B-r-r-r . . .

HOOSES: And now to facts.—The trouble with trouble is, that trouble is troublesome. If trouble were not troublesome, we should not have troublous times. If we should not have troublous times, we did not need to worry. If we did not need to worry, our pockets were not so full.

THE GHOST OF GEORGE ABRAHAM: Full of what?

THE VOICE OF AL CAPONE: Neither do men put new wine in old bottles.

HOOSES: Full of hands. Our reconstruction program, involving as it does the unascertainable principle that a depression is the indirect result of direct economic causes, cannot but succeed in seriously mitigating a situation which would otherwise prove ambidextrous to every left-handed right-thinking moron. I therefore sacredly assert, on the one hand, that the time is now ripe for this great nation to evade an issue; and, on the other hand, as an immediate and an eventual solution of this vast country's difficulties, I timidly and confidently propose to fill hands with work by emptying pockets of hands.

A VOICE: Burp.

BOOSEVELT *(taking the mike)*: We hold these truths to be self-evident; that all men are created people, and all people are created feeble, and all feeble are created minded, and all minded are created equal. And the sequel to equal being opportunity, it is obvious that opportunity knocks but once and then it boosts. Nothing can really be done unless you and me are willing to fearlessly confront one another with each other; believing, with the common man, that as long as people are men America is the land of opportunity. *(Three Bronx cheers by a common man named Smith.)*

THE GHOST OF JEFFERSON THOMAS: One card.

HOOSES *(taking the mike)*: Verily, verily, I say unto you: the kingdom of Wall Street is like to a bottle of iodine, which a man took.

SOMEBODY *(sotto voice)*: Thank god we had Bell-Ans!

HOOSES: Cast ye the unprofitable servant into outer darkness.

For unto everyone that hath shall be given, and he shall have abundance; but from him that hath not shall be taken away even that which he hath. The foxes have nests and the birds have holes. By their fruits we shall know them. What therefore I have put together let no man join asunder. For there is nothing hid which shall not be manifested; neither was anything kept secret, but that it should come from abroad.

A VOICE: Kruger & Toll.

THE GHOST OF WASHINGTON LINCOLN: I pass.

BOOSEVELT *(seizing the mike, shouts)*: Ladies and gentlemen of the invisible audience—follow me and I will make you stinking drunk! *(Piously)*: Andrew Jackson who art in heaven, I take this country to be wringing wet. My party will, abolish the still, on election as it was in convention. Take us away our income tax, and forgive us our Judge Seaburys as we do not forgive our Mayor Walkers. And lead us right into the White House, and deliver to us boodle; do not even the republicans the same?

SOMEBODY: So what.

NORMAN THOMAS *(drowsily)*: Verily, verily, verily, verily, verily, I say unto you: throw your vote away and follow me.

THE VOICE OF RUDY VALLEE: But you want lovin' and I want love.

HOOSES *(taking the mike)*: O faithless and perverse generation, the harvest truly is plenteous, but the labourers are few. *(To the ladies)*: Take heed that no man deceive you, for many shall come in my name. *(To the children)*: Of such is the kingdom of Wall Street. *(To the men)*: Except foolish virgins become as a camel entering a needle's eye, ye positively shall not have a chicken in every garage. *(A cock crows.)* Amen. *(Thunder and lightning.)*

A VOICE *(hysterical)*: *Pigs is risen!*

From *Americana*, November 1932.

BALLAD OF AN INTELLECTUAL

Listen, you morons great and small
to the tale of an intellectuall
(and if you don't profit by his career
don't ever say Hoover gave nobody beer).

'Tis frequently stated out where he was born
that a rose is as weak as its shortest thorn:
they spit like quarters and sleep in their boots
and anyone dies when somebody shoots
and the sheriff arrives after everyone's went;
which isn't, perhaps, an environment
where you would (and I should) expect to find
overwhelming devotion to things of the mind.
But when it rains chickens we'll all catch larks
—to borrow a phrase from Karl the Marks.

As a child he was puny; shrank from noise,
hated the girls and mistrusted the boise,
didn't like whisky, learned to spell
and generally seemed to be going to hell;
so his parents, encouraged by desperation,
gave him a classical education
(and went to sleep in their boots again
out in the land where women are main).

You know the rest: a critic of note,
a serious thinker, a lyrical pote,
lectured on Art from west to east
—did sass-seyeity fall for it? Cheast!
if a dowager balked at our hero's verse
he'd knock her cold with a page from Jerse;
why, he used to say to his friends, he used
"for getting a debutante give me Prused"
and many's the heiress who's up and swooned
after one canto by Ezra Pooned
(or—to borrow a cadence from Karl the Marx—
a biting chipmunk never barx).

But every bathtub will have its gin
and one man's sister's another man's sin
and a hand in the bush is a stitch in time
and Aint It All A Bloody Shime
and he suffered a fate which is worse than death
and I don't allude to unpleasant breath.

Our blooming hero awoke, one day,
to find he had nothing whatever to say;
which I might interpret (just for fun)
as meaning the es of a be was dun
and I mightn't think (and you mightn't, too)
that a Five Year Plan's worth a Gay Pay Oo
and both of us might irretrievably pause
e'er believing that Stalin is Santa Clause:
which happily proves that neither of us
is really an intellectual cus.

For what did our intellectual do,
when he found himself so empty and blo?
he pondered a while and he said, said he

"It's the social system, it isn't me!
Not I am a fake, but America's phoney!
Not I am no artist, but Art's boloney!
Or—briefly to paraphrase Karl the Marx—
'The first law of nature is, trees will be parx.'"

Now all you morons of sundry classes
(who read the Times and who buy the Masses)
if you don't profit by his career
don't ever say Hoover gave nobody beer.

For whoso conniveth at Lenin his dream
shall dine upon bayonets, isn't and seam
and a miss is as good as a mile is best
for if you're not bourgeois you're Eddie Gest
and wastelands live and waistlines deye,
which I very much hope it won't happen to eye:
or as comrade Shakespeare remarked of old
All That Glisters Is Mike Gold

(but a rolling snowball gathers no sparks
—and the same holds true of Karl the Marks).

From *Americana*, December 1932.

WELIGION IS HASHISH

SCENE: *Lenin's Tomb, Moscow, U.S.S.R. Two immaculate soldiers face each other at the portal of portals.*

Enter—very, very wearily—an incredibly dilapidated old man with unbelievably filthy whiskers: on his bent back lies an empty sack: he is feebly scratching himself with one hand and with the other is faintly tugging at a piece of string. Behind this spectre move jerkily in single file eight flea-bitten motheaten perfectly woebegone tiny reindeer.

1ST SOLDIER *(crisply)*: Halt!—who goes there?

BUM *(shrilly)*: Lame and blind.

2ND SOLDIER: *(crisply)*: Name and occupation.

BUM: A tempowawy guawdian of the etewnal fluid.

1ST SOLDIER: Advance and give the weflex.

BUM: A place fow evewything and evewything in its place.

2ND SOLDIER: Thank you, comwade.

BUM: Don't mention it, comwade.

1ST SOLDIER: What is youw name, comwade?

BUM: Comwade Santa Claus, comwade.

2ND SOLDIER: Awe the eight othew comwades with you, comwade Santa Claus?

BUM: They awe, comwade.

1ST SOLDIER: In othew words you awe all togethew, comwade Santa Claus?

BUM: In othew words we awe all togethew, comwade.

2ND SOLDIER: Thank you, comwade.

BUM: Don't mention it, comwade.

1ST SOLDIER: Awe you all togethew hewe incidentially ow on puwpose, comwade?

BUM: We awe all togethew on puwpose, comwade.

2ND SOLDIER: Sewiously, comwade?

BUM: Extwemly sewiously, comwade.

1ST SOLDIER: How sewiously, comwade?

BUM: Almost fatally, comwade.

2ND SOLDIER: Not weally, comwade!

BUM: Absolutely, comwade.

1ST SOLDIER: And what may youw puwpose be, comwade?

BUM: I'm looking fow something, comwade.

2ND SOLDIER: Something you lost, comwade?

BUM: Not exactly, comwade.

1ST SOLDIER: And what may you be looking fow, comwade?

BUM: I may be looking fow a woom and a bathos, comwade.

2ND SOLDIER: A woom and a bathos, comwade!

BUM: You heawd me, comwade.

1ST SOLDIER: You don't mean one whole woom and one whole bathos, comwade?

BUM: Even so, comwade.

2ND SOLDIER: But thewe awe only nine of you altogethew, comwade!

BUM: What do you mean thewe awe only nine of me altogethew, comwade?

1ST SOLDIER: He means, comwade, that comwade Stalin has decweed that thewe must be no mowe wooms with or without bathos.

BUM: But I simply must have a bathos fow myself and a woom fow these othew comwades, comwade!

2ND SOLDIER: But don't you see that we can't any of us have wooms, comwade?

1ST SOLDIER: Ask comwade Stalin, comwade.

BUM: Whewe is comwade Stalin, comwade?

1ST SOLDIER: One moment, comwade. *(Whispers, to* 2ND SOLDIER*)*: —Comwade Bunk!

2ND SOLDIER *(Whispers, to* 1ST*)*: —Yes, comwade Baldewdash!

1ST SOLDIER:—Is comwade Stalin in his woom?

2ND SOLDIER: Don't be silly!

1ST SOLDIER:—Is he in Comwade Lenin's woom?

2ND SOLDIER:—Wath-ew.

1ST SOLDIER: Thank you, comwade Bunk!

2ND SOLDIER:—Don't mention it, comwade Baldewdash!

1ST SOLDIER *(to Bum)*: I'm sowwy, comwade Santa Claus, but comwades Stalin and Lenin awe in confewence. *(The Tomb opens: emitting a thug.)*

BOTH SOLDIERS: Good comwade mowning, comwade Stalin!

THUG: Good comwade mowning, comwades Bunk and Baldewdash!

BOTH SOLDIERS: Thewe's a comwade hewe to see you, comwade Stalin!

THUG: A com—. *(Catching sight of* BUM, *recoils . . . staring, panic-stricken, seizes his head in both hands.)*

BOTH *(starting, trembling)* SOLDIERS: W-w-what's the mattew, comwade Stalin?

STALIN *(impotently pointing to Santa Clause, cries out hysterically)*: —Marx!

From *Americana*, January 1933.

IN MEMORIAM

A roxy is a fabulous birdy. What is a fabulous birdy? An elephancy is not a fabulous birdy.

Fabulous is not big. Fabulous is not bigger. Fabulous is not biggest. Fabulous is bigger-than biggest.

Here is something else. You and I may ask the elephancy to perform a miracle. Any miracle will do. The elephancy looks very sad. The elephancy looks very sad because it must refuse. The elephancy must refuse because no elephancy can perform any miracle.

Now pay strict attention. You and I may not ask the roxy to perform a miracle. Only a roxyfeller may do that. When a roxyfeller asks a roxy, the roxy does not look very sad. The roxy does not look very sad because the roxy can perform any miracle which the roxyfeller asks it to perform. It is a fabulous bird.

Birdies lay eggs. Ordinary birdies lay ordinary eggs.

Roxies are fabulous birdies. Roxies lay eggs.

Roxy eggs are not ordinary eggs.

Look! Here is an egg.

Is the egg an ordinary egg?—I do not think so.—Why do you not think so?—I do not think so because I never saw an egg like the egg.—Do you think the egg may be an elephancy egg? I do not think the egg may be.—Why do you not think the egg may be?—I do not think the egg may be because I do not think that elephancies can lay eggs.—Well then, what do you think the egg may be?—A fabulous egg.

You are right: the egg is a fabulous egg.

Is the fabulous egg bigger-than-biggest?—The fabulous egg is bigger-than-biggest.—Is the bigger-than-biggest, fabulous egg miraculous?—It is miraculous.—How do you think the bigger-than-biggest, fabulous, miraculous egg came here?—I think that somebody must have laid that egg.—Who do you think must have laid it?—I do not think.—Why do you not think?—Because I know.—What do you know?—I know that roxy laid the fabulous egg.

Let us now look at roxy's egg.

It is hollow inside, like a housey. It is made of two parts. Each part is hollow. Each part is a housey. Each housey is empty. The first hollow, empty housey is the bigger-than-biggest housey of representatives and the second hollow, empty housey is the sennet. The representatives are said to lend variety to the first housey. The second housey is said to be an intimate housey because it is bigger than an elephancy's housey, which is bigger than anybody's housey, which is bigger than your housey, which is bigger than my housey, which is not founded upon a roxy.

What is now going on in both parts of the fabulous roxy egg?—Something.—Something what?—Something miraculous.—Something just miraculous?—Something miraculous and fabulous.—Something just miraculous and fabulous?—Something miraculous and fabulous and bigger-than-biggest.—What is something miraculous and fabulous and bigger-than-biggest?—Art.—Do you think anybody makes Art?—O yes.—Who?—Artists.—Are the Artists who make roxy Art bigger-than-biggest Artists?—O yes, they are the bigger-than biggest Artists of all roxy time.—Why are the Artists who make roxy Art the bigger-than-biggest Artists of all roxy time?—Because they are K.O.—Why?—Because the acoustics are perfect.—What is an acoustic?—Damned if I know.—Why are the acoustics perfect?—Because roxyfeller asked roxy.—Do you know what the bigger-than-biggest Artists of all roxy time who make roxy Art and who are K.O. do?—O yes.—What?—Put us to sleep.—And what do we do?—Go to the powder room.—To the powder room?—Da da da.—

What powder room?—Why, roxy's powder room.—Where is roxy's powder room?—O, everywhere is roxy's powder room.

Now pay strict attention.

Look around you very, very, very, carefully and tell me: what is in roxy's powder room?—I am.—Why are you in roxy's powder room?—Because I am hiding from the miraculous and fabulous and bigger-than biggest Art of all roxy time.—And are you also hiding from roxy?—O yes.—Why?—Because I am roxy.—Who am I, then?—I guess you must be roxy, too.—You mean that we are both of us roxy?—We.

Here is something else.

What about the bigger-than-biggest Artists of all roxy time who make the bigger-than-biggest Art of all roxy time which is now going on in both fabulous parts of roxy's fabulous egg?—O, they are all roxy.—What about the fabulous gadgets for making mountains out of molehills and what about the fabulous murals and urals and what about the goosegirl and the loose-girl and what about whathaveyou and what about everything?—O, that's all roxy.—What about the roxyfeller?—O, the roxyfeller's all roxy.—What about God?—O, He's all roxy.—God?—Didn't you know? He's the roxy of ages.

Amen.

Hark! did you hear a simply frightful noise?—O yes.—Do you think the simply frightful noise may have been a social revolution?—I do not think.—Do you think the simply frightful noise might have been a pin dropping?—I do not think.—Do you think the simply frightful noise can have been a bigger-than-biggest variety star whispering to its bigger-than-biggest variety self a hundred thousand million billion variety light-years away?—I do not think.—Do you think the simply frightful noise could have been an intimate talking moving picture hero brushing his intimate moving talking picture teeth?—I do not think.—Speak, speak, thou fearful guest! what do you think the bigger-than-biggest, the intimater than intimatest, the absolutely fabulous and perfectly miraculous and most irrevocably immeasurable and inimitably illimitable and altogether quite inconceivably so to speak roxiest noise of all noises was?—I do not think.—Why do you not think?—Because I know.—What do you know?—I know it was Those Roxy-Bottom Blues.

From *Americana*, March 1933. Samuel "Roxy" Rothafel's Radio City Music Hall opened on December 27, 1932, as a two-a-day vaudeville house; and closed one week later. When it reopened, movies and a stage show were featured in place of vaudeville.

EXIT THE BOOB

This guy says just kick the dictators in the patoot, boys, and live, live, live your life

More than a great many simple folks, for some none-too-obscure unreason, know that they know what's good for you and me. Royally basking in his painfully acquired ignorance of whatever makes life livable, this "share the wealth" prophet butters platitudes for an invisible and immeasurable audience endowed with a simplicity so perfectly prehistoric as to be positively mythical. Quote every man a king unquote. Meanwhile a visible number of merely simplest folks surround that anonymous hater of human values who, busily raving under the peaceful stars, tells mankind just why it must come unto Doctor Marx to be goosed with a "class struggle." Pantspressers of the world unite! you have nothing to lose but your pants, Etcetera, ad infinitum: yet (oddly enough) humanity survives. Individualism flourishes. Millions upon millions of men and women have toothaches. Thousands upon thousands of authentic sadists hope that (as one of them tactlessly assured myself) "someday I'll be in the mouths of the best people."

What ample zest! What copious verve! What abundant enthusiasm! What boundless bonhommerie! It's actually hard to imagine that there really was a time when everything wasn't known to be known and everybody didn't know that they knew it. But science says that a time there was; and science is an honourable man. A time there was when even the most omnipotent emperor didn't know that he knew and he never could know that he had

B.O.—and can't you imagine his ill-starred consort, mounting her dazzling throne with a hideous case of Morning Mouth? Sure an' 'tis a merciful miracle our mysterious mothers and fabulous fathers got themselves born at all at all. Hail, hail, the Civilization's all here . . . although one rather suspects that something must be not far from wrong when every punk can't automatically become Albert Lincoln or Abraham Einstein, merely by letting a button press itself or (if there must be such a thing as imperfection) by throwing a switch: am I right? Wouldn't a ducky invention like that simplify the whole horrid complicated unemployment problem rather nicely? Answer me, you twenty-five-hundred-dollar-a-week apotheosis of cinematographic idiocy. Or (if you prefer) just try to lift those already lifted eyebrows. Hoot, lass, 'tis not a Nude Eel in my sporran either way.

Note that the stalwart champion of Civilization, the dulcet handmaid of Progress, the omnipotent Genie of the uncorked Unknown—science—has succeeded in shrinking our socalled world until it doesn't fit anybody. But there's something stranger still: the fact that any number of simple folks, no matter how mutually antagonistic they may seem to you and me, can (and do) inhabit one and the same microscopic blunder—the blunder of "thinking" that "people" can be "improved." Believe it or not, each of these cranks knows that each of them knows that he, she or it has the absolutely only authentic dope on how to better its, her or his socalled neighbour. Well and bad: but as long as that neighbour equals X, Y probably doesn't mind; and as long as it doesn't equal X, X possibly doesn't mind. Nobody really minds perhaps, until that neighbour becomes XY—

Did you ever share an otherwise palatial dungheap with much too many other vividly stinking human beings? Did you ever (attired in all the majesty of a wilted monkey, with sixty-odd pounds of erroneously distributed junk banging your coccyx) go foolishly limping and funnily hobbling up and down a river of feebly melting tar entitled "company street?" Did you, accidentally, ever exchange your hard-earned right to visit freedom for the doubtful privilege of policing latrines; just because you'd failed—as a warrior can't and mayn't—to grunt loudly at the exact moment when those red hands of yours stuck that real bayonet of Uncle Sam's into an imaginary fellowman? Ah, the ecstasy of it all! And the rapturous ritual of standing in line (here, by the by, we can use what writers, who know that they know, call "a blazing sun") waiting and waiting and waiting and waiting to partially submerge one slipperiest plate in one stickiest kettle of lukewarm once-upon-a-time water, through which meander lazily something like two hundred remains of something which somebody said was supposed to have once upon a time been tapioca pudding . . .

Well, anyhow—the socalled fascist styles for a not too distant future look simply fascinating. Off with your earmuffs, ladies fair, and hear what your well-dressed man will wear. And you, upstanding nonpareil of American masculinity, lend me your auditory appendages. You will wear (sic) mud and you will wear gas and at least three kinds of lice and you will wear terror and agony and hatred and disgust and shrapnel and (without knowing it) a funny little foolish little feeble little fairylike grinless grin. Yes indeedy. Big though you be, big boy, you'll carry that tiny faggoty feeble foolish funny thingless thing wherever you go—all the while never so much as suspecting you've quietly turned into somebody else.

"Who in hell is this s. o. b. to tell me what I'll do?" an outraged sample of the more widely circulated brand of intellectual snob cordially inquires.

Now let said outraged sample keep his shirt on; if he thinks we despise fighting, he's agreebly mistaken. We don't. But neither do we ignore the obvious and incredible fact that, if individuals are organisms, multitudes are mechanisms. Courage we consider whatever is most important on earth; and multitudes do not have courage. A "soldier" who prefers going over the top to being shot in the back by his superior officer is not a man. A man is an entirety, not a fraction of something. A man has courage.

As for who ourselves are: we honestly feel that they couldn't be trusted to furnish the outraged sample with a correct answer—not that he wants a correct answer; far from it. What he wants is a simple answer, which happens to be completely different. The business of a correct answer is to ask a question. The business of a simple answer is the business of a machine gun bullet: to know that it knows.

I do not know that I know—I merely feel deeply—that your correspondent is no mechanism. He is not a "nasty" and he is not a "red" and he is not a "jingo" and he is not a "pacifist" and he is not a "solar engine" and he is not any other form of simple answer. He is alive. What is more, he enjoys nothing so much as being alive. What is most, he would not (so far as an ignorant bloke like him can guess) willingly exchange the worst spontaneous complexity of life for the best premeditated simplicity of something else. Artists are odd, that way. In the immortal words of no less modest a specimen of complexity than the Polish artist Marcoussis "we are living in an Apocalypse. It is necessary to be very intelligent." Certainly not quite oddly enough, a very great many prophets, cranks, busybodies, snobs, opportunists, simple folks (and other nonartists) do not know that they do not know precisely what the word Apocalypse means.

By God, a good dictionary ought to get up on its hind legs and tell them, sometime.

Just a moment (interrupts somebody whom, for the sake of brevity, we'll call Z). I heartily disapprove of cranks (Z comfortingly continues) but there's something of which I disapprove even more heartily; and that's a supercrank. What do I mean by a supercrank? I mean the world's only extant Total Loss: The Art For Art's Sake guy. At least cranks care enough about their fellow men to try to influence them. Not so your Artist With A Capital A. O no: He lives in an Ivory Tower; and He sings hymns to Abstract Beauty; and He doesn't give a hoot in Hell if the whole human race goes to the dogs. He expects mere human beings to appreciate His "genius." Absolutely: and He wonders why out-and-out honest-to-God flesh-and-blood men and women, who don't shirk their responsibilities to the community and who'd rather drop dead than lead the parasitic existence which He idolizes, somehow can't afford to waste their meagre leisure pulling three or four stale ideas out of several tons of affected gibberish which He, forsooth, calls His "work!" See what I'm driving at? Huh? Get the illusion? Speak up!

I think you mean "allusion," my friend; but let that pass. You apparently dislike snobs; so do I. And of snobs there are many varieties.

Only the other day, for instance, I was talking to a variety of snob which might fairly be called the supersnob. Listen (I said to this supersnob) here's a coin, called a "nickel"; it has two sides, "heads" and "tails." Now if I should feel a supreme urge to gamble—as I very well might, particularly if the drinks were on myself—I'd flip this "nickel." And if I did flip it, the question would be: "heads" or "tails"? If, on the other hand, I felt like taking the El to 125th Street, the question would be, not "heads" or "tails," but is it a "nickel" or isn't it? Very well. Now for a metaphor: there is a coin called "dictatorship"; it has two sides, "fascism" and "communism." If you're a guy who thinks he's lucky, you get all excited over the question: which side up will "dictatorship" land—shall we have "communism" or "fascism"? If, however, you're a man who wants to get somewhere—and if "dictatorship" is your last coin—and if you find that "dictatorship" fails to produce the desired result, that it hasn't the value it claims to have, that it simply doesn't turn the trick, that (in short) it's a dud—then what do you do? You grin, baby, and you walk. That's what I said to the supersnob. And he answered: but it might rain.

Fortunately, there still exist persons for whom living means something more complex than keeping out of the rain. Some of these backward, unscientific, possibly even idiotic, persons are artists; the vast majority are not. None of these insufficiently mechanized monsters can possibly be called snobs or supersnobs or Ivory Tower lads. Maybe these pitifully outmoded reactionaries, who haven't forgotten what feet are for, constitute "forgotten men"; I wouldn't know that I knew. One of them, in Biblical parlance, is my neighbour. He resides near me, in a town called Silver Lake, in the state of New Hampshire; and his incomparable name is actually Mike Frost.

Now, ladies and gents, having handed the socalled institution of modern warfare some dirty cracks, I shall (with your permission) allow Mike Frost to lay a sweet bouquet upon the socalled altar of freedom. Listen—

Mike Frost is no slouch. By which I mean that, if he fought the recent war (alias the great war, alias the war to end wars) on his socalled native hearth, it was Uncle Sam's fault for not getting Mike Frost any farther away from Silver Lake, New Hampshire, than Portsmouth, New Hampshire—which was nevertheless a Big Change. Mike Frost, alias my neighbour, was grateful to Uncle Sam for the Big Change. What is more, Mike Frost enjoyed every inch of the War With a Capital W. What is most, that well nigh fatal crusade to end all attempts to make this socalled world safe for anything whatever—by furnishing my neighbour, Mike Frost, with such otherwise unattainable complexities as Travel and Irresponsibility—equals until this very hour the biggest, if not the only, socalled thing in the socalled life of a socalled human being.

Verbum sap.

From *Esquire*, June 1935.

BURLESQUE, I LOVE IT!

Enlightened scholars have doubtless written learned treatises on the relation of burlesque to the satyr choruses, to *The Frogs* and *The Birds*, to Roman comedy, to Punchinello and Brighella, to the "afterpieces" of the minstrel show, to the whole fundamental structure of uncivilized and civilized theatre from prehistoric Then to scientific Now; if they haven't, they ought to be ashamed of themselves. As for your shameless correspondent, he's never even looked up "burlesque" in an encyclopedia and he never intends to. I've seen, in the past thirty years of my proletarian life, a lot of burlesque shows (and I hope to see a lot more) but for no other reason than that burlesque appeals to me. If it doesn't appeal to you, by all means don't read any farther.

Boston's Howard Athenaeum emanated, about 1912, a filth which may never again be equalled—a filth which bore somewhat the same relationship to mere "dirt" that a sunset does to a lighted match. The unparalleled intensity of this filth was due, I imagine, to suppression: that quaintly exaggerated sense of civic virtue which produced a certain Mr. Sumner and a certain Watch and Ward Society, and, in particular, a day when Gertrude Hoffman and her young dancers were ordered to disport themselves in nothing less than wrist-and-ankle-length underwear. Even so, she was called Dirty Gertie.

Less extraordinary than the Howard's filth was the ugliness of its girls—but not much less. Your correspondent used to sit up in the Non Si Fuma and even there they'd make your eyes wince.

Yet so differently were these harpies deformed, I swear that in all my experience with the Old Howard (as it was affectionately called) I never saw one member of a chorus who in any way, shape, or manner resembled another member. The era of interchangeable parts had not put in its standardizing appearance. Those were indeed Ye Goode Olde Days.

Most significantly, the filth and ugliness of the Howard performed a very definite function. This function consisted in the framing of a mammoth collective picture of Mother with a capital M. Never have I seen and heard the maternal instinct glorified with such boundless, not to say delirious, enthusiasm, as in that unholy of unholies. The very bozo who had just distorted a harmless popular ditty to include all known forms of human perversion would, without any warning whatever—that, of course, was the whole trick—plunge himself and us into a monologue whose reeking sentimentality made the Christmas Carol seem positively cynical. Immediately and to a man, those selfsame muckers who had roared themselves hoarse over sin, shame and sorrow would swell and bloat, and then snivel and finally even sob with unfeigned adoration of maternity. A better instance of the emotional versatility of the proletariat would be difficult to conceive.

Burlesque-lovers are faithful; and it took a world-war-to-end-world-wars to blast me out of the Howard and into the National Winter Garden. This gaudy and tawdry institution was located at the very end of Second Avenue, New York City. Having reached the very end, you rose heavenward in something never quite approximating a freight elevator. Alighting in heaven, you passed through a mistranslation of Dante—or did that come later?—and you found Jack Shargel. Shargel was a Jew comedian, sandwiched between oversize derby and oversize shoes, who combined unlimited lasciviousness with a velocity so inscrutable as to suggest only the incomparable Con Colleano of Ringling's. To say that Shargel was a great artist is to put it mildly.

Around Aristophanes Jack (and later, his myth) there hung

very loosely some authentic *commedia dell'arte*, ranging from subtle sketches of the Face on the Bar Room Floor type, to mammillary and abdominal calisthenics by a Juno called Cleo. When I say *commedia* I mean *commedia*. Ray, the straight, used to boast to his devoted and enraptured proletariat that the whole show was "hokum by which I mean that we make it up as we go along." And what a proletariat that proletariat was!

Burlesque audiences are more demanding than most people can realize. Unlike your average theatregoer, your proletarian knows what he wants and won't be happy till he gets it. What he wants (and what he gets) is a show. To give him that show has been, at one time or another, the aim of David Warfield, Lillian Russell, Marie Dressler, Fanny Brice, Willie and Eugene Howard, Bert Lahr, Jack Pearl, Jim Barton, Eddie Cantor, Joe Cook, Mae West and W. C. Fields. But I wouldn't swop any of them for Shargel, whom I never saw except on a burlesque stage. And as for Shargel's audience—it was not only peculiarly demanding, it was extraordinarily well mannered. I have not sat, and I never hope to sit, with tougher or more courteous people.

After being pinched over and over again, the National Winter Garden folded. Its devotees were, very naturally, disconsolate. But every cloud has a silver lining to those who love burlesque. One fine day, John Dos Passos advised me to doff my mourning and pay a visit to the Irving Place Theatre. And lo! here, in its full flower, was strip-teasing.

What would have happened (even to the most seasoned proletarian) if any of the Old Howard's corps de ballet had ever even partially disrobed, heaven alone knows. At the National Winter Garden, whose females bore more than a slight resemblance to females, I seem to recall a glittering runway which now and again served as an auction block and on which more or less living statues were deprived of "lan-joo-ray" for the proletariat's benefit. But Irving Place was a phenomenon of another color. Gone was the plaster nymph of yesteryear and banished to oblivion were the hideous harpies of Ye Goode Olde Days. Pulchritude had entered burlesque. And, with the advent of pulchritude, the focus of burlesque had shifted.

Whereas, formerly, sketches and comedians had constituted a *pièce de résistance* for which soi-disant sex appeal served as trimming, sketches and comedians now served as trimming for Sex with a capital S. Sentimentality had diminished. Humor, filth, slapstick and satire were all present, but they functioned primarily to enhance the Eternal Feminine. And when you saw that Feminine you understood why. It was no static concept, that pulchritude. It moved, and in moving it revealed itself, and in revealing itself it performed such prodigies of innuendo as made the best belly dancer of the *Folies Bergère* entr'acte look like a statue of liberty.

The essence of the Old Howard epoch had been subhuman, neuter, and collective. The essence of the National Winter Garden era had been human, masculine, and Jack Shargel. The essence of the Irving Place burlesque was, is, and I hope will continue to be, *Das Ewigweibliche*—alias Miss June St. Clare. And I beg to state that I speak as a poet and a painter, neither of whom is a press agent.

To see June St. Clare walk the length of the Irving Place stage, or the Apollo stage, or any other stage, is to rejoice that a lost art has been revived. There have been epidemics of women who swam when they walked and of women who floated when they walked. When Miss St. Clare walks, she walks. But when she does something else, she very easily becomes all the animals who ever came out of the ark, rolled into one. Most people move by not keeping still; a very few move by moving; she does neither. She propagates—that is perhaps the word for it—a literally miraculous synthesis of flying and swimming and floating and rising and darting and gliding and pouncing and falling and creeping and every other conceivable way of moving; and all these merely conceivable ways are mysteriously controlled by an inconceivable way which is hers alone. The personality of a Gypsy Rose Lee is where personalities generally are, in the present. The personality of a June St.

Clare wanders from prehistoric Then to posthistoric When, but is most at home in timelessness; and if you think I exaggerate, one of two things is a fact. Either you haven't seen her, or you didn't deserve to.

From *Stage*, March 1936.

SPEECH FROM AN UNFINISHED PLAY: I

Solely as an experiment: stop thinking. Forget, nobly and purely, everything. Undo, graciously relax, break yourselves out of a thousand pieces, and come together. Can you feel (proudly or minutely, humbly or enormously feel) what's coming into this world? Not anything unknown—someone, everyone, even an economizing politician with his life at the end of a leadpencil and his arse on the clouds, can predict that. Not something dreamed—no one, anyone, can guess that; even a physicking mathematician with his hand on the square root of minus one and his mind at the back of his own neck. O no; what's arriving is as unlike meaning, or anything I and somebody and you and everybody didn't dream and nobody knows, as a child's breathing is like geography: form never was where, between them air is; I say it. I say it; which does not tell you. Give a woman's eyes the right man and they'll tell you; rhythm invents when—what's coming is not to compare and include and discuss. What's coming is not to tremble at, to stand up and scream about, to gasp one's heart out for and vomit all over the new rug about. Don't worry; don't try to imagine, the stars know; and the trees even when bursting with buds, sometimes if bending under snow. Wave your voice, make people die, hide in the nonexistence of an atom, get the garbage concession tovarich—that makes no difference; only flowers understand. O little, O most very little civilization, pull your eyes in and kiss all your beautiful machines goodnight; yesterday was another day, which doesn't matter—roses are roses. I swear to you by my immortal head: if sunsets are magnificent (though leaves fall, smiles pass) there shall arrive a whisper—but after the whisper, wonder; and next, death; then laughter (O, all the world will laugh—you never smelled such a world): finally, beginning; a bird beyond every bird, oceans young like mountains, universe absurdly beyond opening universe opening, freedom, function of impossibility, the philo-psycho-socialistico-losophers curl up; you die, I melt—only we may happen, suddenly who by disappearing perfectly into destiny are fatally alive. Be alive therefore; generously explode and be born, be like the sea, resemble mountains, dance; it shall not be forgiven you—open your soul as if it were a window and with a not visible cry bravely (through this immeasurable intensely how silent yesterday) fall upon the skilful thunderously and small awful unmeaning and the joy and upon the new inexcusably tomorrowing immensity of flowers.

From *The New American Caravan* (New York: W. W. Norton, 1936).

SPEECH FROM AN UNFINISHED PLAY: II

by virtue of by virtue, I,
by hereby virtue of the hereby powers vested in hereby me,
do hereby declare and say that in the opinion of this court you are completely guilty of any crime or crimes of which you are absolutely innocent;
and in the name of this great hypocrisy,
which, as you hereby know, can do no wrong,
being a society based upon the equality of importunity, irrespective of andsoforth andsoforth or andsoforth, with liberty and justice for all,
I hereby affirm that to the best of my knowledge and belief you have been conclusively proved,
in flagrante delicto, with full benefit of testimony,
to have committed a foul degenerate heinous and inhuman offense against your innocent and unsuspecting fellowcitizens, not to mention their lives their fortunes and their sacred andsoforth,
namely and to wit,
that hereby you were black in colour at the time of your hereby birth.
In consideration of which, I,
by hereby virtue of andsoforth,
do hereby extend to hereby you, on behalf of the government of the Benighted States of Hysterica, that glorious andsoforth alternative which is the illustrious andsoforth prerogative of every andsoforth citizen; and which is in accordance with

the dictates of justice and of mercy, as revealed to our forefathers in the Declaration of Interdependence; and which, in the ultraenlightened opinion of the supercivilized majority of the hyperhuman andsoforth race, constitutes a glowing andsoforth nucleus andsoforth of radiant andsoforth andsoforth:
e pluribus eunuch, or to make a long story brief,
I give you the choice of either being dead or of not being alive, nolens volens, whichever you prefer.
And in the sacred name of commonsense, I,
by hereby virtue and by hereby andsoforth and by hereby whathaveyou,
do hereby pronounce and decree that hereby you shall be punished for said crime or crimes according to that unwritten law which, according to all rightthinking people, governs the actions of all rightthinking people;
namely and to wit,
that you shall have your right eye suitably excised with a very dull penknife, and placed in your mouth which has previously been opened with a hatchet;
that you shall be soaked with gasoline,
hanged with a rope,
lighted with a match,
cut down while you are alive,
slit up the middle by good women,
stamped on by little children,
and made to kiss the flag by strong men.
Finally: it is the irrevocable verdict of this impeccable court, in due session assembled, that your organ of generation, having been suitably tinged and bedewed with the liquid and solid excrement of all lawabiding citizens in general and of all patriotic persons in particular, shall be forcefully proffered to your own mother, who shall immediately and joyfully eat thereof under penalty of death.
In Hoke signo:

God save the people From the people!
God save All of the people for Some of the people!
God save Some of the people All of the time, and all of the people will take care of themselves.
AMEN

From the *Partisan Review*, March 1938.

SPEECH FROM AN UNFINISHED PLAY: III

O my voices, don't forget me; voices, come to me, I am afraid, I am nothing, nothing without you—you are myself which I shall never know, for to know is to hold: O but you are what everyone may not keep, the poor are not poorer than the rich, the sick are not weak and the well are not strong and captains are soldiers of this who will never be commanded; but this is you, you—and it is much brighter than everything will be very dark and not anyone believes me: women are not so women and men so men that they may imagine the wonder of it, and without wonder they are no one; for this wonder is themselves: all of them can be less than nothing; but each may be more than any someone, each may be everywhere and forever and each may be alive: each of them may become this wonder wholly and the here of this wonderful now and its beautiful moving—O my voices, not all the boys who shall ever die can take you from all the girls who were ever born; and if the young moon sleeps your hands are under her sky (but without you the first star does not breathe) and your fingers are waking the earth

. . . silence.

Then carefully I'll remember how I found you; it was a summer day, the earth was made of sky and the sun was full of bells but in the bells are cries, and then into the air came another brightness; everything around me climbed and fell like a heart, my life flew and swam. She was a little girl, my life. After a while it was a summer day; then she stood, she did not swim and fly, she was not trembling for she was me; and near me were my animals, who are kind and who are not afraid, who do not hate and who cannot lie because their minds are in their eyes. "Jehanne is going" my life tells them "someone is calling me, his name is Michael, he is slender and shining and his armour fits him like water; beside him are two ladies who live before the altar sometimes, they are very beautifully tall but I know their names, Margaret and Catharine. If these three speak to a little girl, she is made of flowers." My animals look at me and look at me and they understand; they are my friends. "Flowers" I tell them "flowers" and their eyes do not need to speak.—But you took me from these friends, O my voices, and you put me on a wide road into the dark world; and I went through cities as if they were clouds, and I came to a silence and in the silence was a fire and men and women stood in this fire. Perhaps the silence was a palace, I don't know; perhaps the fire was torches, fifty torches, a thousand, a hundred, I don't know; I only looked and looked: and in the center of the fire moved men and women beautifully dressed. Then someone whispered "where is he whom you seek?" and now those three who are my voices came to me bright and clear—brighter, much brighter, than music and a little brighter than the morning; they are so bright, no one but me can see their words: they are so clear, no one but me can hear this light who sings "don't fear, Jehanne, for the fire is not a man, Jehanne, but in the fire is the only man." And (smiling) someone who I am went up into it and flames are all above me and all around her, but we are not afraid, for she sees him only, although he was dressed like the others, he has no crown and no sceptre: but I knew she had found him. And I stand before that man. And I say "you are the king."

Silence . . .

ah—how they laughed: the haters, not men and not women; the goddams, which do not fear or dare, the English; which are awake if they are asleep and asleep if they are awake: swarming under a blue steep sky by thousands of tens of thousands they come, laughing and laughing; laughing because we are so few, so very few—yes: but beyond this colour you are breathing and above it is a silence, and I tell you the silence is full of armies and these armies are my armies; I tell you my armies are hundreds of thousands and thousands of hundreds of thousands: I say "you cannot see them; these armies are so huge, only I can see these armies." Yes, the few around me are amazed; breathing, they stare and stare at nothing and at nothing: the air is the air; these men can breathe but these men cannot see, and they are less amazed than I who see and do not breathe. No—it is a dream: no; only blue air is shining and is shining and before me the lice of England come laughing. Her men look at Jehanne. And (trembling) I ask my life "who has spoken?" and my life answers "me."—Then Jehanne The Maid cries to her soldiers "do you believe?" and all together like one man these men answer her "yes!" and the world spoke arrows and a bird sang and the earth opened. Who rides first, in clear armour, lifting high the whiteness of a banner which is wings? Jehanne: and around Jehanne men without wings live to their shoulders in the smoke of bursting bellies, and behind Jehanne men who cannot swim skate on the ice of English brains; and beyond me and above me perfectly are charging millions whom no life but only mine has dreamed. . . . Then how those haters leaped through their laughter and tripped—look, the lines writhe; see: the shapes wince and cringe—now they run: everywhere before us not women who are not men are running, they are running; stumbling, are tumbling; as we lop hit and chop stab smite until down down they go bubbling and down screaming whose flesh wilts under us (their heads are not laughing these teeth bite through these necks) and why? This has no why: this now is more than ours, here we are not some shadows called ourselves, now we are in God together you and I; His are such armies as will fill our blood with always: this is His meaning and our own, my friends; now we are made of one secret. —O for those armies over me again and over you, my soldiers; you thrusting yanking you grappling hacking mowing you diving through dead laughter, you and the good stink of you and the tough blaze of your eyes, yes; and a yell of steel split and clean wriggling of bright flags all grabbed with new sunlight and all the roaring of a high battle around us all with souls dying and walls falling, and the floating of a black horse under me!

. . . silence . . .

someone is lost, someone I must find. Where is she; where? I only look and look, but there is nothing and this nothing neither moves nor does not move—and then within this nothing is another, a nothing which is something. Or someone? It has eyes. Hush. Speak very softly: whisper: can this be the someone whom you seek? No. No; for my someone was made of flowers, and they move—flowers grow and open and they close and disappear; this someone does not die or live, this someone only seems: it cannot grow. Only this something is not asleep but it is dreaming; it is dreaming but it is speaking—I hear words; hark: I hear it saying "Jehanne who has knocked big-fisted knights out of their armour, Jehanne who has smashed princes into smithereens, Jehanne who has seen a man kneeling and a king rising and him, only him, standing: crowned with a crown and sceptred with a sceptre, while people cried and laughed and danced and fell down and the bells swung out into the mountains and the rivers of France melted." These are the words I hear in its dream; and I am afraid.—You less than no one; you something within a nothing: where are my good friends gone, my true kind friends who cannot hate and who do not fear? It dreams, but it speaks.—where have they gone, and their eyes which cannot lie, only who understand me and whom I understand: where? It looks, but it does not see. Answer: who are you?—Me? No—! Don't look: take your eyes into your eyes again! You not—you it—could you have been . . . my Jehanne? O can I have dreamed a king? Were those bells crashing and were those dancers living in my head and falling down and were those people laughing in my heart and crying? Creatures which are not men and are not women—have I dreamed them? Was there ever any fire and any silence and any summer day? You—you with the murdered hair—tell me; was there once any someone in armour like water and ladies much taller than sunlight, calling to me gently and very sweetly crying, until a little girl is made of flowers?

silence.

—But they believed! My soldiers did not see, no; they could only breathe, yes; but they believed. Now I can only breathe; now I can believe: I am a soldier now; I am not a dream—someone else is gone, someone else is dead and the someone who I am is all alone: no . . . no, now she can hear a little girl crying and crying, and saying "help me—I am lost: I am standing in a dark place, I am terribly afraid of this dark, I am my heart falling and climbing but everywhere is dark; dark—speak to me, my voices! O speak! The great doctors have faces like books and I cannot read: speak: —O my voices, their faces which are not faces hate me only because I love you: these are not dead, they are not even English—they are things: I am in the power of things which have no hands and no feet: things follow me everywhere; they listen to my dreaming when I am asleep, things are picking my one red life into large little pieces; hear me, my voices—things undress me with their deaf eyes and I am cold when they cover me with questions.

Tell me—it is Jehanne—speak to her, you voices: have I come to die among things because I would not become a thing?" —So the little girl cries and cries; and I am not dead. Once upon a time she was made of flowers. Therefore the big faces which I cannot read will eat me. And still I shall not read. I shall not know. Ever; for to know is to hold. I shall only understand . . . quietly. —But you shall live, but nothing shall ever hurt you, my voices, who are everything beautiful and everything free; perfectly you are gladness and singing, you are spring when she touches the first tree with her eyes and the fields dance, you are all the white brooks who laugh and cry and the green hills who grow—anywhere sun and stars and the moon are only alive because your light is their light and they play in your day, which is always much nearer than near, nearer than is, nearer than nearer and nearest and now and nearer than how the birds swim through the air and why the fish fly through the sea.

—Thanks!

O I am not afraid, my voices! You shall be very proud of me, for I will be very beautiful for you: I will dress myself carefully in thick red fire and in sharp white fire and in round blue cool fire. Now it is not dark and there is no world: perfectly begins to grow a brighter brightness than all of the sky and of the sea and of the earth; everywhere Jehanne only is alive, everywhere this climbing wonderfully mighty only colour is her gladness. And in her gladness rising, taller than everyone than everything than nothing, stands He Whom she may know: hark—to only Him, to Him, her life is calling and crying and singing "my Love! my Love! out of all this light which is my joy comes to You a woman who is more than every queen: look, her wings begin to open—King Of All Kings, put your great eyes around me as I climb beyond the steepest flower which breathes—see; now all of the little flames are lifting me higher than tomorrow in all of their hands—Man Who Is God! take from these alive fingers quickly one shining bird"

From *Furioso*, Summer 1941; also *This Is My Best* (New York: The Dial Press, 1942).

. . . please honour my contribution by surrounding it with a little silence. Silence is lively; and deathful is doubletalk, eg la guerre

—EEC'S
Silver Lake, N.H.
Aug. 1942

FAIR WARNING

Here is a thing.

To one somebody, this "thing" is a totally flourishing universal joyous particular happening deep amazing miraculous indivisible being.

To another somebody, this "same" thing means something which, if sawed in two at the base, will tell you how old it is.

To somebody else, this "selfsame" thing doesn't exist because there isn't a thunderstorm; but if there were a thunderstorm, this "selfsame" thing would merely exist as something to be especially avoided.

To a fourth somebody, this "very selfsame" thing, properly maltreated, represents something called "lumber"; which, improperly maltreated, represents something else called "money"; which represents something else called (more likely than not) "dear."

Somebody number one is a poet. Actually he is alive. His address is: Now. All the other somebodies are unpoets. They all aren't alive. They all merely are not unexisting—in a kind of an unkind of real unreality or When. Here is another thing: whatever happens, everybody cannot turn the Nowman's Now into When; whatever doesn't, nobody can turn the Whenmen's When into Now.

From the *Junior League Magazine*, May 1938.

WHAT ABOUT IT?

I frankly admit that if I should meet the man who designed the first flying machine, or the Egyptian pyramids, or La Normandie, I should not be tempted to tell him how much better my Aunt Jemima could have turned the selfsame trick with two cracked teaspoons and a withered hairpin. Not because this would constitute a breach of good manners, nor because such a statement might injure my reputation for sanity, but because a poet and painter can always learn something—especially from someone who is neither. I further confess that if the aforesaid poet and painter should find himself face to face with aerial raids, or statues by Lachaise, or tidal waves, or anything equally unbelievable, he would not feel an overwhelming desire to cry "fake!" On the contrary; he would be bowled over, not to mention under and around, by a feeling which can rightly be called "aesthetic." This feeling isn't in the least mysterious. This feeling is merely incredible. It is as if two feelings—the feeling of exaltation and the feeling of humility—should completely mingle while remaining perfectly separate. Anyone who has ever begun-to-begin falling seventy feet in the Cyclone rollercoaster at Coney Island knows what I mean.

And will this anyone kindly tell me why it's okay for Good Americans to enjoy great rollercoasters, whereas no Good American can enjoy first-rate works of art? Why, I demand to know, has "aesthetic"—the one word which stands for whatever is true and unexpected and beautiful and universal in this or any other life—come to be regarded as a symbol of everything which is timidly premeditated and pompously insignificant and pretentiously exclusive? Above all, why should the very people who recoil so violently from "aesthetic" values (attributing thereto God knows what obscurity and affectation) tumble all over each other worshipping science in general and superscience in particular?

Suppose I remarked at this point that the symbolic circumlocutions of an Einstein are child's play, compared with the creative activity of a great, i.e. first-rate, artist. "Liar!" someone would yell "a moment ago you said that art was universal and could be enjoyed by anybody; now you are claiming that art is more mysterious than something which only a handful of people in the whole world pretend to understand.—Fool!" someone else would shout "what right have you to talk condescendingly, let alone disparagingly, about a world-renowned contemporary oracle? How can you, a mere scribbler and dauber, possibly judge anything so abstruse as mathematical physics?—Hypocrite" a third compatriot would bellow "didn't you tell us you felt humble and exalted when you found yourself in the presence of something unbelievable? Well, how about a fourth dimension? Could anything be more unbelievable than that?"

It might be observed *sotto voce* that this same world-renowned mathematical physicist has contradicted and reversed himself, as only an honest worker in a dishonest medium can and must do. Einstein worshippers might also be reminded that their deity had predecessors: Newton and Ptolemy, to name just a couple, benefitted by some pretty slick advertising in their respective days . . . and did you ever read a book by Charles Fort? As for the matter at hand: yes, I did call "aesthetic" experience universal (which it is). But no, I did not state that it could be enjoyed by anybody. I seem to have met, in the course of my life, people who were incapable of enjoying anything; let alone universality or beauty or truth or freedom or themselves. What I did infer, if I did not say it, was that our socalled souls desire and deserve a break just as much as, or more than, our socalled bodies; and if intelligence consists in getting what you want, the Good American body is vastly more intelligent than the Good American soul. I may be wrong, I may very easily be (and very often have been) a fool. But a hypocrite I am not. When I feel that a non-Euclidean continuum doesn't hold a candle to a Renoir, I say so frankly.

Which brings us again to "aesthetic."

And what might be the opposite of this extraordinarily misunderstood word? My reason for asking is simple. If "aesthetic" gives most of my compatriots a pain, then the word which is the opposite of "aesthetic" must imply something altogether painless. By way of discovering this altogether painless opposite, let us make a little pilgrimage to never-never land via the air-conditioned cinema express. What happens when a photograph of Mr. Righto—having taken a most imposing photograph of a nose-dive—is flicked around a photograph of the corner per a photograph of someone's eighteen-cylinder Cadillac at a photograph of some ninety miles an hour and tossed, in a photograph of almost (but not quite) all our hero's stalwart manhood, on a photograph of a nice clean operating table? Answer: Miss You Know Who, the ravishing nurse with the starry eyes, bending deliciously over that once-boyish face contorted by unmitigated heroism, gently but firmly applies an—that's it. "Anaesthetic" is what we were looking for.

No wonder this little stranger arrived by courtesy of a celluloid stork! Like radio (and unlike art) the talkies are a concrete manifestation of mythical superscience. If radio is Public Anaesthetic Number 1, the talkies are Number Two. Poor old bestsellers, despite the benevolent efforts of their worthy publishers, hobble home a feeble third: why? Obviously because the reading of even completely villainous trash requires a slight, a negligible, an almost imperceptible but nevertheless real, effort. By definition, however, any "anaesthetic" succeeds in proportion to the patient's entire effortlessness, to his total submission, to the absolute paralysis of his will. Certain foolish folks have been heard to murmur brightly, now and again, that Man is not a fundamentally rational animal; but I'd like to know what could be more rational than (1) perfecting a painful state of affairs and (2) inventing all sorts of ways of not feeling the painfulness. If that isn't being rational, being rational doesn't consist in advancing boldly to court disaster with one foot and running away with the other as fast as you aren't able to.

Tell me: must our world in general, and our native land in particular, be more and more dangerously and more and more uncomfortably filled to overflowing with gadgets designed to eliminate every vestige of discomfort and of danger including superfluous hair and the human soul? A little bird answers that, if and when discomfort, superfluous hair, danger and the human soul are eliminated, they will recur. He sings (and he means it) that the future holds more for man- and woman-kind than perfect security, utter materialism, prenatal luxury and baldness. This may sound suspiciously reassuring, but it might possibly be true. It would certainly be true if, as some folks (including the wisest folks) have more than once darkly hinted, socalled human beings are essentially and instinctively selfish.

I'm aware that the word "selfish" is strictly taboo just now, like the word "aesthetic." A very popular word just now is "altruistic"; which means, being someone else. Of course if you're already someone else (and the Lord knows exactly how many people are) then you've got to be everybody else. Which (in case you don't know) will be the millennium. Meanwhile, please do me a perfectly huge favour. Try to imagine what would happen if—anywhere in our almost, but thank Heaven not quite, successfully anaesthetized universe—a single living breathing laughing crying loving hating human individual, with no collective axe to grind, should stand straight up in his life, his fortune, his sacred honour and his boots, and cry out "by God! this is good and true and beautiful, and I'm all for this: that is bad and false and ugly, and to hell with that!" I say, just try to imagine. . . .

Such a selfish act wouldn't be in the least mysterious. Such a selfish act would be merely incredible. It would be somewhat as if our nose-diving talkie hero should very unexpectedly (not to say suddenly) hop clean off the operating table—with his stalwart manhood in one hand and his unmitigated heroism in the other—and give that ravishing female anaesthetist with the starry eyes a redhot ripsnorting You Know What, right in front of tooler mond. And there wouldn't be any comfort and there wouldn't be any security and there wouldn't be any prenatal luxury in protesting "but people don't really do such things!" because somebody would have, actually or miraculously, behaved like a man and done something heartily and mightily and thoroughly; as only a man should and can do.

That, enemies and friends, is all for the socalled nonce. I am closing the daubing chest and pocketing the scribbling iron. Now I scram. With me scram just a few more foolish queries than would thoroughly and mightily and heartily plug all the greedily gaping holes in all the comfortably foolproof theories in all this socalled world. But, because I love and hate you, I leave with you neither a query nor a theory; neither anything useful nor everything useless. I leave with you something valuable: a challenge. And here it is—

Can you lose time and experiment with yourselves, or must you lose yourselves and let time do the experimenting? Will you take a poke at fate before you have to pawn your poker? Are you for aesthetics, or are you for anaesthetics? Would you rather wake up while you're you, or afterwards?

How about it!

From *Twice A Year*, Fall–Winter 1938.

RE EZRA POUND: I

John, viii, 7.

So now let us talk about something else. This is a free country because compulsory education. This is a free country because nobody has to eat. This is a free country because not any other country was is or ever will be free. So now you know and knowledge is power.

An interesting fact when you come right down to it is that simple people like complex things. But what amounts to an extraordinary coincidence is mediocre people liking firstrate things. The explanation can't be because complex things are simple. It must be because mediocre people are firstrate.

So now let us pull the wool over each other's toes and go to Hell.
John, viii, 7.

From *We Moderns*, Catalogue 42 of The Gotham Book Mart, N.Y.C. 1940.

RE EZRA POUND: II

Re Ezra Pound—poetry happens to be an art; and artists happen to be human beings.

An artist doesn't live in some geographical abstraction, superimposed on a part of this beautiful earth by the non-imagination of unanimals and dedicated to the proposition that massacre is a social virtue because murder is an individual vice. Nor does an artist live in some soi-disant world, nor does he live in some socalled universe, nor does he live in any number of "worlds" or in any number of "universes." As for a few trifling delusions like the "past" and "present" and "future" of quote mankind unquote, they may be big enough for a couple of billion super mechanized submorons but they're much too small for one human being.

Every artist's strictly illimitable country is himself.

An artist who plays that country false has committed suicide; and even a good lawyer cannot kill the dead. But a human being who's true to himself—whoever himself may be—is immortal; and all the atomic bombs of all the antiartists in spacetime will never civilize immortality.

From *PM*, Sunday, November 25, 1945; also *The Case of Ezra Pound* (New York: The Bodley Press, 1948).

FOREWORD TO AN EXHIBIT: I

Simple people, people who don't exist, prefer things which don't exist, simple things.

"Good" and "bad" are simple things. You bomb me = "bad." I bomb you = "good." Simple people (who, incidentally, run this socalled world) know this (they know everything) whereas complex people—people who feel something—are very, very ignorant and really don't know anything.

Nothing, for simple knowing people, is more dangerous than ignorance. Why?

Because to feel something is to be alive.

"War" and "peace" are not dangerous or alive: far from it. "Peace" is the inefficiency of science. "War" is the science of inefficiency. And science is knowing and knowing is measuring.

Ignorant people really must be educated; that is, they must be made to stop feeling something, and compelled to begin knowing or measuring everything. Then (then only) they won't threaten the very nonexistence of what all simple people call civilization.

Very luckily for you and me, the uncivilized sun mysteriously shines on "good" and "bad" alike. He is an artist.

Art is a mystery.

A mystery is something immeasurable.

In so far as every child and woman and man may be immeasurable, art is the mystery of every man and woman and child. In so far as a human being is an artist, skies and mountains and oceans and thunderbolts and butterflies are immeasurable; and art is every mystery of nature. Nothing measurable can be alive; nothing which is not alive can be art; nothing which cannot be art is true: and everything untrue doesn't matter a very good God damn . . .

item: it is my complex hope that the pictures here exhibited are neither "good" nor "bad," neither peacelike nor warful—that (on the contrary) they are living.

From the catalogue of a onemanshow at the American British Art Center, N.Y.C., March 1944.

FOREWORD TO AN EXHIBIT: II

Are you the author of The Enormous Room?
Eimi.
A me?
I am.
Oh—is that Latin?
Greek.
Well, I'd like to ask you a few questions in English.
How about American?
All right; in American.
Fine and dandy.
Why do you paint?
For exactly the same reason I breathe.
That's not an answer.
There isn't any answer.
How long hasn't there been any answer?
As long as I can remember.
And how long have you written?
As long as I can remember.
I mean poetry.
So do I.
Tell me, doesn't your painting interfere with your writing?
Quite the contrary: they love each other dearly.
They're very different.
Very: one is painting and one is writing.

But your poems are rather hard to understand, whereas your paintings are so easy.

Easy?

Of course—you paint flowers and girls and sunsets; things that everybody understands.

I never met him.

Who?

Everybody.

Did you ever hear of nonrepresentational painting?

I am.

Pardon me?

I am a painter, and painting is nonrepresentational.

Not all painting.

No: housepainting is representational.

And what does a housepainter represent?

Ten dollars an hour.

In other words, you don't want to be serious—

It takes two to be serious.

Well, let me see . . . oh yes, one more question: where will you live after this war is over?

In China; as usual.

China?

Of course.

Whereabouts in China?

Where a painter is a poet.

From the catalogue of a onemanshow at the Memorial Gallery, Rochester, N.Y., May 1945.

FOREWORD TO AN EXHIBIT: III

Sold (as Santa Claus learned from Death) a strictly not giveable epoch—whose bag is out of the cat and whose horse is in the saddle and whose anybody is anybody else (because religion is the opium, and peace! it's fission, and come let us adjust until the whole world's an infrahuman ultrafamily of supersubmorons delightedly drowning in telejukemovieradiovision) and whose hyperscientific miracles can never stop happening (because every day without exception must be christmas or else those three wise salesmen might stop laying their more and more de luxe millenniums at the common feet of the forgotten babe joe blow incorporated)—I have the very great honour to remind you, through one of the arts of silence, that "Life" (as Miss Weird taught Him) "is a matter of being born"; but "Art is a question of being alive"

From the catalogue of a onemanshow at the American British Art Center, N.Y.C., May 1949.

FOREWORD TO AN EXHIBIT: IV

"We are living in a time of plague" said Fritz Wittels; when I mentioned something called an atomic era "so, like the story-tellers of the Decameron, we must find salvation in ourselves."

Many unregenerate years ago, before everybody was a little better than everybody else, New York City boasted a phenomenon entitled The Society of Independent Artists; whose yearly exhibitions opened with near riots—partly on account of the fantastic number of exhibitors (for membership fees were moderate) but chiefly because (since no jury existed) an "Independent show" was sure to comprise every not imaginable variety of artfulness and artlessness; plus occasionally a work (or play) of art.

I was wrestling some peculiarly jovial mob of sightseers at possibly the least orthodox of all Independent "openings," when out of nowhere the sculptor Lachaise gently materialized. "Hello Cumming" his serene voice (addressing me, as always, in the singular) sang above chaos "have you see one litel cat?" I shook my head. He beckoned—and shoulder to shoulder we gradually corkscrewed through several huge rooms; crammed with eccentricities of inspiration and teeming with miscalled humanity. Eventually we paused. He pointed. And I found myself face to face with a small canvas depicting a kitten.

During that distant epoch, pictures which couldn't be labelled either "academic" or "experimental" were usually pronounced "naive." But the healthily spontaneous little painting opposite me transcended classification. Bombarded by chromatic atrocities ranging all the way from lifeless nonrepresentationality to deathful anecdotalism, it remained completely and charmingly itself.

"Dis ting" Lachaise reverently affirmed (in the course of what remotely resembled a lull) "is paint with love."

From the catalogue of a onemanshow at the University of Rochester, May 1957.

IS SOMETHING WRONG?

"Is something wrong with America's socalled creative artists? Why don't our poets and painters and composers and so forth glorify the war effort? Are they Good Americans or are they not?"

First: are they Good Americans. . . .

when I was a boy, Good Americans were—believe it or don't—adoring the Japanese and loathing the Russians; now, Good Americans are adoring the Russians and loathing the Japanese. Furthermore (in case you were born yesterday) yesterday Good Americans were adoring the Finns; today Good Americans are either loathing the Finns or completely forgetting that Finland exists. Not even the fact that twice during my lifetime Good Americans have succeeded in disliking the Germans can convince me that any human being (such as an artist) is a Good American.

Second: why don't they glorify. . . .

when you confuse art with propaganda, you confuse an act of God with something which can be turned on and off like the hot water faucet. If "God" means nothing to you (or less than nothing) I'll cheerfully substitute one of your own favourite words, "freedom." You confuse freedom—the only freedom—with absolute tyranny. Let me, incidentally, opine that absolute tyranny is what most of you are really after; that your socalled ideal isn't America at all and never was America at all: that you'll never be satisfied until what Father Abraham called "a new nation, conceived in liberty" becomes just another subhuman superstate (like the "great freedom-loving democracy" of Comrade Stalin) where an artist—

or any other human being—either does as he's told or turns into fertilizer.

Third: is something wrong. . . .

all over a socalled world, hundreds of millions of servile and insolent inhuman unbeings are busily rolling and unrolling in the enlightenment of propaganda. So what? There are still a few erect human beings in the socalled world. Proudly and humbly, I say to these human beings:

"O my fellow citizens, many an honest man believes a lie. Though you are as honest as the day, fear and hate the liar. Fear and hate him when he should be feared and hated: now. Fear and hate him where he should be feared and hated: in yourselves.

"Do not hate and fear the artist in yourselves, my fellow citizens. Honour him and love him. Love him truly—do not try to possess him. Trust him as nobly as you trust tomorrow.

"Only the artist in yourselves is more truthful than the night."

From *Harper's Magazine*, April 1945; also *The War Poets* (New York: The John Day Company, 1945).

A FOREWORD TO KRAZY

Twenty years ago, a celebration happened—the celebration of Krazy Kat by Gilbert Seldes. It happened in a book called *The Seven Lively Arts*; and it happened so wisely, so lovingly, so joyously, that recelebrating Krazy would be like teaching penguins to fly. Penguins (as a lot of people don't realize) do fly—not through the sea of the sky but through the sky of the sea—and my present ambition is merely, with our celebrated friend's assistance, to show how their flying affects every non-penguin.

What concerns me fundamentally is a meteoric burlesk melodrama, born of the immemorial adage *love will find a way.* This frank frenzy (encouraged by a strictly irrational landscape in perpetual metamorphosis) generates three protagonists and a plot. Two of the protagonists are easily recognized as a cynical brick-throwing mouse and a sentimental policeman-dog. The third protagonist—whose ambiguous gender doesn't disguise the good news that here comes our heroine—may be described as a humbly poetic, gently clownlike, supremely innocent and illimitably affectionate creature (slightly resembling a child's drawing of a cat, but gifted with the secret grace and obvious clumsiness of a penguin on terra firma) who is never so happy as when egoist-mouse, thwarting altruist-dog, hits her in the head with a brick. Dog hates mouse and worships "cat," mouse despises "cat" and hates dog, "cat" hates no one and loves mouse.

Ignatz Mouse and Offissa Pupp are opposite sides of the same coin. Is Offissa Pupp kind? Only in so far as Ignatz Mouse is cruel.

If you're a twofisted, spineless progressive (a mighty fashionable stance nowadays) Offissa Pupp, who forcefully asserts the will of socalled society, becomes a cosmic angel; while Ignatz Mouse, who forcefully defies society's socalled will by asserting his authentic own, becomes a demon of anarchy and a fiend of chaos. But if—whisper it—you're a 100% hidebound reactionary, the foot's in the other shoe. Ignatz Mouse then stands forth as a hero, pluckily struggling to keep the flag of free will flying; while Offissa Pupp assumes the monstrous mien of a Goliath, satanically bullying a tiny but indomitable David. Well, let's flip the coin—so: and lo! Offissa Pupp comes up. That makes Ignatz Mouse "tails." Now we have a hero whose heart has gone to his head and a villain whose head has gone to his heart.

This hero and this villain no more understand Krazy Kat than the mythical denizens of a twodimensional realm understand some threedimensional intruder. The world of Offissa Pupp and Ignatz Mouse is a knowledgeable power-world, in terms of which our unknowledgeable heroine is powerlessness personified. The sensical law of this world is *might makes right*; the nonsensical law of our heroine is *love conquers all*. To put the oak in the acorn: Ignatz Mouse and Offissa Pupp (each completely convinced that his own particular brand of might makes right) are simple-minded—Krazy isn't—therefore, to Offissa Pupp and Ignatz Mouse, Krazy is. But if both our hero and our villain don't and can't understand our heroine, each of them can and each of them does misunderstand her differently. To our softheaded altruist, she is the adorably helpless incarnation of saintliness. To our hardhearted egoist, she is the puzzlingly indestructible embodiment of idiocy. The benevolent overdog sees her as an inspired weakling. The malevolent undermouse views her as a born target. Meanwhile Krazy Kat, through this double misunderstanding, fulfills her joyous destiny.

Let's make no mistake about Krazy. A lot of people "love" because, and a lot of people "love" although, and a few individuals love. Love is something illimitable; and a lot of people spend their limited lives trying to prevent anything illimitable from happening to them. Krazy, however, is not a lot of people. Krazy is herself. Krazy is illimitable—she loves. She loves in the only way anyone can love: illimitably. She isn't morbid and she isn't longsuffering; she doesn't "love" someone because he hurts her and she doesn't "love" someone although he hurts her. She doesn't, moreover, "love" someone who hurts her. Quite the contrary: she loves someone who gives her unmitigated joy. How? By always trying his limited worst to make her unlove him, and always failing—not that our heroine is insensitive (for a more sensitive heroine never existed) but that our villain's every effort to limit her love with his unlove ends by a transforming of his limitation into her illimitability. If you're going to pity anyone, the last anyone to pity is our loving heroine, Krazy Kat. You might better pity that doggedly idolatrous imbecile, our hero; who policemanfully strives to protect his idol from catastrophic desecration at the paws of our iconoclastic villain—never suspecting that this very desecration becomes, through our transcending heroine, a consecration; and that this consecration reveals the ultimate meaning of existence. But the person to really pity (if really pity you must) is Ignatz. Poor villain! All his malevolence turns to beneficence at contact with Krazy's head. By profaning the temple of altruism, alias law and order, he worships (entirely against his will) at the shrine of love.

I repeat: let's make no mistake about Krazy. Her helplessness, as we have just seen, is merely sensical—nonsensically she's a triumphant, not to say invincible, phenomenon. As for this invincible phenomenon's supposed idiocy, it doesn't even begin to fool nonsensical you and me. Life, to a lot of people, means either the triumph of mind over matter or the triumph of matter over mind; but you and I aren't a lot of people. We understand that, just as there is something—love—infinitely more significant than brute force, there is something—wisdom—infinitely more significant than mental prowess. A remarkably developed intelligence impresses us about as much as a sixteen-inch bicep. If we know anything, we know that a lot of people can learn knowledge (which is the same thing as unlearning ignorance) but that none can learn wisdom. Wisdom, like love, is a spiritual gift. And Krazy happens to be extra ordinarily gifted. She has not only the gift of love, but the gift of wisdom as well. Her unknowledgeable wisdom blossoms in almost every episode of our meteoric burlesk melodrama; the supreme blossom, perhaps, being a tribute to Offissa Pupp and Ignatz Mouse—who (as she observes) are playing a little game together. Right! The game they're playing, willy-nilly, is the exciting democratic game of *cat loves mouse*; the game which a lot of highly moral people all over the socalled world consider uncivilized. I refer (of course) to those red-brown-and-blackshirted Puritans who want us all to scrap democracy and adopt their modernized version of *follow the leader*—a strictly ultraprogressive and superbenevolent affair which begins with the liquidation of Ignatz Mouse by Offissa Pupp. But (objects Krazy, in her innocent democratic way) Ignatz Mouse and Offissa Pupp are having fun. Right again! And—from the Puritan point of view—nothing could be worse. Fun, to Puritans, is something wicked: an invention of The Devil Himself. That's why all these superbenevolent collectivists are so hyperspinelessly keen on having us play their ultraprogressive game. The first superbenevolent rule of their ultraprogressive game is *thou shalt not play*.

If only the devilish game of democracy were exclusively concerned with such mindful matters as ignorance and knowledge, crime and punishment, cruelty and kindness, collectivists would really have something on the ball. But it so happens that democracy involves the spiritual values of wisdom, love, and joy. Democracy isn't democracy because or although Ignatz Mouse and Offissa Pupp are fighting a peaceful war. Democracy is democracy in so far as our villain and our hero—by having their fun, by playing their brutal little game—happen (despite their worst and best efforts) to be fulfilling our heroine's immeasurable destiny. Joy is her destiny: and joy comes through Ignatz—via Offissa Pupp; since it's our villain's loathing for law which gives him the strength of ten when he hurls his blissyielding brick. Let's not forget that. And let's be perfectly sure about something else. Even if Offissa Pupp should go crazy and start chasing Krazy, and even if Krazy should go crazy and start chasing Ignatz, and even if crazy Krazy should swallow crazy Ignatz and crazy Offissa Pupp should swallow crazy Krazy and it was the millennium—there'd still be the brick. And (having nothing else to swallow) Offissa Pupp would then swallow the brick. Whereupon, as the brick hit Krazy, Krazy would be happy.

Alas for sensical reformers! Never can they realize that penguins do fly; that Krazy's idiocy and helplessness in terms of a world—any world—are as nothing to the *n*th power, by comparison with a world's—any world's—helplessness and idiocy in terms of Krazy. Yet the truth of truths lies here and nowhere else. Always (no matter what's real) Krazy is no mere reality. She is a living ideal. She is a spiritual force, inhabiting a merely real world—and the realer a merely real world happens to be, the more this living ideal becomes herself. Hence—needless to add—the brick. Only if, and whenever, that kind reality (cruelly wielded by our heroic villain, Ignatz Mouse, in despite of our villainous hero, Offissa Pupp) smites Krazy—fairly and squarely—does the joyous symbol of Love Fulfilled appear above our triumphantly unknowledgeable heroine. And now do we understand the meaning of democracy? If we don't, a poet-painter called George Herriman most certainly cannot be blamed. Democracy, he tells us again and again and again, isn't some ultraprogressive myth of a superbenevolent World As Should Be. The meteoric burlesk melodrama of democracy is a struggle between society (Offissa Pupp) and the individual (Ignatz Mouse) over an ideal (our heroine)—a struggle from which, again and again and again, emerges one stupendous fact; namely, that the ideal of democracy fulfills herself only if, and whenever, society fails to suppress the individual.

Could anything possibly be clearer?

Nothing—unless it's the kindred fact that our illimitably affectionate Krazy has no connection with the oldfashioned heroine of common or garden melodrama. That prosaically "virtuous" puppet couldn't bat a decorously "innocent" eyelash without immediately provoking some utterly estimable Mr. Righto to liquidate some perfectly wicked Mr. Wrongo. In her hyperspineless puritanical simplicity, she desired nothing quite so much as an ultraprogressive and superbenevolent substitute for human nature. Democracy's merciful leading lady, on the other hand, is a fundamentally complex being who demands the whole mystery of life. Krazy Kat—who, with every mangled word and murdered gesture, translates a mangling and murdering world into Peace And Good Will—is the only original and authentic revolutionary protagonist. All blood-and-thunder Worlds As Should Be cannot comprise this immeasureably generous heroine of the strictly unmitigated future.

She has no fear—even of a mouse.

From *The Sewanee Review*, Spring 1946; also *Krazy Kat* (New York: Henry Holt, 1946).

WORDS INTO PICTURES (*VERBUM ETC.*)

Perhaps a few individuals may enjoy my pictures. Possibly a few may enjoy my poems.

And if yes, what could be better?

Equidistant from such wonderful luck—with a distance not reckonable by mere lightyears—are the naying and the yeaing of numberless televisionary unindividuals: movieloving each blinder than radioactive any is deaf.

Were I a critic, should probably add that "academic" (i.e. un-) art resembles every good coin, which it isn't, in having two sides. One side can be called "photographic realism" or even "naturalism"; the other, "nonrepresentational" or "abstract" sic "painting." And your stupid wiseguy doing his worst to deny Nature equals your clever fool who did his best to possess Her.

χαîρε

From *Art News*, May 1949.

JOTTINGS

1
knowledge is a polite word for dead but not buried imagination
2
everything near water looks better
3
it takes three to make a child
4
only as long as we can laugh at ourselves are we nobody else
5
the expression of a clown is mostly in his knees
6
private property began the instant somebody had a mind of his own
7
don't stand under whispers
8
brother, that's not a buck to you: that's a century to me
9
ends are beginnings with their hats on
10
never put off till today what you can do yesterday
11
a poet is a penguin—his wings are to swim with
12
nothing recedes like progress

13
of course Bacon wrote Shakespeare; but so did everybody else, including (luckily) Shakespeare
14
not that she wasn't a faithful husband
15
a chain is no weaker than its missing link
16
many parents wouldn't exist if their children had been a little more careful
17
let rolling stones lie
18
great men burn bridges before they come to them
19
when Americans stop being themselves they start behaving each other
20
you can't ef the statue of liberty
21
false is alike. False teeth
22
enter labor, with an itching heart and a palm of gold: leading (by the nose) humanity, in a unionsuit
23
the pigpen is mightier than the sword
24
item: our unworld has just heaved a sigh of belief
25
people who live in steel houses should pull down the lightning
26
hatred bounces
27
il faut de l'espace pour être un homme

28
most people are perfectly afraid of silence

29
think twice before you think

30
an intelligent person fights for lost causes, realizing that others are merely effects

31
equality is what does not exist among equals

32
it may be dreadful to be old but it's worse not to be young

33
sleep is the mother of courage

From *Wake* No. 10, 1951.

VIDELICET

by E. E. Cummings

For more than half a hundred years, the oversigned's twin obsessions have been painting and writing.

Several decades ago (when Academic Unart was exactly as representational as it now isn't) an eminent art critic described my most recent picture as "hardly the sort of thing you would care to live with."

Earlier still, if memory serves, the notable promoter of a book called The Enormous Room had remaindered its first edition at thirty cents a copy; and I'd scarcely prevented the author's enthusiatic father from purchasing more than sixty copies.

Long before an epoch of disillusionment became an era of dehumanization—and about the time a play called Him, by my "lower-case" self, was dramacritically deplored as "exactly like stepping on something extremely nasty in the dark"—our prenonobjectivist realized that denying Nature's imagination meant renouncing my own; and joyfully hurdled Jehovah's anaesthetic commandment *"Thou shalt not make unto thee any graven image, or any likeness of any thing that is in the heaven above, or that is in the earth beneath, or that is in the water under the earth."* (Exodus XX 4).

Some years later Eimi—the diary of a pilgrimage to Marxist Russia—was dutifully damned by America's fellow-travelling literary gangsters. Still later, learning that fourteen publishers had refused a collection of poems aptly entitled No Thanks, my serenely confident mother requested the privilege of ensuring its unwelcome appearance.

Came the forties; and culture (lucely translated You Never Had It So Good) leaped like a weed. Education of the not educable speedily outranked all other national rackets: college degrees, crowning any activity from stagelighting to piecrust-rolling, were sold as freely as pardons during the middle ages. Television antennae blossomed from the poorest housetops; and moviestars, no longer content with a Cézanne in the toilet, hastily acquired livingroomsize Picassos. Nobody and nothing escaped The New Look: children of parents who'd honestly hated my writing were taught how to pity my painting instead. For a voice like unto the cooing of A-bombs had spoken, saying "EVERYBODY SHALL BE EVERYBODYELSE!" and (after a period of anxiety, during which The Nonforgotten Man pretty nearly suspected that he'd been properly frigged) it was revealed—amid everybody's surprise and delight—that everybodyelse was an artist.

Let me only add that one human being considers himself immeasurably lucky to enjoy, both as a painter and as a writer, the affectionate respect of a few human beings.

From *Arts Digest*, December 1, 1954.

A POET'S ADVICE TO STUDENTS

A poet is somebody who feels, and who expresses his feeling through words.

This may sound easy. It isn't.

A lot of people think or believe or know they feel—but that's thinking or believing or knowing; not feeling. And poetry is feeling—not knowing or believing or thinking.

Almost anybody can learn to think or believe or know, but not a single human being can be taught to feel. Why? Because whenever you think or you believe or you know, you're a lot of other people: but the moment you feel, you're nobody-but-yourself.

To be nobody-but-yourself—in a world which is doing its best, night and day, to make you everybody else—means to fight the hardest battle which any human being can fight; and never stop fighting.

As for expressing nobody-but-yourself in words, that means working just a little harder than anybody who isn't a poet can possibly imagine. Why? Because nothing is quite as easy as using words like somebody else. We all of us do exactly this nearly all of the time—and whenever we do it, we're not poets.

If, at the end of your first ten or fifteen years of fighting and working and feeling, you find you've written one line of one poem, you'll be very lucky indeed.

And so my advice to all young people who wish to become poets is: do something easy, like learning how to blow up the world—unless you're not only willing, but glad, to feel and work and fight till you die.

Does this sound dismal? It isn't.

It's the most wonderful life on earth.

Or so I feel.

From the Ottawa Hills *Spectator*, October 26, 1955.

Matters of Choice

Puerto Rican Women's Struggle for Reproductive Freedom

IRIS LOPEZ

RUTGERS UNIVERSITY PRESS
NEW BRUNSWICK, NEW JERSEY, AND LONDON

Library of Congress Cataloging-in-Publication Data

López, Iris Ofelia.
Matters of choice : Puerto Rican women's struggle for reproductive freedom / Iris Lopez.
p. cm.
Includes bibliographical references and index.
ISBN 978–0-8135–4372–7 (hardcover : alk. paper)
ISBN 978–0-8135–4373–4 (pbk. : alk. paper)
1. Birth control—Puerto Rico—History. 2. Poor women—Puerto Rico—Social conditions. 3. Poor—Puerto Rico—Economic conditions. I. Title.
HQ766.5.P8L66 2008
363.9'7097295—dc22 2008000883

A British Cataloging-in-Publication record for this book is available from the British Library.

Visit our Web site: http://rutgerspress.rutgers.edu

Manufactured in the United States of America